PHILLIPSBURG LIBRARY

6748 9100 030 821 1

DATE DUE

12 17 02   96

D0064892

Theatre of Wonders:
Six Contemporary American Plays

THEATRE OF WONDERS:
Six Contemporary American Plays

by

Len Jenkin
Jeffrey Jones
Des McAnuff
Elizabeth Wray
Mac Wellman

Edited, with a Foreword by Mac Wellman

WITHDRAWN
Phillipsburg Free Public Library
PHILLIPSBURG, N. J.

Sun & Moon Press
Los Angeles, CA

812.54
THE

Wonders, introduction and editorial matter © Sun & , 1985

Len Jenkin, 1977, 1985
seventy Scenes of Halloween," © Jeffrey Jones, 1980, 1985
"Leave It to Beaver Is Dead," © Des McAnuff, 1976, 1979, 1985
"Border," © Elizabeth Wray, 1981, 1985
"Forecast," © Elizabeth Wray, 1982, 1985
"The Professional Frenchman," © John Wellman, 1983, 1985

Cover: Susan Magnus

All rights reserved.
No part of this publication may be reproduced or transmitted in any form or by any means, electronic or mechanical, including photocopy, recording, or any information storage or retrieval system now known or to be invented, without permission in writing from the publishers and/or the authors and their representatives, except by a reviewer who wishes to quote brief passages in connection with a review written for inclusion in a magazine, newspaper, or broadcast. For production rights, refer to the individual plays.

Library of Congress Cataloging in Publication Data

Wellman, John
    Theater of wonders

    (American Theatre and Performance Series; no. 1)

    ISBN: 0-940650-38-X (cloth)
    ISBN: 0-940650-39-8 (pbk)

FIRST EDITION
10 9 8 7 6 5 4 3 2 1

Publication of this book has been made possible, in part, by a matching grant from the National Endowment for the Arts, Washington, D.C., a federal agency, and by contributions to The Contemporary Arts Educational Project, Inc., a nonprofit corporation.

Sun & Moon Press
P.O. Box 481170
Los Angeles, CA 90048

Contents

A Theatre of Wonders

The old word *wonder* with its associations of the unexpected, the "awe-full," the premonitory, and the marvelous occurred to me as I assembled the collection of plays before you. The idea was suggested by critic Bonnie Marranca's excellent notion of a theatre of images, which she developed to discuss the seminal works of Richard Foreman, Robert Wilson, and Lee Breuer. Indeed, much of the work contained here reveals a debt to these three notable members of the New York avant-garde. Yet, I thought to emphasize in my selection what were primarily written works, *plays* rather than anomalous texts, assemblages, or notated improvisations. These are plays that can be performed and produced by any theatre with a sense of adventure and a little imagination.

Another fact I wished to emphasize through my title was that, contrary to the often repeated canard of fretful critics in the daily press, a truly distinctive and imaginative body of dramatic literature does exist in this country. Surely the writing of plays is a most arduous and exacting activity, and the climate of bad press, hostility, and contempt that has prevailed in America in recent decades has only made the situation appear more grim.

It was, and is, my conviction that fine writing—by which I do *not* mean writing performed to the sterile dictates of last year's second-best attempt to portray "real life"—is discoverable. One need only look for it. The fact that such plays are infrequently produced is quite another question. The extreme defensiveness of American theatre, and the chronic loser's mentality of the typical American producer do not conduce to the task of producing anything novel, unconventional, or in any way "wondrous."

I wanted—and got—authors who each had a unique "take" on the matter of the times, and the degree of integrity necessary to grapple with it, each after his or her own measure. What fills me with delight as I look over the plays I have collected is how sharp they are! All the wild anomalies and contradictions of our times find expression here. And what fine contempt for everything that is commonplace, unthinkingly compromised, and complacently for sale.

I wanted—and got—plays with passion, plays with a life inimitable, and not imitating.

—*Mac Wellman*

Gogol
A Mystery Play

by
Len Jenkin

© Len Jenkin, 1977
CAUTION: No performances or readings of this work may be given without the express authorization of the author or his agent. For production rights, contact Flora Roberts, Inc., 157 West 57th Street, Penthouse A, New York, NY 10019.

Gogol was originally performed in the New York Shakespeare Festival at The Public Theatre in May 1978, with the following cast:

Resurrection Man .... Richard Bright

Inspector Bucket .... Clarence Felder

Mistress .... Robyn Goodman

Girl with Pig .... Carol Kane

Man .... Charles Levin

Dr. Tarr .... Leland Moss

Professor Fether .... Larry Pine

Gogol .... Frederick Neumann

Mesmer .... Andrew Robinson

Patient .... Rebecca Stanley

Pontius Pilate .... D. J. Sullivan

Nurse .... Dee Victor

Chained Woman .... Margaret Whitton

Producer: Joe Papp
Director: Len Jenkin

"Something further may follow of this masquerade."
—Herman Melville, *The Confidence Man*

The author's thanks to John
Webster for the misquotations.

Part the First
Prologue: Gogol Alone
The Healing Bath
Mesmer Alone
The Invitation
Street Scene
In the Office of Inspector Bucket
At the Theatre
The House of Gogol
Before the Party

Part the Second
The Party: Some Conversations
Mr. Gogol Brings On the Theatricals
"The Porker Pundit"
"Stanley in Africa"
"Here in the Castle"
"Pontius Pilate Thinks It Over"

PART I

[Bare stage, or drawn curtain. An older man enters in formal dress.]

PROLOGUE: GOGOL ALONE

GOGOL: Welcome. I am Gogol. I am not lights and shadows. I am not the mountain, or the lake below. I am not a stick, not the ashes. I am not an ape. I am not a hummingbird. I was born a man, and that has not changed, no matter what I do.

I am not mother. I am not teacher. I am not a hero or a thief. I do not make paper snowflakes or count stars. I am not funny. I am not poisonous. I am not joking.

I am Gogol, cloud and mud. I am extinct. I run the roller-coaster at night. I am a go-go dancer and a fool.

I have an excellent notion of why you've come here. Let me assure you that each thing you expect to happen, will happen. And less. And more. I am Gogol. Believe that, and I will tell you another one.

I have certain final business to conduct, to wind up my affairs *[He mimes turning a crank]*, in preparation for departure. *[He begins to imitate a train, moving about a bit]* Chooo! Chooooo! Chucka chucka chucka chucka chucka...Woo Wooo! *[He stops the imitation abruptly]* I'm certain you'll find it all amusing. I'm hosting a little party for a friend. Not a friend, exactly...an acquaintance, a pen-pal, a colleague. To be honest, I've never met the man. I doubt that all will go smoothly.

There's already been an accident. I've been wounded. A slipup backstage, some weeks ago, in this very theater.

Propmen were shelving the spears from a production of *Hamlet* as I was walking out on stage to rehearse these opening remarks to you, and I gained a wound in my side.

It still bleeds. [*He reaches inside his tuxedo jacket, feels the wound gingerly.*] You think that's a lie. You actually believe I'd waste my time and yours feigning injury. What interest would I have in making fools of you? Do you think I do parlor tricks as well?

I'm only sorry that due to my . . . illness, the events you are about to witness will not be everything they might have been. Yet, of course, if it wasn't for this weakness, these events would not exist. [*Gogol again reaches his hand inside his jacket. This time it comes out bloody.*]

I wish you an enjoyable evening. I shall have one, one way or the other. If you find you don't care for the events displayed, please make every effort to moderate your feelings and pay attention. The drama you will witness depicts the world as it is. If what appears seems false to you, please take the opportunity to reexamine this impression in the full light of the play. Kind ladies and gentlemen, we begin. [*Blood begins welling through Gogol's shirt and coat from the wound in his side. He grimaces slightly, presses the wound with one hand.*]

Let me repeat. I am Gogol. There has been an accident. A series of accidents. But I believe we can continue. You will not be disappointed. Enjoy yourselves.

Gogol lifts his bloody hand up to his face, and draws on himself in blood, a bright red circle on each cheek. He smears his face over with blood. He laughs. A giant turtle enters, moving very slowly. It has a small saddle on its back. As it passes behind Gogol, he mounts it, facing the audience. The turtle, never varying its pace, carries him off. The stage is bare. It darkens.

THE HEALING BATH

Music. . . Mozart from a string quartet. Lights come up, or the curtain is opened, revealing the quartet playing in front of a red curtain that fills the small portion of the stage, center. They have music stands, tuxedos, the works. A potted palm. A chandelier. Medical charts. A skeleton. This is Dr. Mesmer's salon. A loud buzzer is heard. The band stops playing abruptly. Dr. Mesmer appears, a young man, formal dress. He has a white robe over his arm. He consults a watch, dismisses the quartet. They exit. Mesmer takes a bow to the audience, and opens the red curtain. Behind it is the healing bath, a large ornate bathtub on a platform. It's foamy, and billowy, and has various scientific and magical apparatus attached to it.

MESMER: Time!

Out of the tub rises a beautiful young woman, nude. Mesmer takes her hand, leads her down marble steps, and robes her. She is the patient.

PATIENT: Doctor Mesmer! Doctor! I'm so light, so perfect, so ready. I'm. . .

MESMER: Shhhh. Please, don't try to talk as yet. The magnetic bath has drained away a lifetime of poisons. Your nerves are like new shoots in spring. . . tender.

PATIENT: I can't help it, doctor. . . It's a miracle. I'm a miracle. The healing bath. . . the magnetic chain. . . the heat in your hands . . . .

MESMER: All this is only the guided operation of natural forces, little known to. . .

PATIENT: Can't you see that I love you?

She throws her arms around him. He embraces her. Passion. Offstage noise of people scuffling, approaching. He pushes her away from him and begins talking. She tries to hang on.

MESMER: The salutary effects will continue, as the magnetic crisis has revitalized the entire organism. A delicate prickling sensation along the nerves is to be expected. You must continue your mesmeric meditations, and see me in. . .

The husband of the patient bursts in, a dignified older man, also in formal dress. The Nurse, a dumpy older woman, is dragging behind him, trying to prevent him from entering.

NURSE: Stop, you! You're not supposed to. . .

PATIENT: George! What are you doing here?

HUSBAND: I demand to know, sir, what you've been doing with my wife. Let me be frank. I don't believe in this mesmeric hogwash. I think, my dear sir, you've hoodwinked the people of Paris, France, and Grand Island, Nebraska. I have my doubts. Serious doubts. Bunk. My wife has nervous trouble. She wanted treatment. But your treatment, young man, is far from ordinary. You've noticed I've refused to call you "Doctor"? I'm a medical man myself, I'm proud to say, and I won't have. . .

PATIENT: Dear, please. Dr. Mesmer has done wonders. [*Nurse exits*] I feel alive again. I feel a love for you this moment that I haven't felt since the first night, in the hotel on Lake Como.

HUSBAND: Shhhh. Young man, my wife seems to have confidence in your methods. But, despite her goodwill, I demand that. . .

MESMER: Quiet. Don't you think it's better to be well? The geraniums in your windowbox flower. Your children want to be near you. When you dig for worms to go fishing, you find them.

HUSBAND: You talk nonsense. We know what you've been doing. You'll be hearing from me, *doctor,* and my colleagues!

MESMER: On your way out, pay the nurse.

HUSBAND: Thief! Mountebank! Dragging the name of medicine in the dirt! [*to wife*] Where are your clothes?

MESMER: I hid them.

PATIENT: They're in the dressing room. This way, dear. Goodbye, Doctor.

MESMER: Get out, both of you. I have work to do. [*They exit*]

MESMER ALONE

I am Franz Anton Mesmer. I am a doctor. This is the truth, I swear in God's name. I would swear it on the True Cross, or the sacred symbol of any other religion, occupation or amusement, now or in the hereafter. I would attest to it in a court of law. I have papers stating these facts [*He shows them to the audience*] signed by certified doctors of medicine. My name is Franz Anton Mesmer. I am a doctor. I heal the sick. I would wager my life on it.

Therefore, to that most dramatic of theatrical questions: [*with a real sense of emergency*] "Is there a doctor in the house?"—the answer is yes. Dr. Mesmer is in the house, and at your service, creeping up the stairs toward the bedroom, prick and fingers tingling, black flag flapping in the breeze. Dr. Mesmer, that's me. Curing them right and left.

I am also a quack. Quack. Quack. A charlatan. Poseur.

A phony. A quack is anyone too dumb to invent a believable explanation for his occasional moment of luck or grace. Listen. If I knew what I was doing, I could sell it on the corner, put my foot in my ass, and get out of town. Not likely.

Snake wine. You know what that is? The Chinamen take a big dead snake and coil him round and round in a jar. Then they fill that jar with alcohol and water. They let it sit. And when that snake starts to rot and turns white as milk, its ready. Snake wine. There's a little spout at the bottom of those jars, and they drain the liquid off into tiny eggshell cups. Nothing better. With snake wine God loves you, and you never cry during the day, and you can get it up for a statue. I'd have to put myself in the jar.

This isn't my idea. It's happening. I could of opened an Orange Julius stand. Healing should be a sideline. Anyone takes it up full time becomes a liar. My motto is "Service" or "Cop and Blow." But the customer. . . the customer is always satisfied. Why not the proprietor? One thing's for sure. I got a talent for this business. Maybe I did something for God without knowing it, and he's paying back in pieces. Or maybe my nurse is playing stinkfinger with the patients in the dressing rooms. . . .

Now you people might want to say: physician, heal thyself. Easier said, my friends, easier said. My disease refuses to develop symptoms. Nothing to cut out of me, that I can see. So I keep on serving the public, and making up stories to tell 'em, and taking their money, and banging one or two between times, and it's hard to tell if I'm making fools of my patients, or they're making a fool of me. Maybe there's not a truthful man or woman among us, in all of Podunk, or Mouseville, or Paree.

I seem to have got the habit, and everybody wants some. Whatever it is that's making this racket work, I know one thing. It's running out. I'm burning it, my friends, at an unprecedented rate, in order to keep warm in this, the coldest winter any of us can remember. [*Nurse enters*]

So stop by soon. Whether it's tongue troubles, or mild depression, or the vague malaise you feel because you're not in touch with the godfoot, I fix 'em. Mend everything but broken hearts. Magnetism, psychic forces, energy channels. You name it, I suck it up and deliver free, except for a small service charge.

THE INVITATION

NURSE: Stop whining and lying. It's an ugly combination. Those two are gone. Do you want the money, or should I tuck it away for a rainy day? Maybe we'll have a hurricane.

MESMER: Save it. Where do you put it anyway?

NURSE: In the toe of my slipper, dear.

MESMER: You have no faith in mesmerism, or me, at all, do you? Why do you work for me?

NURSE: You're no worse than the others. I've seen a bit more of doctors than the young ladies who come for you to take them swimming. I like you. By the bye, champ, you have a visitor, and she's a looker. Bring her in?

MESMER: I thought the day was over.

NURSE: From the looks of this one, not by a long shot.

Nurse exits, and returns with Gogol's mistress, an extremely attractive woman of indeterminate age, in a black floor-length dress. She holds a large white envelope.

MESMER: Madam?

MISTRESS: Dr. Mesmer. You don't know me. I'm an associate of Mr. Gogol, a gentleman of this city, who requests your presence this evening at a...

An old peasant woman, long ragged dress, babushka, rushes in and throws herself at Mesmer, embracing his knees.

PEASANT WOMAN: O God that this could be the day! Doctor how I prayed all night for you. Doctor! Doctor, make me a miracle for little Franz red hot for three days his eyes yellow as cat piss and burning. We never forget you forever. Forever. Lord God comforter let me touch you for strength. We have no money. Mercy, doctor, and the magnets will stop his little legs from twitching... [*Nurse enters*]

MESMER: Get this woman off of me! And take care of her.

NURSE: [*grabbing woman*] Come on, Momma. He's a hardhearted bastard [*pulling her out along the floor*] but I got a little something in my purse. Come on...

PEASANT WOMAN: [*being dragged offstage*] Doctor! Doctor! We're dying! Give me one touch of your...

MESMER: [*to mistress*] I'm sorry. These things happen.

MISTRESS: So they do. Gogol and I would like your company this evening at a little gathering we're having at home. All the instructions are enclosed. [*She hands him the envelope*]

MESMER: I don't go to parties. Even when I'm invited.

MISTRESS: Mr. Gogol will tell you what you need to know, and has a gift for you. [*She turns to go*] We hope you will attend. [*She exits, and the Nurse enters*]

NURSE: She's a hot one. I'll bet you're gonna make it to that little affair. Drum up some business, will you? Tips have been lousy.

MESMER: Keep your mouth to yourself, or you'll be back in the pissoirs.

NURSE: Not a chance. After working for you, I know a little too much about certain people in this town. And remember, doctor, that we better pile it up while it's flying in the window. We're in plenty of trouble around here. The way we're going, we may have to catch the hurry bus to Sioux City one of these days. Midnight coach.

MESMER: Are you worried?

NURSE: Are you?

MESMER: I can feel it. We are about busted, for better or worse.

NURSE: My view exactly. Be careful when you go out. They could put the police on it, despite the scandal. Where are you going?

MESMER: Walking. And perhaps that little party. My cloak and hat, if you're not too fancy for that sort of thing.

NURSE: Coming up, O healer of souls. [*She hands him his cloak and hat*] And don't forget. They don't know what a harmless idiot you are. That doctor today was a beauty. Can't keep your hands off, can you?

MESMER: That's none of your business.

NURSE: We are really in it, doctor.

MESMER: So we are. [*He exits. Nurse alone.*]

NURSE: That gentleman is in more trouble than he's likely to get out of alive and sane. He's the toast of Tokyo, and every captain and first mate, not to mention the whores, want to get a little treatment and talk about it over dinner at Booboo's. Yesterday thirty people linked themselves in a magnetic chain around a tree in the park and chanted his name for half an hour till the cops broke it up. I'm on his side, but I'm not sure he knows it. . . That's enough talk from me. I'm not supposed to give the speeches here. That's for the good doctor, and Mr. Gogol. I'm just the nurse. I better clean up the place, and if I had any brains I'd make a couple plane reservations for Rio...me and my boy. We'll see, won't we ....

[*Lights fade on the Nurse and Mesmer's salon*]

STREET SCENE

Night. Old fashioned street lamp, perhaps a dimly lighted window floating toward the rear, with the shade drawn. The Resurrection Man enters, wet, bent, stringy hair, in rags. He carries a shovel and a large wooden mallet. On a rope he drags the corpse of a young woman, blonde hair hanging about her. She is in a torn grave shroud, and spotted with mud, as in the Resurrection Man himself. He stops stage center.

RESURRECTION MAN: Rain's wet. Sucks. They're biting at my heels. Featherfuckers. They'd get me if I wasn't light as a goose and half as quick. I ain't responsible. Servant of science, that's my name, and a bit for the pot if you please. A man's got to do the work he's made for, according to his tastes and peecooliarities. Each man a man. Indivisible. I used to have a hat, but I lost it.

I am drunk enough. I got to drink to do my work, and I got to do my work to get the scum to drink to do my work. Howse them for posies in the street? Howse that for a tune-up, friend? Sucks. I been doing this for years. There ain't no one better, and that ain't no consolation. You hear me, fishfaces? Why you always sucking in air like that, walk through the bloody lobby like you was drowning? Like you was trying to suck the world in through a straw. Like you was pulling your last come in through a straw. Bloody bastards. The dead don't bother. They look up calm at you, and don't care who comes knocking. Hospitable. They no longer got their tastes and peecooliarities. Missing, you might say, along with the grease on their bones...

Here comes the good doctor himself. The man I'm looking for... [*Mesmer enters, walking rapidly*] Doctor Mesmer! My old partner in research, out in the nighttime! I got a fine one tonight, doctor. Ten bucks will fetch her. Got a tumor as big as an apple in her side. Fascinating to a man of science...

MESMER: I'm not interested in stacking my surgery with the corpses of your chance acquaintances. Drag her to a tavern and stand her up in the corner. Or perhaps you can pimp for her. Your friends won't know the difference. Kindly get out of my way.

RESURRECTION MAN: You bought from me once, young doctor, and you'll buy from me again. They all do... Hippocrates, Galileo, Gogol...

MESMER: I choose to learn from the living.

RESURRECTION MAN: So you say, Doctor Mesmer. But this one's a beauty. I cried at her funeral this very afternoon. Who knows the secrets you'll find in her? The lives saved... send a stranger to kill the cock. It's on the table, tasty, and don't sing no more. We all eat of it, and who knows who did the diddle...

MESMER: No, I tell you.

RESURRECTION MAN: She'd fit between your sheets, Blondie would. She's barely cold.

MESMER: I don't indulge.

RESURRECTION MAN: We all have our peecooliarities, doctor. You have yours, and I have mine. Take a look at her. Take a look and I'll tell you a secret. . . [*Mesmer looks quickly, turns away*]

MESMER: Why don't the two of you crawl off together. I am going.

RESURRECTION MAN: Better go fast, doctor. I hear things. They've gone to Bucket, they have.

MESMER: Who is Bucket?

RESURRECTION MAN: Get indoors, doctor. Safe and warm. And don't go home. I wouldn't, if I was you. Somebody's tired of your tricks and your manners. Pay me a penny, will you? They're green, they are, and you've diddled them. Buy from me, will you? And I'll get home before Old John and his horses.

MESMER: I don't want her. I have trouble enough. Where can I. . .?

RESURRECTION MAN: Why don't you drop in to the theatre, doctor? [*A sign reading theatre in bright yellow letters suddenly appears behind them*] Safe and warm. Watch the show and think it over. I'll be where you can find me.

Mesmer turns, looks around, and runs "into the theatre," disappearing from view. The Resurrection Man's corpse begins to sit up. He bops it with his mallet. It collapses, and he begins to drag it off.

I bet there's nighttime folks about who'd like to know where Doctor Mesmer sits tonight. Pay me a penny, Blondie, and I'll whisper it to you. . .

[*He exits, dragging the corpse, who rises up a bit as she is hauled offstage. Lights dim.*]

IN THE OFFICE OF INSPECTOR BUCKET

A hatrack perhaps, and an umbrella stand. A swivel chair.
Three formally attired and elderly doctors have come to
see Bucket. Inspector Bucket is loudly dressed.

BUCKET: You insult me, gentlemen, and doctors all. But being
without knowledge in this, however wise you be in plucking the vena cava from a corpse, I forgive you. Neither
time nor space binds Inspector Bucket. Their hold on me
is, at best, tenuous, Ten-u-us. A wink and a flick of the
pinky and I'm gone, ranging through the four quarters in
search of the man.

Charlie Chan, Mike Hammer, Boston Blackie, all plan-
etbound trash. In the twists and twists of the asteroid belt,
or the windings of our municipal sewer system, Bucket
never fails. Snow, sleet, hurricane, fire or flood are
nothing to me. Once the miscreant knows his every step
is haunted by Bucket, his garbage sniffed, his dreams
monitored and filed, his heartbeats numbered—he turns
himself in. Even the Bulletproof Belgian came begging to
be nailed, and you think this Mesmer could cause difficulty. Pish! Piffle!

DOCTOR ONE: We must have him, body and soul.

DOCTOR TWO: Ego and Id.

DOCTOR THREE: Essence and senescense.

DOCTOR ONE: Fingers and toes.

BUCKET: You think that Bucket will take your money to hunt
a man, and bring back meat? You will have everything
you wish from him. Once he turns himself in, the job
begins. He will be drained, then empty, then never have
exited to trouble your dreams. Meanwhile, Tarr and
Fether.

Dr. Tarr and Prof. Fether enter. They are identical in dress, but can be very different body types. They are dignified, but so much so as to be comic, or frightening. They move together, though not particularly mechanically, and not always.

Gentlemen, my most valued assistants, Dr. Tarr [*He bows*] and Professor Fether [*He bows*]. When the type of offender you describe faces Tarr and Fether he cowers, he cringes, he begs to follow them home.

TARR AND FETHER: So true!

DOCTOR ONE: They don't look like the kind of investigators we. . .

BUCKET: Pish! Leave the luring of deviants to me, gentlemen. I do it for a living. I know my job. My windups know their jobs.

DOCTOR ONE: Windups?

BUCKET: Are you prejudiced, sir?

DOCTOR TWO: We'll remember you for this, Inspector. Bring that quack to his knees, and you'll have the thanks of every decent-thinking person in Los Angeles.

BUCKET: I already have certain information, my friends. My eyes are everywhere. Now! To put my windups in service! [*Bucket steps behind the back of Tarr, and whispers in his ear. He does the same for Fether.*] My faithful assistants, to the theatre! To the theatre! It's almost showtime!

TARR AND FETHER: So true! So true! [*They exit*]

BUCKET: Gentles all, he's doomed. Place your faith in my palm. I'll keep it warm until the job is done. Now, away!

DOCTOR ONE: Bring him to his knees.

DOCTOR TWO: Break him like a clock.

DOCTOR THREE: Crack his egg and feed us with the yellow meat.

Tear his. . .

BUCKET: I am Bucket. That is all I need say. Away! [*He shoos the doctors offstage. Bucket turns to the audience*]

The things I do for a dollar would make a grown man puke. I'm used to it. Did divorce business. Don't even get any on my vest anymore. I pass through it all like piss through a waterfall. Never touches me. Mesmer, however, is a problem. Mr. Gogol will not like it, to say the least. Ah, well, in the meantime my fee from those jealous incompetents allows the purchase of a few chop suey dinners. . .

Bucket takes a wad of bills out of his pocket, thumbs it, replaces it. Lights dim on Bucket in serious thought.

AT THE THEATRE

Mesmer is seated alone onstage, in the center one of a row of three red plush theatre seats, facing the show, which is stage rear. Lights up. It is a girlie show, burlesque. The two actresses we will see later as part of Gogol's company are doing bumps and grinds in gaudy sequinned costumes, flanked by the two actors, dressed as baggypants comedians. They stare and point at the girls. Mesmer is interested. Striptease music is played, with a lot of wrong notes, by the string quartet. The music ends, the girls exit, and the comics come forward.

COMIC ONE: Say, didn't I see you in the graveyard last night with one of those babes?

COMIC TWO: Yep, that was me all right.

COMIC ONE: What the hell were you doing with her in the graveyard?

COMIC TWO: I was burying a stiff. [*Dr. Tarr appears alongside Comic One, Prof. Fether alongside Comic Two*].

TARR: [*to Comic One*] Pardon me, but there's a man backstage who urgently wants to see you. He's got six weeks for you in Vegas as the warmup act for Elvis. [*Comic One rushes offstage*]

FETHER: [*to Comic Two*] Excuse me, but you've got an important phone call from Florida. Seems your mother's mobile home is on fire. Hurry!

> *Comic Two rushes off quickly. They have been replaced by Tarr and Fether, who take up their positions, and do an odd energetic little dance. They stop dancing abruptly.*

FETHER: Good evening, Dr. Tarr.

TARR: Good evening, Professor Fether. Any trouble getting to the theatre tonight?

FETHER: Yes, indeed. I was run over by a beer truck.

TARR: You don't say.

FETHER: Yes, indeed. My skull looked like a white waffle covered with hairy red syrup. But I just tossed my severed leg over my shoulder, and dragged my broken spine and my splint liver over to Doctor Mesmer's place. He magnetized me in a jiffy with those magic hands, and here I am. Good as new. [*Tarr and Fether again break into their dance, and stop abruptly*]

> Dr. Tarr, how is your wife these days? I heard she was ill.

TARR: Ill? I should say not. She's livelier than ever since her mesmeric treatments. If I didn't know that Doctor Mesmer knew what he was doing, I might think she had an overdose of magnetic fluid.

FETHER: Sir! Doctor Mesmer is the most responsible and far-sighted practitioner in town. Whatever makes you think she had an overdose?

TARR: Little green leaves grow out of her ears, and I can't get her to come down off the chandelier!

They take another dance break which ends with a flourish. Mesmer writhes a bit in his seat.

TARR: Did you hear about Mr. Holofernes? Always depressed, out of touch, a victim of illusion and fear?

FETHER: Always groaning with weight of birth and death. A bore.

TARR: He visited Dr. Mesmer and now he hums the music of the spheres as he strolls down Bourbon Street. His eyes shine like shoebuttons. The whores unzip his fly for him. He's right, tight, lit up like a good humor truck, and he loves us all!

FETHER: Holy! Holy! Holy!

TARR: Wonderful! Wonderful!

FETHER: That reminds me. . . Ready?

Tarr and Fether sing, to the traditional tune, the following, performing a grotesque parody of religious ecstasy, ending by falling to their knees. They sing it through twice.

TARR AND FETHER: Wonderful, wonderful, Mesmer is to me
Councillor, Prince of Peace, Mighty doctor he
Helping me, keeping me, free from doubt and pain
Wonderful is Doctor Mesmer, praised be his name!

As they finish, Mesmer gets up and rapidly leaves the theatre. Tarr and Fether call after him.

TARR AND FETHER: Wait! Wait, doctor! We've hardly begun!
Lights go dark.

THE HOUSE OF GOGOL

Mozart is played by the string quartet, who are now placed in one rear corner of the stage: hired musicians for a party. Candles in ornate candelabra, perhaps a stained glass window lighted from behind. A central space that can serve as a dance floor. To the rear a red curtain conceals a small stage. An effect of depth to the space. Gogol's mistress in onstage alone, seated. She is in a black evening gown, very beautiful.

MISTRESS: In the morning, when I was small, I would be given an egg to eat. A white egg in a blue cup. I would eat it, and compare the color of the yolk to the sun outside the window. If they matched I felt lucky. When I finished, if I hadn't cracked the two halves of the eggshell into little pieces, my mother would sing:

> You must break the shell to bits, for fear
> The witches should make it a boat, my dear
> For over the sea, away from home
> Far by night the witches roam.

I liked the idea of tiny witches in eggshell boats, out on the ocean. It seemed brave of them. I hid the shells from mother. I never knew that the witches were as big as trees, and their power made the shell grow into a great white barge, where they sailed among pointed teeth. They are after me still.

To hide from them while I grow stronger, I travel. Travel is. . . entertaining. I always try to be somewhere else. Do you like riddles? Here's one Gogol taught me: How does the Czar of Russia go to sleep? Oh—it's time for your lesson! I almost forgot. Geography. Circumnavigation. GLOBE!

A large globe appears near Gogol's mistress. Within it is the head of Magellan. He has a pointed beard, ruffled collar. The continents and oceans can be seen outlined on the transparent surface that surrounds the head.

Before we begin, have you seen Gogol? This is his place. I'm his mistress. We have guests this evening.

The figure of Mesmer, walking rapidly through night-time streets, occasionally looking behind him in paranoia, appears in the distance. He pauses, takes out the letter the mistress gave him, glances at the address. He hurries onward. The mistress watches him. He is gone. She continues.

You won't be disappointed. When we have a little evening's entertainment, everyone gets what they want, just the way they want it—or what they need, just the way they need it. There's no accounting for taste. I spent a weekend in New Guinea once, and I. . .

MAGELLAN'S HEAD: [*Spanish accent, very violently*] The geography lesson! Now! You insolent whore! Do you think your sexual history is more important than the globe of the earth?

MISTRESS: Poor Magellan wants me to come to the point. [*She takes up a classroom pointer and delicately touches the globe with its tip.*] The lesson! You forget Mr. Gogol's instructions so easily. Is that how you found the Indies?

MAGELLAN: No! No!

MISTRESS: We'll do without you. [*She pops the globe like a balloon. It disappears, along with Magellan's head.*] His English is lousy anyway. I must ask Gogol to provide me with less excitable teachers.

Geography is a subject I've learned through necessity. When I was twenty, I'd run, and then be somewhere, and stop running. I'd spend a month, and I was bored. The older I became the sooner that boredom appeared, and I'd find I wanted to leave wherever I was. When I was twenty-two it was three weeks, in whatever company. Then two weeks, a week, a day. Now its down to two hours. I can just about get through this performance without screaming. I'm not joking. [*She begins a horrendous scream, cuts it off abruptly*] The obvious result is, I've been everywhere. More than once. And I've learned the secrets of geography. It begins with a geography of the body. Circumnavigation.

She moves to stage rear, to the red curtain. She draws the curtain and a small stage is revealed. On this stage is the set of a dungeon of large stones, crudely painted on cardboard. Chained to the wall, with cardboard chains, is an attractive young woman. This is one of the two actresses in Gogol's troupe. She is wearing modern casual dress, jeans and a top, but both are torn in places. She is passive throughout what follows. Gogol's mistress refers to her with the pointer, moving it slowly from her head, down over one breast to the waist as she speaks.

The polar cap. . . the continents and the seas. . . The equator at last! The center, the eye that binds [*pointer on naval*]. Hot spot.

She drops her pointer and advances toward the girl, forgetting her audience. The curtain is suddenly drawn between them, and there is a low growl. A large brown bear, walking on its hindlegs, has closed the curtain, and now steps out and waggles a hairy paw at Gogol's mistress, a clear signal that she is forbidden to do what she was about to do.

MISTRESS: What do you think you're doing? [*The bear gestures*

offstage, indicating that others are coming] Goddammit,
you think we're embarked on the good ship Lollypop here.
All right. I'll be good. But as long as I am, you're to do
as I tell you, or Gogol will let me whip you for my birth-
day. [*She addresses the audience again*] Mamma always
said, when you greet company, make a little curtsey.

*She does so, beautifully, with the bear standing by her,
tossing her hair, and bringing up her face with a wicked
smile on it. She stands quite still. Gogol enters, accom-
panied by a smaller bear than the one his mistress has been
arguing with, and a bald man in a baggy suit and rimless
glasses. This is Mordecai, the accountant.*

GOGOL: My dear, what exactly do you think this is? Coming
attractions?

MISTRESS: I was only trying to be encouraging, darling.

GOGOL: You'll be encouraging later. That is the order of things.
Now you will be fairly quiet and not interfere with rehear-
sals. Roots, then branches, then almost anything you can
imagine. Meanwhile, have they [*gesture toward audience*]
learned anything?

MISTRESS: Don't make jokes. I refuse to let you be the only one
playing comedy.

GOGOL: Comedy? It's a pity you are indispensable. [*To smaller
bear*] Bring out the books. Mordecai wants to examine
them. Last analysis.

MORDECAI: [*with groans of passion*] Books! Books!

*The smaller bear fetches large account books. Mordecai
grabs them and rubs himself up against them.*

MISTRESS: I wish you'd get another accountant.

*Mordecai retires to the rear of the stage with the books.
There is a small table, where he lights a candle and begins
to examine them.*

GOGOL: I have a wound in my side. It's hardly necessary, but
    it's showy.

MISTRESS: So do I.

GOGOL: You hurt yourself?

MISTRESS: A baby, still unborn, is gnawing at me.

GOGOL: You're too sensitive. Have you set the theatricals?

MISTRESS: Your actors will be ready. The sets are painted. The
    orchestra is tuning up.

GOGOL: And the invitation?

MISTRESS: Personally placed in his healing hands. He's pretty.

GOGOL: Well done. Mesmer will be here, and either he'll cure
    me, or, as I suspect will be the case, I'll cure him. Where
    are the police?

MISTRESS: In the fog.

GOGOL: Once Mesmer has arrived, electrify the gates, alarm the
    alarms. We can't be disturbed until the time is right. Where
    is Inspector Bucket?

MISTRESS: Everywhere, as usual. Close.

GOGOL: We must rely on the Inspector's sense of balance, his
    curious pride. I would hate to compel him to do anything.

MISTRESS: Your affair. I have no influence on the Inspector, or
    his creatures.

   In the distance, the Resurrection Man can be seen walk-
   ing through the same midnight street Doctor Mesmer did,
   following him, bopping his corpse when it rises, and whist-
   ling to himself. Mistress and Gogol watch disinterestedly.
   He stops, looks carefully after Mesmer, decides something
   for himself, and then turns about and goes off in the direc-
   tion he came in.

GOGOL: And the actors?

MISTRESS: Your usual troupe, dressing with us in a moment.
    Meanwhile, KISS ME!

GOGOL: Now? When I'm about to . . .

MISTRESS: Yes, at this golden moment, on the banks of the Orinoco! Wild and tangled memories throng my heart! [*She brings up her arm to mask her face.*] Have you any idea who I really am?

GOGOL: Yes. Enough for now.

MISTRESS: Please. We'll be serious soon enough.

GOGOL: The evening is wearing on.

MISTRESS: Dear Gogol, please. Tell me. How does the Czar of Russia eat potatoes?

GOGOL: You want to recite your lessons?

MISTRESS: I'm asking a serious question. The kind you like.

GOGOL: You want to impress the audience with your skill at riddles.

MISTRESS: Yes.

GOGOL: You know the answer. I taught you.

MISTRESS: Please . . .

GOGOL: We will be at the end before *you* know it.

MISTRESS: Soon I'll be still, and help at the party, and do what I'm told, and laugh and cry when I'm told, and love whom I'm told.

GOGOL: Quickly, then.

MISTRESS: How does the Czar of Russia eat potatoes?

GOGOL: I don't know.

MISTRESS: Good. The Czar orders his golden throne placed on the great lawn before the Winter Palace. He seats himself, and the soldiers of the fourth army begin to build a wall of yellow butter between him and a Schmeisser cannon aimed directly at his mouth. The wall is built, ten feet high. The cannon is loaded with the finest Idaho homegrown, tamped down with salt. The world is still. FIRE! The explosion echoes through Mother Russia. The potato, warm from the blast, rockets through the wall of butter into the open mouth of the Czar. His mouth clangs shut on it like the gates of Hell. The cannon is trundled away through the dusk, and as the moon rises, the Czar sits alone on his throne, on the great lawn of the Winter Palace, chewing.

GOGOL: Fine. Are you done?

MORDECAI: [*Rushing up from stage rear*] Done! The books are done! Balanced, like an eagle on a crag, like a beachball on the nose of a seal, like a...

GOGOL: Good. Mordecai, take the books home with you and burn them.

MORDECAI: Burn? Burn Books?

GOGOL: Burn them. We're starting over tonight. [*calling*] Show him out.

MORDECAI: Very good... [*The small bear enters, takes Mordecai's hand, leads him out, holding all the books.*] Burn with matches... burn... [*Mordecai is gone.*]

BEFORE THE PARTY

The actors enter, two men and two women, the men in tux and tails, the women very beautiful and elegant in evening gowns. They form the center of a group that includes the Mistress, the two bears, and the turtle. Gogol addresses them all.

GOGOL: My loves! My actors! In the time I was a playwright and we performed in Bucharest, Buenos Aires and Belgrave Square: in the time of the burning of the manuscripts; and in the theatricals held here, for us alone, you were with me. Tonight is our last performance together. Some of it you have rehearsed, and much of it is ex tempore. I want you to burn your brightest. Fire in the belly, sweethearts, all night long. The audience, though rather small, is perceptive and critical, far more so than he seems. Take care, play well, joy in your bones, the glow of your bodies even and warm. Swirl! Swirl!

All turn about, except Gogol, in a quick little dance. As they whirl, in the distance, Inspector Bucket, Tarr and Fether enter to him, heads hung in defeat. He turns them around, points them back into the night, after whispering in their ears. They exit. Bucket alone. The scene fades. The dance is done.

My loves, each of you is burdened tonight with parts within parts, and your training has prepared you. But I also ask you to recall for a moment with me a great performer of the past, who split himself seven ways to please. Let the memory of my teacher, who the older members of our little company have seen on this very stage, strengthen your spirit. My teacher! The great biloquist, improvisatore, prince of wizards, master of the secrets of ancient magic; my teacher, whose show included the Hypnotic Minstrels, the Cake of Death, and wondrous tableaux vivants, delineated masterfully by the company under his direction: "Vishnu and his Mother Kali," "The Destruction of Nineveh," "Aeolus Whispering to Venus the Secret of the Winds"; and all followed by a drama of inconceivable interest: *The Polish Exiles*; and as a finale, a comic dance by the master himself. Let the soul of this genius return from cloud nine, and goose you to the peak of your art.

And for tonight, my loves, my eyes and hands over these years, forget the usual tools of the actor's trade: the grimace, the take, the shout, the eyes rolling distraught, the joy buzzer, the whoopee cushion, the squirting flower and the X-ray specs. Leave this arsenal in your dressing rooms. Bring yourselves alone, play the evening itself, you yourselves. I want you all to play so well that each of you believes that he or she is the only actor. All the others are real, and you alone fear to alter the action with a misplaced word, a pause that lasts too long. Remember that our audience, Doctor Mesmer, is himself a powerful performer, though very rough in spots. I will be here, as always, alongside you. You have prepared yourselves. It is time. [*A loud knock is heard from offstage.*] Places, please! That is Doctor Mesmer now.

The actors, Gogol, the animals, all take places in a casual party grouping, the animals as servants. Tableau. Another loud knocking from offstage, this a little desperate. Suddenly, Mozart. The actors swirl into a dance, formal and quick, in a circle around center stage. Gogol gestures to the large bear to go to the door. The bear moves slowly toward it. Then, darkness. The Mozart builds. House lights up, music gone.

PART II

THE PARTY: SOME CONVERSATIONS

At Gogol's. Onstage are the four actors as they were in the previous scene, tuxedos and evening gowns. The two bears are present as servants. The small stage is still at the rear, red curtain drawn across it. The string quartet

plays. Gogol's Mistress is seated to one side, still. The act-
ors talk animatedly in a group. Doctor Mesmer is near
them.

ACTRESS ONE: Wealthy? My dear, I believe Mr. Gogol is the richest man in this part of Alaska.

ACTOR ONE: Rich as Croesus!

ACTRESS TWO: Rich as Midas!

ACTOR: Rich as Onassis!

ACTOR ONE: Where does all his money come from? Is he in business?

ACTRESS ONE: I don't know if I should be saying this, but I've heard that Gogol's money doesn't quite come from legal sources. In fact, they say he's a gangster.

ACTOR: Narcotics.

ACTRESS TWO: You must be kidding. Mr. Gogol is the sole owner of Consolidated Aerospace Industries. He's the man who made the Venus landing possible.

ACTOR ONE: I believe you have him confused with Mr. Sogol. Our host, Gogol, is a ne'er-do-well, inherited it all from his mother, some kind of countess. Quite a playboy in his youth, I hear.

ACTRESS ONE: That's the motorcycle racing champion, Bogol. Mr. Gogol is nothing that exciting. He's in the poultry business. Acres of chickens. Sells the parts to those chain stores. Couldn't get along without him.

ACTRESS TWO: I don't know. I'm certain he's connected with sports in some way. Isn't he the most valuable player in the professional punchball league? What do you think, Doctor Mesmer?

MESMER: I . . .

ACTRESS ONE: I've got it! I wasn't sure when I received the invitation, but now . . . Gogol made his first million in nuts and bolts, then he invested heavily in the stock of a company manufacturing plastic internal organs, has some money in pet cemeteries, and he's in on a lot of boondoggles and crusades.

ACTOR ONE: Loot! That's it! He's the man who plundered the Saracens.

ACTRESS TWO: Really? How romantic.

ACTOR: Relax, darling. He's just an investment banker, or a phony medium who works the geriatric circuit. What do you think, Doctor Mesmer?

MESMER: I . . .

ACTRESS TWO: Our host is a very sick man, I hear.

ACTOR ONE: When I told some friends at lunch I was invited here tonight, they told me he had yellow fever.

ACTRESS ONE: Nothing so tame, I'm afraid. The man is incurably syphilitic. It's eating his brain away. I read it in the papers.

ACTOR TWO: They'll print anything, darling. Gogol happens to be ill with scurvy, which he contracted on a recent tropical expedition. Only one of his party to survive, I believe. I'm surprised he's socializing at all in his condition.

ACTRESS TWO: You are all mistaken. It's the plague. First case on this island in four hundred years. What do you think, Doctor Mesmer?

MESMER: I . . .

> *Mistress has risen before Mesmer begins speaking, comes over and, before he can speak to the other "guests," takes his arm and draws him away.*

MISTRESS: And the really fabulous thing about Gogol is his love affairs. The man just never stops doing it. But I don't need to tell his secrets to you. You're his doctor.

MESMER: No, I never have . . .

MISTRESS: I'm his mistress, but I won't be for long. I'm nobody.

I was swimming in the sea, and Gogol scooped me up in a net and wouldn't throw me back. But before me there was the Duchess of Bilgewater...

ACTRESS ONE: And Carmelita Pepita, the Bolivian Bombshell!

ACTOR ONE: The Dowager Empress of China!

ACTOR TWO: Sweet Rosy O'Grady!

ACTRESS TWO: And the Wicked Witch of the West!

MISTRESS: And so you see, he's a man of experience.

ACTRESS ONE: Of finesse!

ACTRESS TWO: Of generosity!

ACTOR ONE: Of courage!

ACTOR TWO: Of innocence!

MESMER: To be honest I never even heard of the man until...

MISTRESS: Hush! Or he'll hear you. He's busy preparing the theatricals. He'll be out to introduce them presently. Let's you and I...

Her voices fades to inaudibility as music rises. It is Mozart, as usual. Mesmer and Mistress dance in a small circle. We hear the actors over the music.

ACTRESS ONE: That's Doctor Mesmer, the wonderworker.

ACTOR ONE: The humbug, you mean.

ACTOR TWO: The fugitive, rather. The police are after him. Searching this very moment.

ACTRESS TWO: How exciting.

All four actors join in the dance, along with Mesmer and Mistress. Inspector Bucket appears in the distance, in his office. The Resurrection Man, drugging his corpse, enters to him. The Mozart is soft, and the dancers whirl slowly.

BUCKET: Well? What you you got for me this time?

RESURRECTION MAN: Something you'll like, Inspector Mesmer.

BUCKET: Where?

RESURRECTION MAN: In the nighttime. He wouldn't buy, Inspector, so I came to you. I can't leave this lovely without a home. I came to you.

BUCKET: Where did he go?

RESURRECTION MAN: I followed him, Inspector, to the big house outside of town. The one with the iron gates made with strange pictures. Makes me feel funny to look at 'em.

BUCKET: Gogol's. What I was afraid of. Thank you, and thank you. You are a servant of justice and a benefactor of the good people of Istanbul. Now, on your way, and take the pale lady with you.

RESURRECTION MAN: Silver, Inspector. Silver's what I came for, silver's what I speak for, and you'll have me here until I taste the metal.

BUCKET: Here, then, and go. [*Bucket hands him silver coins, then sits down, thinking.*]

RESURRECTION MAN: Inspector, get him! Don't sit there waiting for him to rise up in front of you like a ghost. My words weren't words for you to sit on 'em.

BUCKET: Still, a little time. He's not ripe yet for plucking. A little while. Go there, and watch over him till I arrive. Keep him safe in your eye . . . .

RESURRECTION MAN: Good Doctor Mesmer thinks I'm a worm under his shoes he does, a man who's done more for science with my back than he's done with his magic hands. I ain't scared on 'em. I'll be there. But before I go, Inspector, if you was thinking to do a little anatomizing on the cold nights, I got a young lady here could help you. Buy from me, sir. It's a wet night and I'm soaked to the bones. Inside the bones is all cold water . . .

BUCKET: Get out! I'll find you when I need you.

RESURRECTION MAN: Come on dearie. [*The corpse rises. He bops it down.*] Quiet now. There'll be a home for you yet. We'll give Doctor Mesmer another try. [*The Resurrection Man exits. Bucket is sunk in contemplation. This scene fades.*]

MR. GOGOL BRINGS ON THE THEATRICALS

Gogol enters. The dancing stops. The music fades. The Mistress leads Mesmer over to Gogol.

MISTRESS: Gogol, Mesmer. Mesmer, Gogol.

MESMER: How do you do.

GOGOL: Doctor Mesmer, we are ready to begin. I know everything about you. You know nothing about me, but you will know all. Don't listen to rumors. The truth is, I'm a simple man, and not well. But you are not here in your professional capacity. Listen. I am an author who has produced, for the past twenty years, silence. Not complete, however. There have been some small theatricals for the entertainment of my staff and guests. These I have written, but it is the work of a moment, a white colt passing by a crack in the wall. Gone. I maintain a small troupe of actors to aid me in this idleness. We shall see their work, don't you think? Lights! [*Animal servants dim lights, candles, etc.*] Be seated, please.

The other "guests" seat themselves quickly as audience for the small red-curtained stage on stage. It is brought forward. The only seat for Mesmer is front and center, in a row by itself. Mesmer takes this seat. Gogol leads his Mistress to a seat in the rear of this little audience.

Come, madam, sit by my side and let the world slip: we shall ne'er be younger. Begin!

After Gogol's announcement to "begin," the curtain does

not open. The scene is as follows: all in the on-stage audience, except for Mesmer, are in darkness. He, at the very front, is in the pool of light, very bright, that shines on the red curtain of the small stage. As soon as darkness permits, the actors ("guests") leave when necessary to change and perform parts in the theatricals. The four of them do all the roles.

From alongside the stage a young girl comes out into the light. She is dressed in rags, and has with her a large pink wooden pig, mounted on wheels, which she drags along after her on a rope. The pig is old and cracked, and in need of a paint job. She is most tender with it at all times, treating it much as a child. She is confused, and finally seems to locate the audience.

GOGOL: And who, may I ask, is that unscheduled urchin? The acts are ordered and set. Why this delay?

MISTRESS: [*Moving into the light.*] She was performing with her pig on streetcorners for pennies, dear Gogol. I found her on my visit to the city, and thought she would be a sweet addition to the theatricals. A little surprise.

GOGOL: Then let her get on with it. [*Mistress returns to her seat.*]

"THE PORKER PUNDIT"

GIRL: I do hope, sirs and ladies, that my pig will be good tonight and tell you, every one, that what you wish in your heart to know. He can do it, and that's why he's called the Porker Pundit, a fancy name to be sure for my own dear piggy, but his own true name, for my father gave it to him, and when he died, he gave piggy to me. Isn't that right, piggy dear? The Porker Pundit can answer any question, so if you'll look into your heart and see there what you most wish to know and ask, he'll answer, and there's no need to throw a penny, for the kind lady has given us already, oh more than we deserve. Isn't that right and true, piggy dear? Who would like to ask a question first? Ask, oh ask! [*Silence, punctuated by coughs, from the audience*]

It's so simple, sirs and ladies, and don't be frightened. Piggy talks inside your head and tells you the answer. Nobody else will know! It helps you to look at him. If you can't hear the Porker Pundit inside your head after you ask your question, I'll help and tell you the answer. It's always in my head, even when I don't know what it means. Spelled out in big letters, like the ones that start the story in picture books. So please, sirs and ladies, ask! [*Silence from the audience on-stage. She turns to Mesmer*] Please, sir, why don't you try? If no one asks a question my part here is done, and I return into the nighttime.

MESMER: What will become of me?

Girl gestures gracefully toward the pig. Silence for about twenty seconds.

GIRL: Did the Pundit speak to you, doctor?

MESMER: How do you know I'm a doctor?

GIRL: Everyone knows Doctor Mesmer. The people tell lies about you in the street.

MESMER: The Pundit said nothing.

GIRL: You didn't hear him.

MESMER: He said nothing.

GIRL: You didn't hear him, even though you are Doctor Mesmer, and I'll just have to tell you.

You're going on a long journey! You're going to Singapore! And Hong Kong! And America.

MESMER: [*getting up*] You're a liar.

GIRL: No! I'm not! I saw it! A long journey. I did make up the places, but the journey I saw. Piggy showed me.

MESMER: You lie again. What did you see? What? The truth!

GIRL: He doesn't believe you, piggy dear. Let's go. Dr. Mesmer, I hope they find you, and they will. Where can you go from here?

Mesmer moves as if to grab her. She backs away from him, mounts her pig, and it goes off under its own power, into the darkness.

GOGOL: Well done, doctor. Such trash shouldn't be allowed to deceive decent people with their tricks. But please, sit back and let the world glide on. Here comes Stanley, Henry M. Stanley, still looking, just where I left him.

A man enters through the closed curtain of the small stage, and moves down onto the space between the stage and Mesmer. He has a moustache, pith helmet, ragged and dirty safari garb, knapsack and binoculars. He looks carefully around.

I doubt he'll find anyone here. Darkest Africa is the place, but the poor man has been wandering for years. . . .

"STANLEY IN AFRICA"

Stanley spots Mesmer, stares, rubs his eyes, begins to pull himself together for their meeting. He is ecstatic, unsure, then certain. He advances towards Mesmer.

STANLEY: Doctor Mesmer, I presume!

MESMER: Yes. But I. . .

STANLEY: Mesmer! Mesmer, old man, it's you, at last! You don't know what its been like. Ten years! The tse-tse fly, the giant worm, the vines. The vines! The natives! Whenever

I asked directions to you the wogs would confuse me with gibberish. Pretending they didn't speak English! But I fooled them! Had the last laugh. Found you after all, eh! Pretty elusive fellow, aren't you?

MESMER: Aren't you searching for Doctor *Livingstone*?

STANLEY: Living who?

MESMER: Livingstone.

STANLEY: [*Fumbling in his knapsack.*] Hmmm. I don't recall that name, but let me see. I've got my orders right here. I'm to interview you for the Iowa City Bugle, you know. Ah... here's my editor's note. [*Stanley looks at scrap of paper.*] No. You're wrong. Clear as a mirror. "Find Dr. Mesmer."

MESMER: Let me see that.

STANLEY: Na na na. No fair peeking. Come now, I've found you fair and square, and we're going to have a lot of fun here in the jungle. I imagine you've gotten to know a few of the dusky beauties who reside hereabouts. Hmmm. Let's stroll around the verandah, shall we, and I'll tell you the news from home. [*Stanley drags Mesmer with him, and they walk about, arm in arm, in front of the stage.*] Your neighbor, Mrs. Gilpin, had twins and they both look the same. Your Uncle Bob lost his job at the slaughterhouse, and the shock treatments don't help. Your old girl friend Rhonda got married and moved to Cloud Cuckoo Land. We got a new traffic light at Main Street, but so many folks are color-blind that it... [*Stanley stops this talk abruptly.*] On second thought, let's you and I go to the theatre, Doctor. There's a little play by Mr. Gogol I believe you'll find quite entertaining, after forty-two years in the land of Mumbo-Jumbo! Just turn around.

   Stanley turns Mesmer around until he is facing the stage,

*and pushes him toward it. At that moment the curtain
opens to reveal the chained woman, and Stanley has disappeared. She is the same chained woman we have seen before, about twenty, and her clothes, torn suggestively, are
modern, jeans and a top. She is barefoot. The cardboard
wall behind her, which is the only thing on the small stage,
is a sloppily painted version of a dungeon cell wall. Her
"chains," which secure her by the wrists but give her some
play from side to side, are also clearly cardboard.*

GOGOL: [*from the darkness*] I hope in this play, at any rate,
someone will remember their lines, and not attempt to save
their abrasive performances by initiating repugnant audience contact. I'm glad you remembered who you were,
Doctor. Please continue.

"HERE IN THE CASTLE"

*Mesmer returns to his seat. There is a bit of music, soft
Mozart, as the girl begins. She wriggles slowly in her
chains, like a woman underwater.*

CHAINED GIRL: Here in the castle, I'm given everything I need
to live. Except the illusion of freedom. I don't need it anymore. In its place, there is love. And safety. I learned to
love all the feelings my body can give me. I used to not
like some of them, but now I love them all. My body is
a wonderful temple. [*Pause, and then in a loud whisper
at first*] That isn't all true. I'm not quite as good as I should
be. I guess I still have more to learn. Right now I have
an itch. I don't love it. I wish it would go away. . . I think
I hate them all, Mr. Gogol and the rest. You're looking
at me. Do you like me? I didn't used to think I was special,

but now I do. Why don't you come up here on stage, so I can see you, too. It's so dark out there, you could be anyone. My body can't. . .

She is suddenly quiet as Mordecai, the accountant, in his business suit, walks on stage. He is shaking his head, as if he is forced to discipline a naughty child. In a very unsensual way, he rips a strip off her blouse, and gags her very tightly with it so she cannot speak. He exits. The audience, excepting Dr. Mesmer, applauds lightly. She writhes slowly in her paper chains, very sexy, and in pain. Mesmer rises from his seat, takes a step toward the stage. He hesitates. In that moment the Resurrection Man comes blinking into the light, into the space between the stage and the audience. He looks at the chained girl, blows his nose, leaves his corpse below the stage, and climbs up onto it. The girl looks at him passively.

GOGOL: What now? It seems this is to be an evening of interruptions.

MISTRESS: It's only the Resurrection Man. . .

RESURRECTION MAN: [*To Chained Girl*] Hello, Miss, I was watching through the window, looking for Dr. Mesmer there, but when I saw you I says to myself, there's the kind of girl Old Jocko likes to do the in and out with, and no mistake. Sweet as honey, and strung up tight. Do you know me, girlie?

During the rest of the speech, the Resurrection Man is pawing and pinching the girl as if she was a horse he was going to buy. Also, Mesmer draws closer to the stage.

I'm the man who brings them back, and a little thing like you would do to chase the cold. Now my labors ain't all that hard, cause the grave is fresh, and ain't had time to pack, and I don't dig up the coffin like some people think.

A man alone, and that is how I works at my labors, dearie, just uncovers the top half of the box, and breaks the lid in with his shovel. Then I slides down in there, and set a rope around my new friend, under the arms, and haul her up. Then I strips the body and put the clothes back into grave. I'm not one for stealing, love. The body goes in the sack. The artistic part is what comes next, where I shows my skill, man and boy, for forty years. The grave's got to be the same. Like nobody touched it. The same dirt goes back into the hole as came out, and every stone, every flower, every blade of grass has got to be back the same as it was. Perfect. When the family comes on Sunday, they can weep without even the tiniest suspicion that the loved one ain't below. Nothing happened. Nothing happened, that's my motto. What's yours?

By this time the Resurrection Man has one hand of hers out of the chains, one hand of his down her pants, and has begun to put her over his shoulder and carry her off. Mesmer leaps onstage, grabs the Resurrection Man by the arm, the girl suddenly screams, and then the voice of Gogol.

GOGOL: Doctor Mesmer, please. It will be taken care of. I appreciate your sentiments, and your lively response to the performance, but you don't think I'd allow my theatre's finest actress to be carted off by that lunatic, who no doubt came here either to spy on you for the police, or to attempt to sell me the corpse he's brought with him. Isn't that so?

RESURRECTION MAN: Now that you say it, Mr. Gogol, the body I have on board is something special. I thought you'd enjoy...

GOGOL: Silence! Doctor, sit down. [*Mesmer does so.*] Continue.

RESURRECTION MAN: Continue?

He begins again to try to walk off with the girl. Pontius Pilate walks out onto the stage [the small stage], a man in high ranking Roman garb. He steps out in front of the curtain line.

PILATE: Close the curtain. They no longer amuse me. Get rid of him, and give her to the legion at Jerusalem Gate, or kill her. Let it be her choice.

The curtain closes behind him. He seats himself on a chair before it, but on the stage. He bows his head. A wine jug is on the floor by his side. Silence. In the distance the figures of Tarr and Fether appear, peering and pointing toward the main action. They rise and bow to each other, fade away, and disappear. Pilate looks up at the audience, onstage and off.

"PONTIUS PILATE THINKS IT OVER"

PILATE: My judges! I'm pleased at your arrival, as I wish this matter to be resolved without delay. I am Pontius Pilate, procurator of Judea, Tetrarch of Galilee, Commander of Valdaran's Green Region and twenty cohorts of assorted cavalry. I am great Caesar's legate here in the desert, among madmen. I am an imperial servant, and demand to be judged with every privilege to which my rank entitles me. Excuse me. [*He drinks wine.*]

Here in Jerusalem, the days are burning, and a twilight damp mists from the Dead Sea fill the streets. The climate is idiotic. It has driven the Jews insane. The rays of the sun lead them to every crank and false prophet who cries "water!" I am troubled, my judges, and my hope is that either you will absolve me so that I may continue to administer this wretched city for the greater glory of Rome, and attempt to put some sense into the minds of these intractable people, or that you will send me home where, under charge or no, I may rest, and present my report in full to Caesar. That my death may also be a solution to the problem my failure to understand the native population may have created for Rome, is for you to judge. Excuse me. [*Drinks wine*]

I am troubled...Decent baths are unknown here, and their construction is secondary, where the streets still run with human filth. The amusements of their simple cookery and simpler women are soon exhausted. If you live long enough in these climes, my judges, the study of the local mystery cults is an answer to your consuming boredom. I have indulged my scholarly appetites. But my memory fails me...

Pilate trails off, is silent. In the distance the figure of Inspector Bucket appears, on the same midnight street we have seen before. He puts his forefinger into his mouth, holds it up in the wind. He shrugs his shoulders in resignation, walks forward along the street, and disappears from view as the scene fades.

Render unto God what is Caesar's, and unto Caesar what is God's. Neither of them is aware of any difference. ...The loaves in the vineyard...the camel and the mustardseed. Seek not, and ye shall find. Knock and it shall be closed against you. A stitch in time saves nine. Every dog has his day. I fear I have murdered the Messiah, the world honored one. I saw it in a dream.

The day before I ordered the execution of Jesus of Nazareth I ordered the execution of Simon bar Nachman, a magician and fortuneteller from Bethany. The day before that

I ordered the crucifixion of a Persian who exhorted the people to go naked and worship the sun. Before that a legionaire from Sicily for gambling. Before that Mithridates, a Hebrew from somewhere to the east, who preached a doctrine of personal freedom that could not coexist with great Caesar's plans for this territory. The man Jesus performed miracles. Juliana the Saracen, a nameless learned Greek, and every man of the Dust Worshippers of Arabia performed miracles as well, and them all I put to the sword. He told me nothing when I questioned him. If he was the Messiah in truth, he could have been sent to Rome, so that Caesar might examine him, and have him teach. If he was the Messiah in truth, he would have held back my hand. These words I say, but I do not believe them. I saw this too, in the dream, as I saw there as well, your judgment. Judge now, quickly, and let me have peace. Be it on your heads.

MISTRESS: Death!

ACTOR ONE: Death!

ACTRESS ONE: Death!

ACTRESS 2: Death!

GOGOL: Death!

PILATE: Well done. I have lived long enough. Here!

> Pilate takes a gun out from under his tunic, tosses it to Mesmer, and kneels. Mesmer rises to catch it.

I need no ceremony, no words. I have heard enough of them, all my life. [*Silence. Mesmer holds the gun down by his side.*]

ACTOR ONE: Kill him!

ACTRESS ONE: Think of his crimes, the people he's murdered!

ACTRESS 2: Go ahead! Can't you see he wants it?

MISTRESS: [*Coming up alongside Mesmer*] Shoot him, Doctor.

You're spoiling the play. They're only blanks anyway.

MESMER: He's not guilty. He should be sent home.

MISTRESS: He has no home. Kill him. That's how it goes.

MESMER: All right. I'll play. [*He raises the gun and points it at Pilate's head.*]

PILATE: Mercy! Mercy! Spare me, doctor. . . I didn't know what I was doing. How could I tell it was him? Could you? He looked just like any other nut off the street. Besides, that gun has real bullets in it. I loaded it myself. Mercy! Mercy! [*Pilate breaks down and sobs uncontrollably.*]

MESMER: Shut up! You've done enough. Your part here is ended.
Mesmer shoots Pilate. Blood, as realistic as possible. Pilate falls. Mesmer is shocked. He drops the gun to the floor.

GOGOL: Well done, and haul that tub of guts into the next room! [*A bear drags Pilate's body off the small stage and away.*] What follows here, as is the custom, is but a little epilogue, wherein the actors thank the audience, and beg their indulgence. It will be brief, and the theatrics are at an end.

"A LITTLE EPILOGUE"

The curtain opens. A middle-aged man, modern beat-up work clothes, steps forward, down off the stage, and stands before it.

MAN: My dog got killed today. Hit by a car. When I got to her the blood was still pumping out onto the highway, right on the white line. I picked her up and she was sticky all over from the blood. I started to carry her to the truck to bring her to the vet, and I laid her on the front seat, and the blood wasn't pumping anymore, and I figured,

that's dumb. She's dead. That's a dead dog I'm looking
at on the front seat of the truck. I closed the door of the
truck, locked it, and I threw the key in the bushes and
started walking. I got here. I remember the car that hit
her. I was standing right there, watching like a blind man
. . . was a new green Chevrolet, man and a woman, didn't
even slow down. If I ever find them, I will cut their hearts
out from their bodies and leave them lying in the sun.
That's the one thing I know. Meanwhile, I guess I'm looking for work. You got a job for a man like me?

*Man holds out one hand, palm up and cupped, and
steps forward. He sees no one.*

Nobody around. I guess I might sit down and rest. [*He
goes up on the small stage*] This field sure is pretty. [*He
sits down, his legs spread in front of him.*] Lots of butter-
cups, and them purple fuzzy ones. And the sun's bright.
It's heating me clear through, and I'm sweating all over.
Lookit that little bird. He's flying up there and his wings
ain't even moving.

Lord Jesus have pity on me. I been left here alone.

There's something. . . moving on the edge of the hill. It's
a woman, and the brush sways and bends as she passes
through. She's flesh like me. Here! Here! [*He waves his
arms, without rising from the floor*] It's all right. When
she gets here, she'll pick me up, and carry me home. . . .

*Man falls silent, staring out. The man's head relaxes,
slumps. Light and tentative applause from the onstage audience. The curtain closes. As it closes, the band (again,
Mozart) strikes up. Gogol silences it with a wave of his
hand. All actors, in their formal dress again, gradually
group themselves with the animals and Gogol's Mistress
so as to form a physical backdrop for what follows.*

"MESMER'S CURE"

GOGOL: My little theatricals have ended, Doctor, and I hope
they have stirred the audience. I hope they have opened
a wound that won't close, a dark space in the center of
the chest, in which darkness, if they look carefully, they
can see the stars.

But now, Doctor Mesmer, it is your turn to perform.
You are here, by my invitation, for a purpose. I am dying. I find this disappointing, and am prepared to deal with
it in one of two ways. This depends on you. I want you
now to cure me. Use those powers which have made you
the talk of New York, and cure me. [*Gogol lowers his
voice.*] If you succeed with me, I plan to run away. They
don't know. I'll get a blackthorn stick and a good pair of
shoes. I wish an old age in which to live behind railroad
stations, and give candy to children as raggedy as myself.
Every man has the right, at the end, to become God's
tramp, and sleep under the hill.

MESMER: It would be my pleasure to provide the tonic of the
magnetic influence. . .

GOGOL: None of your bullshit! Even yet, you don't see. You
are here. I could turn you over to the police, who even
now are drifting through the streets, sniffing for you,
waiting by your laboratory door. Your nurse is a particular
friend of mine. I know you, Mesmer. I can help you. Cure
me, and anything may follow.

MESMER: My treatments require the. . .

GOGOL: Stop! I don't want your excuses, or your equipment.
I am dying, do you understand that? I want you to take
my death by the hand, and lead it from me. Now.

MESMER: That would be a joke. I can't help you, Mr. Gogol.

You'll have to just crawl off in a corner and die. It would be a blind exercise. I'm a liar and a thief, and it's over. The police are waiting. I can't go home, or back to my laboratory. I've played my hand for too much, and it never held anything at all. My cures have been good fortune, an accident of my nervous system, electricity from heaven, the dumb faith of my patients, god knows what else. I'm done.

GOGOL: You are a doctor.

MESMER: I made myself a doctor.

GOGOL: Then you can't desert your profession. Listen, good Doctor Mesmer. Listen to me. You don't know what you are. You don't know you are a fraud, a quack. You don't know you are a healer. You don't know. If you fail, I will walk the road I would walk if you had never lived. Let me be your final case.

MESMER: You are not a young woman with a nervous condition. It would be a mockery.

GOGOL: Let it be that, then. Besides, what's a party without bringing someone back from the dead? You will try, and if you succeed, you will have given the world another senile old loon to wander its streets and country lanes. A great deed. If you fail, you will have done nothing but perform a little charade with me. Begin!

MESMER: Why not? We will commence, and end, your treatment now.

Gogol gestures. The turtle enters, with a broad platform on his back. He halts stage center, and collapses to a shell. Gogol mounts the platform and seats himself on the single chair on it. Mesmer also mounts the platform and stands by him. Mesmer begins to examine Gogol.

MESMER: Where is the pain.

GOGOL: There is none. I have no pain.

MESMER: Then what is wrong with you, that you brought me here to heal you?

GOGOL: Wrong? Nothing. I told you. It is just that I am dying. My death has come for me, and takes various forms. A raw wound in my side as big as an apple. Blood congealing around my heart. Dizziness. Wandering in a dark valley, and voices speak to me from mountains far away. That which moves my body has gathered into light at the top of my skull, ready to burst the bone.

MESMER: It seems to me you will live yet for years.

GOGOL: If you don't cure me I will die. This I swear, and you will see it through tonight. Don't be a fool. I am Gogol. I await my death with patience and skill. You are an accident here, and perhaps that changes things. Cure me of fading away beneath my skin. Cure me of this transparency. Light and air fill me up, meat and blood are gone. Inside me grows an empty room, dusty, quiet, no one has disturbed its peace for years. Thin beams of light enter it through my eyes and ears, bright spots on the floor. Thin. Criss cross. I am a shell, ready to fly. Hold me down, doctor, if you can.

MESMER: It's your party. [*To all but Gogol*] Please clasp hands firmly, and link yourselves in a ring about us, so that the magnetic influence will be sealed and unbroken.

Done. This is the circle. They obey, so that around and below Gogol and Mesmer are the remaining figures onstage (Four actors, Mistress, two bears) hand in hand, circling the platform on the turtle's back as slowly as possible. They should complete one full circle by the time the goings on above them are done. Soft music, which fades.

Do you want the words as well?

GOGOL: All of it.

MESMER: The magnetic current, with its sources in the depths of the earth and the depths of space, is channeled through me, and by me, through my hands. I first will pass them over you at a distance from your body, so as to send the initial currents through you gently. You should feel the healing vibrations almost immediately.

GOGOL: Get on with it, Doctor.

> *Mesmer passes his hands about Gogol's upper body. He is in a posture of extreme tension. Gogol is relaxed.*

MESMER: Did you feel anything?

GOGOL: Definite and clear. You are quite extraordinary, doctor. Pray go on.

MESMER: When I touch you, you may feel burning at first, but this will change to a healing warmth and vibration that will penetrate every cell of your body, cell by cell. . . Now.

> *Mesmer reaches out, touches Gogol's temples, and staggers back as if he has had an electric shock. He tries again. Again the shock, which throws him violently off the platform and to the floor of the stage. His body breaks the circle.*

GOGOL: Try again, doctor.

MESMER: What are you doing to me? You're the lightning—

GOGOL: [*stepping down off the platform.*] I am letting you feel the charge of my death, and you cannot hold it, or drain it away. So be it.

> *Gogol waves a hand. The actors, Mistress, bears, take more casual positions in the space. The turtle with the platform moves off.*

I have no choice. It is now necessary that *I* cure *you*.

MESMER: I'm fine, thank you.

GOGOL: Doctor, do you know that for twenty million years,

more than there are hairs in the beard of God, the gentle brontosaurus munched watery cabbage in the muck. He was strong and he was dumb. He had two brains, one in his head to blink his great eyelids, and one in his tail to help him wiggle it. He thought the world was made of blood and steam. And sometimes, Doctor Mesmer, when the moon rolled over his head like a fat yellow stone, he thought of you, sitting in your office, scheming and scaring yourself. He dreamed you one way in his tiny head, and another in his tail. And that is you. That's all. You're a double dream in a dead dinosaur. You're Doctor Mesmer. You're a fly buzzing around my pisspot. You're this and that and something else, and you're so busy being things and wanting to be things that you're nothing at all. Good. Otherwise, we couldn't even begin. And you're in luck. There's no need for you to find out who you are. I've done it for you. [*Gogol makes boxing motions, not comically, and not directed at Mesmer.*] The referee has reached nine, sir, but I'm about to ring the bell.

TARR AND FETHER INTERVENE

Tarr and Fether rush onstage, in between Gogol and Mesmer. They bow to Gogol.

GOGOL: Good evening. My favorite comedians, Doctor Tarr and Professor Fether.

TARR: Sorry to disturb you, Mr. Gogol.

FETHER: We don't mean any harm, Mr. Gogol. We do as we're told.

TARR: Yes, indeed. As we're told. Inspector Bucket sent us.

GOGOL: Get on with it, then.

TARR AND FETHER: Thank you, Mr. Gogol.

GOGOL: Dr. Mesmer, they're all yours. [*Gogol backs away.*]

TARR: Good evening, Doctor Mesmer.

FETHER: Good evening, Doctor Mesmer. Would you like to know our jobs?

TARR: Professor Fether is a mirror. And I'm a mirror of his mirror. So we're all mirrors together. That's our job.

FETHER: We were sent for you.

MESMER: Gogol, get rid of them. [*Tarr and Fether close in on Mesmer.*]

TARR: I'm good.

FETHER: I'm bad.

TARR: I'm shit.

FETHER: I'm shining light.

TARR: I'm wonderful.

FETHER: God's pet.

TARR: Mother's calling.

FETHER: My nervous system is a finely tuned arabesque.

TARR: Gogol is crazy.

FETHER: Gogol wants my pajamas.

TARR: I'm better than everyone else.

FETHER: Why is that muscle in my back twitching?

TARR: She doesn't like me.

FETHER: I'm a faker.

TARR: A robber.

FETHER: A stealer of souls.

TARR: A wonder worker.

FETHER: The world is doomed.

TARR: If the people from Mars only get here on time, they'll take care of everything.

FETHER: It's hopeless. I'll flee to Zurich and break the stock exchange.

TARR: I'll get a job with the circus.

FETHER: I remember this girl from High School...

TARR: One large with mushrooms and pepperoni, and a pack of Luckies.

FETHER: God is gonna get my name in the papers.

TARR: I'm noble, and everyone else is mean.

FETHER: If I just breathe deeply and focus on my...

TARR: Let me out of here!

FETHER: Maybe this Gogol character will slip me a few bucks and I can hop the 11:15 to Cincinnati.

TARR: Maybe this Gogol character is with the police.

FETHER: Maybe this Gogol character is going to kill me.

GOGOL: Get rid of them, Doctor. They're driving me mad in the bargain.

MESMER: How?

GOGOL: Why don't you knock their heads together?

> *Mesmer grabs Dr. Tarr and Prof. Fether and knocks their heads together. There is a loud metallic gong at the moment of impact. They fall in a heap.*

Well done, Doctor. But Inspector Bucket can't be far behind. You won't get rid of him so easily. [*To Mistress*] Give these two to the Resurrection Man. He can haul them to the junkyard.

> *The Mistress beckons to the two bears, who drag Tarr and Fether offstage, and return.*

MESMER: I believe I better get out of here.

GOGOL'S CURE

GOGOL: We have arrived at the point where we are forgetting what you believe. I have already forgotten it. I advise you

to follow my example. I don't need your notions about
yourself to help us. I need you.

MESMER: What are you? Are you one of the doctors?

GOGOL: I'm the jack-of-all-trades, and I am about to retire.
Listen. Certain men are seed-men. You are one, but this
does not mean that you have not stupidly gotten yourself
known, and become mildly useful, and displayed your talent as if it was something you had earned. You have been
a fool. This will cease. You are to become my cup. This
has its compensations, for a man in your position. [*Sings*]
When Gogol drinks, Mesmer gets tipsy. When Mesmer
stumbles, Gogol falls. . .

MESMER: What do you think you're going to do with me? What
is the big idea?

GOGOL: I am going to let you out.

MESMER: Out? There's nowhere left for me to go. Out where?
*The two bears move to either side of Mesmer, ready
to hold him if he should run. They do not touch him.*

GOGOL: Let me put it simply. I am going to hide you forever.
You can stop thinking of escape. You can stop weighing
your chances. I am not the police. I am your refuge and
your hope.

MESMER: I failed to cure you. I'm nothing to you. No one. You
are going to do me a favor it seems, a great favor. I don't
trust it. Help me. What do you want out of this?

GOGOL: I want to die.

MESMER: You've changed your mind.

GOGOL: No.

MESMER: That is your affair. What have I to do with it?

GOGOL: You have nothing to do with it. It will just happen.
And your safety and your life will come to you. I can't
imagine more than a moment of doubt before you crack

your shell.

MESMER: [*Looking at bears on either side of him*] I don't have a choice.

GOGOL: You made it long ago. [*He takes a step toward the audience.*] Now we can proceed to the climax of the evening: my death. Don't send flowers. However, there's to be some little formality. Leaving a place as pleasant as this round ball of ours requires some little grace note. I've barely gotten used to it . . . .

Some little direction, Doctor Mesmer, for yourself, though you'll find your way well enough. It's like a summer birdcage in a garden. The birds that are without despair to get in, and the birds that are within despair that they shall never get out. You are not a bird. Don't despair. Don't wobble. Don't make a fool of yourself. Now, let me die.

Gogol takes a seated position stage center. All the others, bears included, gather around him. Mistress chants, half-song, half speech.

MISTRESS: Call for the robin redbreast and the wren
Where over shady groves they rise
And with leaves and flowers disguise
The bodies of unburied men.
Call unto the funeral house
The ant, the glowworm, and the mouse
To build him chambers that will keep him warm
And draw the circle that keeps him from harm.
Invite the silent wolf, that's foe to men
For with his nails he brings them up again.
The best I could with such short notice. Goodbye,
love.

GOGOL: Goodbye, and goodbye all, and goodbye to you, Doctor Mesmer. You had mercy, and you killed Pilate, but the weapon was fake. This is real [*Gogol produces a dagger from his clothes.*], but before you do me that favor...

MESMER: No. For whatever reasons, I cannot...

GOGOL: No reasons. None of them could do this for me. Believe it. You will save us both. You will. I see it. The last thing I see.

But before you do me that favor, a practice I learned from you. The healing bath!

A bear sneaks up behind Mesmer with a bucket of water, and dumps it over his head.

Good. Now, my damp executioner, drive the point of this blade through the top of my skull. One stroke, and clean. I don't wish to flop about like a fish. Break the shell for me, doctor, and let the light in.

Mesmer moves behind Gogol, so that the audience can see them both clearly, one above the other. Mesmer raises the dagger with both hands, brings it down through the top of Gogol's skull, withdraws it. Gogol goes limp, falls forward onto the floor. Silence. There is blood. One by one, all turn to look at Mesmer. One of the bears nuzzles him.

BUCKET AT LAST

MESMER: Leave him there.

MISTRESS: The charm is firm and good. Well done. [*She comes closer to Mesmer*] I'll take the dagger. We may need it again some day.

MESMER: We'll be having a visitor in a moment. Prepare yourselves, all.

Mesmer seats himself in the chair. He waves a hand. All present form a tableau about him. The corpse is alone. Music rises. Mozart. Doors crash open. The music stops. Inspector Bucket strolls in alone. He faces them.

BUCKET: I know you. You know me. I am Inspector Bucket. I extend my fingers, and at the end of them... [*He looks around carefully, then calls out.*] Doctor Tarr! Professor Fether! Where are my associates?

MISTRESS: In the scrapyard, face up, in the rain.

BUCKET: You don't say. I have been walking the midnight streets. Time and space are toys to Inspector Bucket. I have arrived. I have come for Mesmer.

Mistress first, then the actors, the bears, then Mesmer himself points to the corpse on the floor.

BUCKET: [*Looking at Mesmer*] This is how it is? This is what Mr. Gogol has for me. I will manage. The decision has been made. I have not been treated fairly, but I will manage. [*Calling*]Come in, and bring your rope![*The Resurrection Man enters with his looped rope. Bucket points to the corpse.*] Take Mesmer away. [*The Resurrection Man goes to the corpse, looks.*]

RESURRECTION MAN: But this is...

BUCKET: [*Screaming*] You don't know this is from that is, you grave grubber. Take the body of Doctor Mesmer away, and sell it in a far country, to anatomists who will leave it in shreds, unrecognizable meat.

RESURRECTION MAN: Come along with me quietly now... [*He loops his rope around the corpse and drags it offstage.*]

BUCKET: [*Looking at Mesmer*] Thank you, Mr. Gogol. I'm sorry to have disturbed you with this business, but this Doctor Mesmer was a dangerous fellow. Putting all sorts of ideas into people's heads. Thank you again, and if I can serve you in the future, let me know and I will come to you. Goodbye, and rest assured that everything will be taken care of to your satisfaction. Inspector Bucket, your servant, sir. [*Bucket bows, exits*]

The tableau around Mesmer is as before. Mistress moves very close to him. He raises one arm high.

MESMER-GOGOL: Music!

The string quartet beings to play Mozart. Mesmer-Gogol and his mistress begin to dance, swirling in slow circles. The two pairs of actors join them. Dance. Sudden darkness. Music continues and builds as the house lights come up.

Seventy Scenes
of Halloween

by
Jeffrey Jones

© Jeffrey Jones, 1980
CAUTION: No performances or readings of this work may be given without the express authorization of the author. For production rights, contact the author c/o New Dramatists, 424 West 44th Street, New York, NY 10036

Seventy Scenes of Halloween was originally performed by Creation Production Company at the Theatre at St. Clement's, New York City, September 18-October 12, 1980, with the following cast:

Jeff .... Christopher McCann

Joan .... Frederikke Meister

Beast .... Kevin O'Rourke

Witch .... Caroline McGee

Director: Matthew Maguire
Designer: Jim Clayburgh
Costumes: Maura Clifford

Dedicated with love and gratitude to Joan Gregorius Jones

GENERAL NOTES

The play consists of the seventy interchangeable scenes arranged in a given sequence. Different arrangements create different "stories" with different "meanings."

All scenes take place in the living room of a rented house. There are entrances from the front hallway, the kitchen and the upstairs. There is also a window with a view of the night outside and a wall closet. The furnishings include two easy chairs and a television set. The television set remains on and audible throughout the entire play.

With a few exceptions, each scene begins as indicated with an audible cue to bring up the lights of the room. Usually this will be done by the stage-manager offstage. Each scene ends with a blackout taken on a silent, visual cue. That the television will partially illuminate the set-up between scenes is intentional.

There are four actors in the play, two men and two women, all in their early thirties. Both men wear an identical basic costume of everyday clothing, as do both women. These are the costumes of the characters of Jeff and Joan, usually played by Actor & Actress 1.

There are also characters called Ghosts. Ghosts are created by draping an actor or actress with a common white bedsheet. Do not cut eyeholes in the sheet. It is usually not important which actor plays a Ghost, and at times it may be expedient to have the stage-manager also become a Ghost.

The other two characters are masked characters, the Beast and the Witch, usually played by Actor and Actress 2. These masks must be machine-made, store-bought Halloween masks. Generally speaking, the desirable ambiguity of these two more symbolic characters will be heightened by selecting more neutral, representational masks instead of grotesque or horrific masks.

The rest of their costumes should be kept simple to facilitate quick changes and should look homemade. It is not important that the underlying basic costume be totally concealed.

The beast has an animal's head (stag?) and wears a bright nylon poncho with bright rubber kitchen gloves. The witch has a woman's face (not necessarily old) and a black cape and gloves with the traditional conical hat.

The birdcall mentioned in the script should be of the variety which produces a chirping sound through the twisting of a metal pin in a wooden shank rather than the kind you blow through. The chicken is available at local supermarkets.

THE FIRST SCENE

s.m.: [*Off*] Scene one—go!

    Lights up: Actor 1 as Jeff is watching TV. He calls:

JEFF: Hey, Joan?

JOAN: [*Off*] What?

JEFF: Do we have any kandy korn?

JOAN: [*Off*] What?

JEFF: Do we have any kandy korn?

JOAN: [*Off*] What?

JEFF: Kandy korn!

    Joan?. . .

JOAN: [*Off*] What?

JEFF: Can you hear me?

JOAN: [*Off*] I can't hear you!

JEFF: DO...WE...HAVE...ANY...KANDY KORN?

JOAN: [*Off*] Kandy korn?

JEFF: Yes!

JOAN: [*Off*] No!

JEFF: Well, why not, God-damn it?

I thought I told you to get some.

(Shit.)

JOAN: [*Off*] What?

JEFF: Never mind!

Actress 1 as Joan enters from kitchen.

JOAN: I can't hear a thing you're saying when I'm out there.

Not one word.

JEFF: I'm sorry.

JOAN: I just hate shouting across the house, I hate it.

JEFF: Sorry.

JOAN: Why, did you want some?

JEFF: It's not important.

Let's forget it.

JOAN: Fine.

BLACKOUT.

THE SECOND SCENE

S.M.: [*Off*] Scene two—go!

*Lights up; Actress 1 as Joan is watching TV. Actor 1
calls from offstage.*

JEFF: [*Off*] Hey, Joan?

JOAN: What?

JEFF: [*Off*] Do we have any kandy korn?

JOAN: In the kitchen.

JEFF: [*Off*] What?

JOAN: In the kitchen!

JEFF: [*Off*] I am in the kitchen!

Did you say it's in the kitchen?

JOAN: Yes!

JEFF: [*Off*] What? I can't hear you.

Joan?. . .

JOAN: Yes!

JEFF: [*Off*] Did you say yes?

JOAN: Yes!

JEFF: [*Off*] Oh. . . okay. . . .

I'm looking for it, but. . . .

JOAN: Look in the cupboard over the sink.

JEFF: [*Off*] What?

JOAN: Look in the cupboard over the sink!

JEFF: [*Off*] I can't hear you!

JOAN: CUPBOARD. . . OVER. . . THE SINK!

JEFF: [*Off*] Wait a minute. . . .

Never mind, I found it. . . .

You know where it was?

It was in the cupboard over the sink.

I don't think that's such a great place for it, though.

Tell you what: I'm going to leave it in the pantry, okay?

Joan, is that okay?

JOAN: Yes!

JEFF: [*Off*] Okay. . . .

The doorbell rings.

Will you get that?

Joan is already going to the door.

Joan?. . .

JOAN: Yes, I'm getting it!

Joan exits towards front door.

BLACKOUT.

THE THIRD SCENE

s.m.: [*Off*] Three—go!

> *Lights up: Actress 1 as Joan is watching television. The doorbell rings.*

JOAN: I'll get it.

JEFF: [*Off*] Will you get that?

JOAN: What?

JEFF: [*Off*] Will you get the door?

JOAN: [*Rising*] That's what I said.

JEFF: [*Off*] Sorry.

JOAN: That's all right.

> *Joan exits toward front door.*
> *The Beast's head appears in the window.*

BLACKOUT.

THE FOURTH SCENE

s.m.: [*Off*] Four—go!

> *The Beast's head is in the window; barestage. From inside the closet comes the faint sound of scratching, then a birdcall. Actor & Actress 1 call from offstage.*

JEFF: [*Off*] Joan?

JOAN: [*Off*] I'm in the kitchen.

JEFF: [*Off*] Do we have any kandy korn?

JOAN: [*Off*] I'm in the kitchen.

JEFF: [*Off*] What?

JOAN: [*Off*] I can't hear you.

JEFF: [*Off*] Can you hear me?. . .

> Joan?. . .
>
> Hello?. . .

Actor 1 as Jeff enters from upstairs; the Beast disappears below window; the sounds stop.

Where are you?...

JOAN: [*Off*] Out in the kitchen.

JEFF: Oh, okay...

Jeff crosses the stage and exits towards kitchen. The Beast reappears and the sounds resume.

BLACKOUT.

THE SIXTH SCENE

S.M.: [*Off*] Six—go!

Lights up: Actor & Actress 1 as Jeff & Joan are watching TV.

JEFF: God-damn it!

Why the fuck didn't you get me that kandy korn like I asked?

JOAN: I'm sorry.

I didn't realize . . . .

JEFF: Didn't I ask you?

Didn't I ask you specifically...?

JOAN: Yes!

I just didn't think it was that big a deal.

JEFF: Not that big a deal?

Jesus Christ!

I ask you specifically to get something and you say it's not that big a deal?

I can't believe it—I fucking can't believe it!

It's like everything else!

It's like living with a fucking mongolian idiot! !

JOAN: Oh, shut up!

How was I supposed to know you wanted it for you?

JEFF: Well, who else...?

JOAN: I thought you just wanted me to get some for the kids!

All you said was: Get some kandy korn.

I thought you wanted it for the kids.

JEFF: So?

JOAN: So it's no good for the kids.

It's not wrapped.

If it's not wrapped they're not supposed to take it.

They even had a thing on the news.

JEFF: (Oh, Jesus!...)

Not you—I mean them. I'd forgotten about that.

JOAN: Besides, they didn't have any at the Pathmark store.

JEFF: Oh.

JOAN: If I'd known you wanted them I'd have looked elsewhere. But you didn't make that clear.

JEFF: I know. I'm sorry.

JOAN: That's all right.

JEFF: You want to watch this program?

JOAN: It's fine.

A Ghost walks swiftly past the window, as:

BLACKOUT.

THE FIFTH SCENE

S.M.: [*Off*] Five—go!

*Lights up: Actor 1 as Jeff is watching TV. Actress 1
as Joan enters from kitchen with large knife.*

JOAN: This knife is too dull, I can't cut with it.

I'm afraid to cut with it this way,

I'm afraid I'll cut myself, it's dangerous.

It's so dull, you know—it cuts,

But I'm afraid of it slipping and cutting my
finger,

They do that sometimes when they get dull.

JEFF: Unh-hunh . . . .

JOAN: So you'll sharpen it?

JEFF: What?

JOAN: You'll sharpen it?

JEFF: Yes.

Just leave it.

JOAN: You want me to leave it here?

Can I leave it here?

I'll leave it for you right here.

Is that okay?

JEFF: Fine.

JOAN: Okay.

I mean. I don't need it right away,

But as soon as you can get to it, that'll be great.

I mean, I could probably go ahead and use it anyway but

I'm afraid to cut myself,

You know?

JEFF: Right.

JOAN: Is there a better place to leave it?

JEFF: I'm watching TV.

JOAN: Oh. Sorry.

BLACKOUT.

THE THIRTY-FIFTH SCENE

S.M.: [Off] Thirty-five—go!

Lights up: Actor & Actress 1 as Jeff & Joan are watching TV. Actor 2 as the Beast looks in from the window, working the birdcall. The Humans do not react as they chant:

BEAST: Sometimes when I look up
HUMANS: in the bare branches
BEAST: I notice the bird
HUMANS: fly up in the branches
BEAST: I notice the branches
HUMANS: in the bare branches
BEAST: I feel the bird call me
HUMANS: out of the branches
BEAST: I feel the bird's eye on me
HUMANS: up in the branches
BEAST: I feel the cold wind
HUMANS: blow through the bare branches
BEAST: I feel very hungry
HUMANS: looking up at the branches
BEAST: I shout up my shout
HUMANS: back into the branches
BEAST: Then I notice the bird fall
HUMANS: out of the branches
BEAST: Then I feel afraid of the bird
    Then I become the bird
HUMANS: Then I feel afraid of the bird
    Then I become the bird
BEAST: Then I am standing alone again underneath the bare
    branches
HUMANS: And the leaves are falling down all around me from
    the bare branches. . .
ALL: OHHHHHHHHHHHHHHH!
    I. . .AM. . .SO. . .HUNGRYYYYYYY!
    YAH!
      A Ghost pops out of the closet and runs briefly about
    the room, fluttering and peeping.
GHOST: Feeeeeeeeed meeeeeeeee. . . . . .

Feeeeeeeed meeeeeeeee......
Feeeeeeeed meeeeeeeee......
BLACKOUT

THE SEVENTH SCENE

S.M.: [Off] Seven—go!

> *Lights up: Actor & Actress 1 as Jeff & Joan watching TV. Beat.*

JEFF: Scared of me?

JOAN: Well, kind of . . . .

But it's not *you*: I just . . . .

I just want to curl up and hide, that's all.

I don't know.

JEFF: Well, shit—I'm no ball of fire myself, sometimes—you know? I mean, I get scared too, I guess. I get squeamish—I guess that's the same thing . . . .

It's like I'm profoundly ambivalent. Either it's Fantasyland, right? You know? Turn-on City, swinging from the chandeliers (I mean, in my mind). Or else it's still something that's somehow degrading and . . . You know, that kind of thing. And I feel: if I could just find a middle ground . . . I mean, your feelings are: it's either this or that—And you have to stop and say to yourself: Now wait, I know it's not *really* like that. Even so, that doesn't automatically change the way you feel. Does this make sense?

JOAN: Unh-hunh.

JEFF: Like that's why I say sometimes, you know: Don't necessarily believe me when I act uninterested. I mean, sometimes I have to be convinced. Like a lot of times, I start out thinking I'm really turned off. And then once I get into it I go: Hey, this is really *great*! So that's what I mean when I say sometimes I have to look to you to start things.

JOAN: I know, but see: when you're not interested it's hard for me to keep going because I don't know, and sometimes I. . . I mean, I don't want to get all excited and then I have no place to go, you know?

The doorbell rings.

JEFF: (I'll get it in a sec.) Right.

JOAN: I guess it goes back to living with Lance: I mean, he used to get me so turned on. We'd be making it for hours, literally, with no clothes on; I would try everything, but he just wouldn't fuck me. I got so frustrated. . . I mean, that's where I learned to shut down.

The doorbell rings.

That's also why, man, when you lose it, that's it for me. I don't want to have to go digging around for it. I'm not begging for it.

JEFF: I gotta get the door—don't forget where we are, I'll be right back.

Jeff exits towards front door.

THE EIGHTH SCENE

S.M.: [*Off*] Eight—go!

Lights up: Actress 1 as Joan is watching TV. Actor 1 as Jeff enters from front door.

JOAN: Well?

JEFF: Just as I suspected, Roderigo:

Another visit from the tiny humanoids.

JOAN: Ahah!

JEFF: Yes, it's true: miniature people.

Midgets, perhaps, or dwarves.

It was hard to tell what they were underneath their sinister disguises.

JOAN: Really?

But, Jeff—what do they want with us?

JEFF: Food, Joan!

Ritual offerings.

Actually, they were extremely direct:

Either I supplied them *tout-suite avec* le grub, or else. . .

JOAN: Yes?

JEFF: There were threats, Joan, let's just say there were threats.

JOAN: I see.

JEFF: Yes.

JOAN: Sounds pretty serious.

JEFF: It was hell.

JOAN: So what happened?

JEFF: Joan—what could I do—I'm a man—I was weak. Quickly assessing their depraved little needs, I proceeded to offer them large amounts of sugary substances. Of course, I knew they had too much already: Their hands, their mouths were sticky with the stuff! But I was reckless—I gave them more, more, *all they wanted!* And then, suddenly, as quickly as they had come, they disappeared into the darkness that spawned them. And tonight, this living nightmare is endlessly replaying itself in every small suburban town somewhere, in the Twilight Zone (Dee-dee dee-dee, dee-dee dee-dee)

So what are you watching? Hunh, baby?

Joan shakes her head. She doesn't know. They both start to laugh.

No?

JOAN: Don't ask me, boy—you know. . . .

I don't know. . . .

JEFF: Nothing, hunh?

Nichts. Not one thing!

JOAN: Nope.

JEFF: I'll bet you don't even know the name of it, do you?
Hunh? Come on, now. . .

JOAN: I do so—it's [name of actual program].

JEFF: Here, let me get you another drink.

Jeff exits towards kitchen with glasses.

JOAN: Sure, baby! I say—let the party begin!

THE NINTH SCENE

S.M.: [*Off*] Nine—go

Lights up: Actress 1 as Joan is watching TV.

JOAN: No—I don't want them either.

Not right now, at any rate—I'm not ready. I've really
made up my mind about that—I mean, for right now.
I was talking to Laura, you know, about this?
(She's so great!)
Anyway, I really realized—I was so *rooked* as a kid—I
mean, forget it, I was never allowed to be a kid. I had
to be this perfect little grown-up, you know?

ACTOR 1: [*Off*] Meanwhile your parents are acting like children,
right?

JOAN: Yeah—so now that I'm grown up,
Now that I've got a house of my own, boy—
I'm gonna be the baby for a while.
I'm basically very selfish, I'm very needy.
I don't need some other human being feeding off of me.
I don't need to get it from both sides.

I just want to be left alone to play.

The doorbell rings.

ACTOR 1: [*Off*] Go away! Go away! There's nobody home and we eat little children!

JOAN: That's okay, I'll get it.

Joan rises and exits towards front door. Beat. Actress 2 calls feebly from inside closet.

ACTRESS 2: [*Off*] Come back...let me out...Help...let me out....

Joooaaaannnnn....

BLACKOUT.

THE TENTH SCENE

S.M.: [*Off*] Ten—go!

Lights up: Actress 2 as Witch, unmasked, stands down center. Another Witch, masked, watches TV throughout scene.

ACTRESS 2: "We had lost our way.

The forest grew darker,

And together we walked hand-in-hand until we came upon a cottage in a clearing.

We knocked on the door; nobody answered.

We peered through the windows; nothing was there.

And so, at last, we lay down together and cried ourselves to sleep.

In the middle of the night, I heard a voice sweetly calling my name.

I saw the inside of the cottage ablaze with light.

I turned back to where we were sleeping, but no one was there.

And when I looked through the door I saw a table piled
    with food and one chair and one plate and one knife.
It seemed however much I ate, I was never full;
And whenever I looked away, there was more on my plate.
At last, a great drowsiness overwhelmed me and I climbed
    the stairs to the four-poster bed,
Falling into a slumber on a great white counterpane.
But when I awoke for the second time, it was in darkness.
I was locked in a room so small I could hardly stand.
I cried for help for hours but nobody came.
And then I knew that I should never see my home again,
And that I had been utterly transformed."

Actor 2 calls from inside closet, pounding on door:

ACTOR 2: Let...me...out!...

BLACKOUT.

THE ELEVENTH SCENE

S.M.: [*Off*] Eleven—go!

    Lights up: Actress 1 as Joan is watching TV. Actor 1
    as Jeff enters from front.

JEFF: ...Pathetic, boy—absolutely *pa*-thetic (piss me off...)

JOAN: What?

JEFF: Oh, this kid that was just out there.

He had all these weird pieces of cardboard stuck on his
body. So I asked him, I said: What are you supposed to
be?

Kid says: I don't know.

So I said: You mean to tell me you make your own costume and you don't even know who you're supposed to
be?

Kid goes: Can I just have my candy now, Mister? Jesus!
(Unbelievable.) I almost didn't give it to him. And his sister
had some dumb Da-Glo painted sheet on—I mean these
are not costumes!

JOAN: Who were they?

JEFF: Oh, just some—I don't know—kids that live in that house
down the—you know.
I've seen them playing on the—you've seen 'em.
If you'd seen them you'd know.
The ones that are always out there?
Kid with the glasses, you know, looks about 45 and
vicious?

JOAN: Unh-hunh. . . .

JEFF: You know the ones I mean?

JOAN: Not really.

JEFF: Ah—forget it, it's not important.
I HATE KIDS!
God! Let's never have any!
All they do is smell funny and scream and yell and fight
and eat and get into trouble and get hurt and make you
spend all your money.
One of Nature's less-good ideas.

JOAN: Well, I can see my sweetie's in a good mood.

JEFF: I'm kidded out, Joan; I'm suffering from Kiddy-Overload.
You ever tried to have a conversation with an eight-year
old? "Hello, children: I'm your adult neighbor, and I'm
only *slightly* lame. . . ."
I mean, they're worse than grown-ups!
At least with grown-ups you don't have to be nice.

JOAN: [Rising] You want another drink? I'll make you one.

JEFF: Please! And make it strong . . . .

Joan exits toward kitchen. The doorbell rings.
WE'RE NOT HOME!

JOAN: [*Off*] I'll get it!

JEFF: You just make the drinks! I'll get it! (Little fuckers!)
Jeff exits towards front door.
BLACKOUT.

THE TWELFTH SCENE

S.M.: [*Off*] Twelve—go!
Lights up: Barestage. The closet door is shut and from inside comes loud pounding. Actor 2 is heard bellowing from inside closet:

ACTOR 2: [*Off*] FEEEEEEEEED MEEEEEEEEE...
FEEEEEEEEEEEEEEED MEEEEEEEEEEEEEEEEE...
I...AM...SO...HUN...GR...
AHHHHHHHHHHHHHHHHHHHHHHHHH!
IIII...AMMMM...SOOO...HUNNNN...GRYYYYY!
Furious pounding.
BLACKOUT.

THE SEVENTEENTH SCENE

S.M.: [*Off*] Seventeen—go!
Lights up: Actor 1 as Jeff is watching TV. He lights a joint; the doorbell rings.

JEFF: [*Calls*] Will you get that?
Actress 1 answers from offstage.

ACTRESS 1: [*Off*] In a minute.

JEFF: [*Calls*] Okay.

> *Beat. The doorbell rings again.*

Joan?

ACTRESS 1: [*Off*] I'm coming, I'm coming. . .

> *Actress 1 as Joan enters from upstairs.*

JEFF: And listen—don't let them in, don't let them smell it, okay? Like, just open the door a crack. Or am I being paranoid?

Can you smell it?

JOAN: Of course.

JEFF: Yeah, but could you like, smell it upstairs?

JOAN: Of course.

JEFF: Shit, what if it's the cops?

JOAN: It's not the cops. It's Tommy and Little Artie, I saw them out the bedroom.

JEFF: Oh.

JOAN: I'll handle it.

> *Joan exits towards front door.*

JEFF: [*Calls*] Or listen, you could just deal with them out on the porch, that would work. Don't you think? Or do you? Maybe it's—or do whatever you want. I'm watching TV. BLACKOUT.

THE EIGHTEENTH SCENE

S.M.: [*Off*] Eighteen—go!

> *Lights up: Actor & Actress 1 as Jeff & Joan are watching TV. Joan rises.*

JEFF: Will you make me one?

JOAN: I wasn't going into the kitchen.

JEFF: Oh. Sorry . . . .

JOAN: Why? Do you need another one?

JEFF: No, no, I'm fine, actually. . . .

> *Joan exits upstairs; Jeff keeps watching TV.*

Oh, wow—look at that! [*Calls*] Joan! Quick! Come look at this!

Hurry, hurry, hurry!

Oh, wait. . . never mind. . . .

> *Joan enters from upstairs.*

JOAN: What is it?

JEFF: That's all right—never mind—I'm sorry. . . There was this thing on TV, I wanted you to see it, but. . . It's gone.

JOAN: Oh. Okay.

> *Joan exits upstairs; Jeff keeps watching TV. Beat.*

JEFF: [*Calls*] It's back!. . . Quick! Joan? If you want to see it, hurry!

> *Joan enters from stairs.*

JOAN: What?

JEFF: No—shit—you just missed it. Don't worry—it'll come right back. Wait a minute—I'm sure they'll cut right back to it now.

JOAN: What is it?

JEFF: Hang on a sec, you'll see. . . (Oh, this is really boring right now. . . .)It's this, this—you'll see, you'll see. . . (Oh, come on!. . .) I can't believe they're not showing it.

JOAN: Well, look, if they do, you can let me know.

> *Joan exits upstairs.*

JEFF: Yeah, I'll holler. Sorry to drag you away. . . .Once you see it, you'll see though: I mean, it's not all that big a deal, but it's still kind of far out, you know what I mean?. . . Joan? Can you hear me. . . ? Hey, Joan?. . .

JOAN: [*Off*] Is it on?

JEFF: No, no, that's all right—it's not on yet! Don't come!

Joan enters from upstairs.

I'm sorry—it was a mistake—it's not on . . . .

JOAN: Well, I thought you were calling me.

BLACKOUT.

THE NINETEENTH SCENE

S.M.: [*Off*] Nineteen—go!

> *Lights up: Actor & Actress 1 as Jeff & Joan are watching TV. The doorbell rings.*

JEFF: Do you mind, or. . .

JOAN: What?

JEFF: Getting the door . . . .

JOAN: No, not really, I guess.

JEFF: Or do you want me to? I mean, I will. . . if you want. . . .

JOAN: No, that's all right.

> *Joan rises.*

JEFF: See, it's just—I've been doing it all night and I'm kind of getting tired of jumping up and down all the time and never getting a chance to relax for a minute.

JOAN: I know.

JEFF: You don't want to have to do it either, right?

JOAN: It's not that big a deal.

JEFF: Yeah, but still—you'd really rather not, right?

JOAN: I don't mind . . . .

> *Joan exits towards front door.*

JEFF: (You're fucking lying to me, Joan . . . .)

BLACKOUT.

THE TWENTIETH SCENE

s.m.: [*Off*] Twenty-go!

> *Lights up: Actor & Actress 1 as Jeff & Joan are watching TV. The doorbell rings.*

JEFF: You want me to get it?

JOAN: No, that's all right.

JEFF: No, you want me to get it, don't you?

JOAN: Except that you don't want to. I know that. It's fine.

JEFF: That's not what I'm asking you, Joan. I'm asking if you want me to go get it, and you do—right? And now you're all mad at me—right? I mean, why do you have to be so passive? Why can't you just say what you want? Sure, I don't particularly like getting the door, but I will; I'd do anything to avoid all this passive-aggressive bullshit!

JOAN: Oh, fuck you! Jesus!

> *Joan storms out toward front door.*

JEFF: [*Calls*] Well now, what? Are you getting the door or what?

> *Beat.*

BLACKOUT.

THE TWENTY-FIRST SCENE

s.m.:[*Off*] Twenty-one—go!

> *Lights up: Actor & Actress 1 as Jeff & Joan are watching TV. The doorbell rings.*

JEFF: . . . I'll get it . . . .

JOAN: Never mind—I'll get it in a minute.

JEFF: I said, I'll get it, Joan.

JOAN: God, can't you just let me sit here a minute without badgering me?!

JEFF: But that's just it, that's just it! I mean, you say you're
     going to get the door and then all you do is just sit around!
     It's driving me crazy! If you want me to get it, say so—
     say so! Why do we have to go through all this weird man-
     ipulation shit?
JOAN: Oh, don't give me that shit! You're the one who's manipu-
     lating! You just want me to take care of it!
JEFF: And you don't want to, do you? That's all I'm trying to
     get you to admit. And then you get all defensive and hos-
     tile! God, I don't know why you keep doing it!
JOAN: Because you're the one who's so fucking hostile all the
     time, and I just keep hoping if I get the god-damned door
     and leave you alone, maybe you'll simmer down!
JEFF: Then get it! Go get it! Why the fuck don't you get it in-
     stead of sitting around? I can't stand it!
     Jeff storms out upstairs. The doorbell rings again.
     BLACKOUT.

THE TWENTY-SECOND SCENE

ACTRESS 1: [*Softly*] Twenty-two—go!
     *Lights up: Actress 1 as Joan is watching TV. Beat. Act-
     or 1 as Jeff appears from closet, screaming in rage.*
JEFF: All right! I fucked her! Is that what you want to hear?
     Is it? You wanted to know, god-damn it, you're going to
     know: Three times I fucked her! One right after the other
     (which we *never* do) And the third time in the morning!
     And I can get hard right now just thinking about it. And,
     yes—I feel guilty—okay? And, yes—I know it's fucking
     everything up—okay? And I'm not saying it's right or it's
     wrong except it's something I've wanted all my life and

now I have the chance for it and I am not going to spend the rest of my life wishing I hadn't let it slip away!

Does this mean anything to you or are you too fucked up with your own self-pity? I mean, look at you—look at you! Nine years! Nine fucking years, Joan, and none of it matters, does it? We might just as well be goddamn assholes like everybody else, you know? I mean, I really thought, I really thought I could be honest with you and you'd understand—not like it, but at least understand—because it was just my trip, it had to do with something I needed. . .It has nothing to do with you! Nothing! But I was wrong, wasn't I? I was a fool! I should have lied to you! I never should have told you anything at all, and it would have been over, and you never would have known. I was a fucking idiot, wasn't I? Oh, for Christ sake, can't you say an-y-thing? An-y-thinggggggg, Joan? HUNH? Oh, Jesus, I hate it when you're like this. Say something! Say something!

JOAN: [*Softly*] I love you. . . .

JEFF: You love me. . .bullshit!

Because your love is like a jail!

Jeff storms out towards kitchen. Beat.

JOAN: [*Softly*] Blackout.

BLACKOUT.

THE FIFTEENTH SCENE

S.M.: [*Off*] Fifteen—go!

Lights up: Actor & Actress 1 as Jeff & Joan are watching TV. A Ghost is just seen disappearing at the window. The doorbell rings.

JEFF: I'll get it.

> *No movement. Beat. Jeff rises and exits towards front door. The closet door slowly opens and Actress 2 calls from within.*

ACTRESS 2: [*Off*] Joooaaannn . . . .

Jooooaaaannnn . . . .

> *Joan rises stiffly, turns, walks towards closet, exiting.*

J o o o o o a a a a a a n n n n n . . . . .

> *Actress 2 cackles from closet.*

BLACKOUT.

THE TWENTY-THIRD SCENE

ACTOR 2: [*Off*] Twenty-three—go!

> *Lights up: Barestage. Knocking from inside closet, and Actress 2 calls from offstage:*

ACTRESS 2: [*Off*] Help!

Let me out!

Let me out of here!

Someone!

Anyone! Help!

If you can hear me, let me out of here! Please!

I'll give you anything! Anything!

Is there anybody out there?

Hello?

Hello?

> *The Beast enters with a kitchen knife raised, approaches closet.*

Who is that?

What are you doing?

No! Noooooooo!Please, no, don't do it, pleeeeeease · · · ·

The Beast sticks the knife into the closet door. Actress 2 screams horribly. The Beast turns and exits.
BLACKOUT.

THE TWENTY-FOURTH SCENE

S.M.: [*Off*] Twenty-four—go!

    Lights up: Actor 1 as Jeff, masked as Beast, and Actress 1 as Joan, masked as Witch, are watching TV. Actor 2 as Beast, unmasked, and Actress 2 as Witch, unmasked, call from outside window.

ACTOR 2 & ACTRESS 2: Hi! Hi!,

    Hi, you guys! Hi!

    Hi, Jeff! Hi, Joan!

    How you doin'?

    Hey, Happy Halloween, you guys!

    Hey, it's us, guys.

    Hey, open up!

    Jeff? Joan?

    (Maybe they can't hear us.)

    Hey—hello in there!

    Hello?

    Hey, come on, let us in.

    Hey, quit fooling around.

    Hey, it's Halloween!

    (They must be ignoring us.)

    Trick or treat!

    Hey, come on, it's getting cold out here!

    (Go see if the front door's open. . .)

    Hey, we're coming on around to the front.

    Actor & Actress 2 disappear.

The doorbell rings.
The doorbell rings.
The doorbell rings.
Jeff & Joan still do not react.
BLACKOUT.

THE TWENTY-FIFTH SCENE

s.m.: [*Off*] Twenty-five—go!
    Lights up: Actress 1 as Joan masked as Witch and Actor
    1 as Jeff masked as Beast are watching TV. Allow a beat.
JOAN: It's getting kind of moist in here . . . .
    Getting all sticky . . . .
JEFF: Damp . . . .
    Very damp . . . .
    Very soggy . . . .
    Suddenly and for no apparent reason, Jeff yells. Beat.
    Joan turns to him.
JOAN: Now what?
JEFF: I keep bumping my eyelashes, it's very uncomfortable.
    My eyelashes, I keep bumping them against something.
    I think it's the edge of the eyehole or something. It's driv-
    ing me crazy.
    Beat. Jeff then pushes the mask around on his face as
    Actress 2 shrieks from within the closet.
    There . . . .
    That's better . . . .
JOAN: [*Pointing at TV*] Who is that actor?
BLACKOUT.

THE TWENTY-SEVENTH SCENE (A & B)

S.M.: [*Off*] Twenty-seven A—go!

> *Lights up: Actor & Actress 1 as Jeff & Joan are watching TV. Actor & Actress 2, as Beast & Witch, are outside window, tapping on the pane, calling "Trick or Treat!" etc., while Jeff & Joan studiously ignore them.*

JEFF: [*Out of the corner of his mouth, sotto voce*] Pretend they're not there . . . .

JOAN: [*Ditto*] I am. . . .

JEFF: [*Ditto*] Driving me crazy. . . .

JOAN: [*As before*] Me too. . . .

> *The doorbell starts to ring.*
>
> *Pictures start rattling on the walls.*
>
> *It gets noisier and noisier.*
>
> *Perhaps the remarks become personal and somewhat obscene. . . .Suddenly Jeff leaps out of his chair and runs towards the front door, yelling:*

JEFF: I am going to KILL THOSE MOTHERFUCKERS!!!!!!!

> *And everything disappears as if on cue.*

JOAN: They're gone.

JEFF: What happened?

> BLACKOUT.

S.M.: [*Off*] . . . and B—go!

> *Lights up: Jeff has crossed to TV to change channels. Joan is looking out the window.*

JOAN: You really think they're gone?

> *Unobserved, part of a Ghost's sheet flutters from closet.*

JEFF: Sure . . . .

> BLACKOUT.

THE FOURTEENTH SCENE

s.m.: [*Off*] Fourteen—go!
Lights up: Actor & Actress 1 as Jeff & Joan are watching TV.

JEFF: Can you imagine what it must be like being eaten by an animal? I was just thinking about that . . . .
I mean, not just the pain (which I'm sure is intense) but the horror . . . .
Joan rises.

JOAN: Yeah? . . . Go ahead, keep talking. . . .
Joan crosses to closet, opens door and exits within.

JEFF: It's like, I was watching this program, this nature program, and it suddenly hit me:
All it was was animals eating each other. They had bugs jumping on other bugs, biting into them with their pincers (and then they always show the juice running out). It was great, they had everything: birds and bugs, frogs and bugs. Lots of bugs. (Bugs get eaten.)
But then—they had this whole sequence where this pack of hyenas surrounded a baby water-buffalo or something, and they were running around, and the mother was trying to chase them away, and finally one of them just grabs it right by the throat and pulls it down on the ground and then they were all over it. They showed one of them running away with the whole hind leg ripped off and bleeding in its mouth . . . .
I mean, *strong* stuff!
But like, the way they present it, it's like they don't even know what they're looking at. It's like weird propaganda, you know? With the bouncy little soundtrack and the dippy announcer going: "And so, life goes on on the Seren-

geti . . .'' And I mean, this is for children? This is so they won't have their minds warped by sex-and-violence? Good, wholesome family entertainment, right? You know what I mean? . . .

Joan? . . .

Actress 2 as Joan walks very quickly from closet to kitchen.

ACTRESS 2: Right.

JEFF: . . . Joanie??? . . .

No sooner does Actress 2 as Joan exit by kitchen than Actress 1 as Joan enters from kitchen—as if she'd just turned around.

JOAN: I heard you—what is it?

JEFF: . . . Nothing. . . .

Forget it . . . .

BLACKOUT.

THE SIXTEENTH SCENE

S.M.: [*Off*] Sixteen—go!

Lights up: Actor 1 as Jeff is watching TV. Actress 1 as Joan leans against wall by the kitchen entrance.

JOAN: We've got ants.

JEFF: Hunh?

JOAN: Ants.

JEFF: Isn't that just what you said?

JOAN: Yeah—we've got ants, they're everywhere. All in the sugar and honey and everywhere.

JEFF: Really?

JOAN: I had to throw them all out.

JEFF: Really? That's so weird. I mean, isn't it too late for ants,

I mean too cold outside? I thought they hibernated or
something. (Maybe not.) Hunh.

JOAN: What's even weirder is they were all inside of jars that
had tops on them too, just solid ants crawling around
on top of each other, just these bottles full of insects. . . .

JEFF: (Gross.)

JOAN: . . . It was gross, I threw them out. I also had to throw
out the flour, there were bugs in it, these little black things,
these little black specks . . . .

JEFF: You sure it wasn't pepper or something?

JOAN: There were wings. I sifted some to see. There was also
this big white soft fat thing that was. . .

JEFF: Please! What a gross-out!

JOAN: It was laying eggs; I think. So then I went to the refrigera-
tor, you know? (Just checking.)

JEFF: Unh-hnh . . . .

JOAN: Well, first of all, there were maggots. Maggots in the
cheese, maggots in the milk, maggots in the eggs, threw
them all out. Then, in the lettuce, those little centipede
things with the jaws? Threw all that out too. Oh—by the
way—there's a whole calf's head in the freezer but the neck
part got stuck to the metal so I thought I'd let you take
care of that. Besides, the closet is full of snakes. You don't
believe me, do you? You think I'm making it all up. Listen—can't you hear them slithering around in there? You
don't believe me? They're this high in there. You want me
to show you? Come here—open it yourself. You open the
door and they'll all come tumbling out all over you. In
fact, when you open the door, be sure you stand off to
one side out of the way. In fact, don't! Don't open the
door. Okay? Don't open it. We'll just keep it shut. I'll get
the snake man in the morning.

Joan exits swiftly towards kitchen.
BLACKOUT.

THE TWENTY-EIGHTH SCENE

S.M.: [*Off*] Twenty-eight—go!

    Lights up: Barestage. The closet door is ajar; birdcall sounds. A Ghost enters tentatively from closet, crossing toward kitchen. Abruptly, Actor 1 calls from offstage:

ACTOR 1: [*Off*] Joan?...

    Where are you?...

    The Ghost immediately runs back into closet.

    Joan?...

    Several other Ghosts run from kitchen into closet. Actor 1 as Jeff enters from kitchen with shoebox.

    Joanieeeeeeee?...

    Jeff crosses and exits upstairs.

ACTRESS 1: [*Off*] What?

ACTOR 1: [*Off*] Where the hell are you?

ACTRESS 1: [*Off*] In here.

ACTOR 1: [*Off*] Where the hell is here?

ACTRESS 1: [*Off*] What?

ACTOR 1: [*Off*] Where are you?

    Actress 1 as Joan enters stealthily from closet, shutting door. She crosses to chair quickly and sits, watching TV.

JOAN: Right here! I'm watching television.

    What do you need?

ACTOR 1: [*Off*] Nothing. Forget it.

    BLACKOUT.

THE THIRTEENTH SCENE

s.m.: [*Off*] Thirteen—go!
        Lights up: Actress 1 as Joan is watching TV. Actor 1
        as Jeff enters from front door with shoebox.
JEFF: Look what I found.
JOAN: What?
JEFF: This was just sitting on the front porch. Somebody must
        have left it . . . (I guess).
JOAN: Just like that? Weird.
        What's inside?
JEFF: I don't know. You want to open it?
JOAN: Not really . . . .
        Jeff weighs box in his hand.
JEFF: Not real heavy . . . .
        Jeff shakes box.
        Doesn't rattle . . . .
        Okay, here we go now . . . .
        Jeff opens box.
        Hunh!
JOAN: What is it?
JEFF: Nothing. There's nothing in here.
JOAN: That's bizarre.
JEFF: Yeah, it's either that or it's very dull, I'll tell you.
        The doorbell rings.
        I'll get it.
        Jeff leaves box behind, exits toward front door. As Joan
        watches TV, the birdcall sounds. Abruptly, She stands up
        and calls:
JOAN: I'll put it in the closet!
        BLACKOUT.

THE THIRTY-FIRST SCENE

s.m.: [*Off*] Thirty-one—go!

> *Lights up: Actress 1 as Joan is watching TV. Actor 1 as Jeff enters from front door with shoebox.*

JEFF: Look at this.

JOAN: What?

JEFF: Found this box out on the porch, like somebody left it out there or something.

JOAN: You mean kids?

JEFF: Maybe.

> It was really—it was placed, you know, right in the middle. Something about the way it was positioned.

JOAN: That's weird.

JEFF: Yeah.

> *Jeff rattles box.*

JOAN: What is it?

JEFF: There's something inside here.

JOAN: I know, but what?

JEFF: How would I know?

> *Jeff opens box; inside is the Beast mask.*

> That's it. That's all there is.

JOAN: Here, let me see it. Let me see the box, too.

> *Joan tries on the mask.*

> How do I look?

JEFF: Hunh?

JOAN: How do I look?

JEFF: No, I'm fine.

JOAN: What?

JEFF: I'll get it.

> *The doorbell rings. Jeff crosses to stairs, climbs and exits.*

JOAN: Do you want me to?

JEFF: No, that's okay.

JOAN: Are you sure?

JEFF: [*Off*] No, it's fine, really.

A Ghost appears in each entrance; birdcall sounds. Joan, masked, rises with box and exits through closet, Ghosts following.

BLACKOUT.

THE THIRTIETH SCENE

S.M.: [*Off*] Thirty—go!

Lights up: Barestage. Actor 1 as Jeff enters from front door with shoebox. He calls:

JEFF: Hey, Joan? Joanie? Look what I found.

ACTRESS 1: [*Off*] What did you say?

JEFF: I found something.

ACTRESS 1: [*Off*] *What?*

Jeff shakes box, opens it, finds a birdcall.

JEFF: Weird: it's a box with a—looks like a birdcall or something in it. . . .

Jeff works the birdcall.

That's what it is all right.

ACTRESS 1: [*Off*] Are you talking to me?

The doorbell rings.

JEFF: I'll get it.

ACTRESS 1: [*Off*] Will you get that?

JEFF: That's what I said.

Jeff exits towards front door. A Ghost enters from closet, removes box and birdcall and returns to closet, closing the door again.

BLACKOUT.

THE THIRTY-SECOND SCENE

s.m.: [*Off*] Thirty-two—go!

> *Lights up: Barestage. Actor 1 as Jeff enters from front*
> *door with shoebox. He calls:*

JEFF: Hey, Joan? Joanie? Look what I found.

ACTRESS 1: [*Off*] I'm in here.

JEFF: I said, I found something.

ACTRESS 1: [*Off*] I'm in here.

> *Jeff shakes box, opens it, finds the kitchen knife.*

I can't hear you.

JEFF: No, I didn't say anything.

ACTRESS 1: [*Off*] I can't hear you.

> *The doorbell rings.*

Did you say you found something? Did you find something? What did you find?

JEFF: I have to get the door, okay? Okay, Joan?

Can you hear me?

ACTRESS 1: [*Off*] I'm in here.

JEFF: Never mind, forget it.

> *Jeff exits towards front door. Joan, masked as Beast,*
> *quickly enters from closet, removes box and knife and re-*
> *turns to closet, closing the door again.*

BLACKOUT.

THE THIRTY-THIRD SCENE

s.m.: [*Off*] Thirty-three—go!

> *Lights up: Barestage.*

ACTRESS 1: [*Off*] Jeff?...

ACTOR 1: [*Off*] What?

ACTRESS 1: [*Off*] Can you come in here quickly please? I think
     I just cut myself pretty badly. . . .
          Actor 1 as Jeff comes running from upstairs.
JEFF: Yeah!
     Where are you?
     Joan?
     Where are you?
          Jeff exits towards kitchen.
     [*Off*] Joanie?. . .
     BLACKOUT.

THE THIRTY-FOURTH SCENE

S.M.: [*Off*] Thirty-four—go!
          *Lights up: Barestage. Actor 1 as Jeff enters from front
     door with shoebox. He calls:*
JEFF: Joan? I found another one . . . .
          Jeff opens box, finds chicken inside.
     There's like a chicken—a dead chicken inside here . . . .
          *Joan, masked as Beast, holding kitchen knife upraised,
     enters from closet and advances silently on Jeff.*
     Here, look at this, this chicken was. . .
     Joan?. . .
     What are you doing, Joan? Jesus, put that knife down!
     JOANNNNNNNNNNNNN!!!
     BLACKOUT.

THE THIRTY-SIXTH SCENE

S.M.: [*Off*] Thirty-six—go!

Lights up: Actor & Actress 1 as Two Ghosts are watching TV.

ACTRESS 1: Is there anything else on?

ACTOR 1: I don't know. Where's the TV Guide?

ACTRESS 1: I don't know.

ACTOR 1: Last time I saw it was on the TV. But it's not there now.

ACTRESS 1: No. Besides, that was last week's.

ACTOR 1: Oh, was that last week's?

ACTRESS 1: UNH-HUNH.

ACTOR 1: Then I guess I haven't seen this week's, I don't think.

ACTRESS 1: Well, it was on the TV the last time I saw it. But it's not there now.

ACTOR 1: Nope.

ACTRESS 1: I don't know where it is. Maybe we threw it out.

ACTOR 1: Could be.

ACTRESS 1: Well, that's okay.

ACTOR 1: Yep. That's life. I threw some stuff out but I'm not looking through the trash.

ACTRESS 1: No—no, no, no.

ACTOR 1: But we can change the channels, see what's on. . . If you want.

ACTRESS 1: No, actually, this is fine.

ACTOR 1: Is this fine with you?

ACTRESS 1: Yeah, this is fine.

ACTOR 1: Yeah, actually, this is fine with me too.

ACTRESS 1: Okay. Fine.

BLACKOUT.

THE THIRTY-SEVENTH SCENE

S.M.: [Off] Thirty-seven—go!
> *Lights up: Actor & Actress 2 as Beast & Witch are calling.*

WITCH: W-o-o-o-o-o-o-o-o-o-o-o-o-o-o-o ......
BEAST: I smell the Mommy,
And I smell the Daddy,
And I smell the blood of the baby boy.
Be they near or be they far,
I'll hunt them down and eat them all!
WITCH: Come here, little children, come out from where you're
hiding! We know you're in here somewhere, and we have
a surprise . . . .
BEAST: HEY! . . .
HEY! . . .
WE'RE HERE . . . .
> *The Beast & Witch begin to talk more normally.*

WITCH: (I don't think they're even home)
BEAST: (Well, they didn't go far if they left the TV set on.)
Boy, I am really starving . . .
WITCH: I just hope they didn't forget.
BEAST: They'll be back, don't worry about it.
Hey, come here.
WITCH: What?
BEAST: Let's play a trick on them when they get back.
Come here, I'll show you . . . .
> *They cross to closet, exit within and hide.*

BLACKOUT.

THE THIRTY-EIGHTH SCENE

s.m.: [*Off*] Thirty-eight—go!
Lights up: Barestage.
Beat.
s.m.: [*Off*] And house up . . . .
Houselights fade up.

INTERMISSION

s.m.: [*Off*] Fade house to half . . .
And house out . . . .
Houselights fade out.
Offstage, sound of the birdcall.
s.m.: [*Off*] And blackout!
BLACKOUT.

THE SIXTY-SEVENTH SCENE

s.m.: [*Off*] Sixty-seven—go!
Lights up: Actor & Actress 2 as Jeff & Joan are watch-
ing TV.
JEFF: Hey, Joan?
JOAN: What?
JEFF: Do we have any kandy korn?

JOAN: I can't hear you.
JEFF: Do we have any kandy korn?
JOAN: What?
JEFF: Can you hear me?
JOAN: I'm in the kitchen.
JEFF: What?
JOAN: What?
JEFF: What?
JOAN: I'm in the kitchen.
JEFF: Can you hear me?
JOAN: I can't hear you.
JEFF: Can you hear me?
JOAN: I can't hear you.
JEFF: Hey, Joan?
JOAN: I can't hear you.
JEFF: Hey, Joan?
JOAN: I can't hear you.
JEFF: Do we have any kandy korn?
JOAN: What?
JEFF: I'm in the kitchen
JOAN: I'm in the kitchen.
JEFF: I'm in the kitchen.
JOAN: What?
JEFF: Hey, Joan?
JOAN: What?
JEFF: Hey, Joan?
JOAN: I can't hear you.
JEFF: What?
JOAN: Hey, Joan?
JEFF: Do we have any kandy korn?
BOTH: I'm in the cupboard over the sink.
    BLACKOUT.

THE TWENTY-SIXTH SCENE

s.m.: [*Off*] Twenty-six—go!
    Lights up: Actor & Actress 1 as Jeff & Joan are watching TV.
JEFF: I'm sorry I yelled at you about the door.
JOAN: That's okay.
    I yelled at you too.
JEFF: No, it's my fault and I'm sorry.
JOAN: It's not all your fault.
JEFF: Well, I think it is.
    But I'm not mad at you any more.
JOAN: No, I'm not mad at you either.
    It's just... when you yell at me...
JEFF: I know, I know, I'm sorry.
    I don't know why I get so angry sometimes.
JOAN: Well, it's partly my fault too for not...
JEFF: No, it's not your fault.
    It's not.
    Okay?
JOAN: Okay.
JEFF: Okay.
    The end.
    Beat.
    Joan rises, crosses to Jeff, kisses him.
BLACKOUT.

THE TWENTY-NINTH SCENE

ACTOR 2: [*Off*] Twenty-nine—go!
    Lights up: Actress 1 as Joan is watching TV. The Beast

enters from upstairs, carrying shoebox.

JOAN: Oh, wow!

Is that your costume? That's great!

You really look scary.

(Actually, you don't, you look like my sweetie, but that's cause I know . . . .)

The Beast hands Joan the shoebox.

What?

What's this?

What is this?

Come on, tell me!

What's in here?

Jeff—how come you won't tell me?

Is there something ooky in here?

There is, isn't there? What?

Tell me!

I'm not opening it (I'll bet there's something gross.)

Why won't you tell me, Hunh?

The Beast turns and exits towards kitchen.

What's wrong?

Sweetie? . . .

I was only kidding . . . .

Jeff . . . .

Joan exits after the Beast, carrying box, as Actor 1 as Jeff enters from closet.

JEFF: Yo? . . .

Jeff sits and watches TV. Actress 1 screams from off stage.

[*Calls*] Anything wrong, sweetie? . . .

BLACKOUT.

THE FORTY-FIFTH SCENE

s.m.: [*Off*] Forty-five—go!
Lights up: Actor 1 as Jeff is watching TV. Actor 2 as
the Beast enters from closet.
BEAST: Psssssssssst!
Hey, buddy.
Hey, Jeff. (See, I know you.)
Look at this. . . .
Beast holds a strange hunched-over pose in which he
seems to be pointing to something very small for a beat;
then:
Right now! And look at this. . . .
Another similar pose held for a beat:
Right now! And look at this. . . .
Another similar pose held for a beat:
Right now! And look at this. . . .
Another similar pose held for a beat:
Right now!
And look at you! (Right now!)
And look at me! (Right now!)
And look at everything! (Right now!)
Runs to chair, pulls shoebox from underneath chair.
And look at this!
What is this?
What is it?
What's inside of it?
Something's inside of it.
But what?
Wouldn't you like to know?
Wouldn't you like a peek?
Wouldn't you like to find out?. . .

Well, too bad—you're not going to . . . .
And Beast runs off to closet carrying box.
BLACKOUT.

THE FIFTY-FIRST SCENE

S.M.: [*Off*] Fifty-one—go!
> *Lights up: Actor & Actress 1 as Jeff & Joan are watching*
> *TV.*

JEFF: Hey, what ever happened to that box?

JOAN: Hunh?

JEFF: The shoebox—you know . . . .
> *Jeff points to the place where Ghost puts shoebox in*
> *Scene 41.*

The white shoebox or whatever it was . . . .
Sitting over there, it's been sitting over there.
I've been staring at the damn thing all night long.
It was yours, right?
I mean, you must have been the one to take it.

JOAN: I don't know what in God's name you are talking about.

JEFF: Hey, I'm not pissed off at you or anything.

JOAN: You're saying you saw one of my shoeboxes over there all night?

JEFF: Is this a put-on?

JOAN: Boy, you've been acting so weird . . . .
> BLACKOUT.

THE FORTY-FIRST SCENE

s.m.: [*Off*] Forty-one—go!
> *Lights up: Barestage, birdcall sound. A Ghost enters stealthily from closet with shoebox. Ghost places box in a fairly conspicuous place, exits through closet.*
> BLACKOUT.

THE FIFTY-FOURTH SCENE

s.m.: [*Off*] Fifty-four—go!
> *Lights up: Actor 1 as Jeff is watching TV. He does not react to Actress 2 as Joan, standing in closet doorway.*

JEFF: [*Calls*] Are you ready?...

ACTRESS 2: [*Softly*] I'm ready....
> *Beat.*

JEFF: [*Calls*] Joan?...
> Are you ready?...

ACTRESS 2: [*Softly*] I was....
> *Actress 2 turns and exits into closet, closing door.*

JEFF: [*Calls*] Joan?...
> ...(Oh, shit....)
> *Jeff puts his head in his hands.*

ACTRESS 2: [*Off*] I'm coming as fast as I can!...
> BLACKOUT.

THE FORTY-FOURTH SCENE

s.m.: [*Off*] Forty-four—go!
> *Lights up: Actor 1 as Jeff is watching TV. Closet door*

opens, Beast peeps out.

BEAST: [*Softly*] I'm in here.

> *Beast pops back in, shutting door; Jeff doesn't react.*

ACTRESS 1: [*Off*] What?

> *Closet door opens, Beast peeps out.*

BEAST: [*Softly*] I'm in here.

> *Beast pops back in, shutting door; Jeff doesn't react.*

ACTRESS 1: [*Off*] What?

> *Closet door opens, Beast peeps out.*

BEAST: [*Softly*] I'm in here.

> *Beast pops back in, shutting door; Jeff doesn't react.*
>
> *Actress 1 as Joan enters carrying overcoats.*

JOAN: Did you say something?

JEFF: No.

Why?

JOAN: Oh, for some reason I thought you were calling me. I thought I'd just hang up our coats and neat up a little.

> *Joan goes to closet and hangs up coats.*

JEFF: Oh, yeah, never know when one of our many friends is going to drop by unannounced . . . .

Certainly wouldn't want to create a bad impression by having a messy house.

JOAN: I know, but even so, there's no reason not to hang our coats up every once in a while.

After all, it's so often we neat up . . . .

> *Something reaches out and pulls Joan into closet. She screams. Jeff doesn't react.*
>
> *Beat.*
>
> *Jeff rises and closes closet door.*

BLACKOUT.

THE FORTIETH SCENE

s.m.: [*Off*] Forty-go!

> *Lights up: Barestage, birdcall sounds. Actor 1 as Jeff, carrying the knife, enters from kitchen and sneaks up on closet door. The birdcall stops. Jeff flings the closet door open and exits inside. Actress 2 as Witch pops in from the nearest entrance and slams closet shut.*

ACTOR 1: [*Off*] Joan?. . .

Hey!

Let me out!

Let me out of here!

Help! Let me out!

HELLLLLLLLLLLLLLP!

> *Loud banging from inside closet; Witch cackles.*

BLACKOUT.

THE SIXTY-THIRD SCENE

s.m.: [*Off*] Sixty-three—go!

> *Lights up: Actress 1 as Joan is watching TV. Two Ghosts stand behind her. Actor 1 calls from offstage.*

ACTOR 1: [*Off*] You know I love you, baby. . . .

You know there could never be anyone like you in my life, don't you baby?

> *The Ghosts slowly shroud Joan with another sheet.*

You're so magnificent.

You're so special to me.

We have something nobody else in the world has.

Let's not ruin it by being possessive.

I feel so close to you and I love to make love to you.

I just want to show you what you mean to me . . . .
I just want to love you . . . .
I love you . . . .
    Actor 1's voice turns into animal noises; pounding from closet.
BLACKOUT.

THE FORTY-THIRD SCENE

S.M.: [*Off*] Forty-three—go!
    Lights up: A Ghost is watching TV. Actor 1 as Jeff enters from kitchen, stands against upstage wall.
JEFF: Why won't you answer me? . . .
Why won't you talk to me? . . .
This is wrong, this is wrong, this is stupid and wrong!
    Ghost rises and slowly walks upstairs.
[*Calling after*] I happen to love you, I'm sorry . . . .
    Jeff sits in the chair but doesn't watch TV.
BLACKOUT.

THE FORTY-SEVENTH SCENE

S.M.: [*Off*] Forty-seven—go!
    Lights up: Actor 1 as Jeff is watching TV. Beat. Actress 2 as Joan bursts out of closet, screaming in rage.
JOAN: I wish I had a dick like a man!
I wish I had that fat thing!
I wish I had something that works!
Because I have nothing!
I have nothing!

So how do you like that?

Why don't you put that in your next play?

Actress 2 exits into closet, slamming door.

BLACKOUT.

THE FORTY-SIXTH SCENE

ACTOR & ACTRESS 2: [*Off*] Forty-six—go!
> *Lights up: Actor 1 as Jeff is watching TV. Actor & Actress 2 as Beast & Witch are upstage.*

BEAST: Do you notice anything?

Do you notice anything different?

Do you notice anything different about her?

WITCH: Don't you notice anything different about me?

Don't you notice anything about me?

Don't you notice anything?...

BEAST: Speak up, there . . . .

WITCH: I pray you, sir, I prithee tell,

Whether my face doth please thee well?

JEFF: Alas, the eyes deceive, I cannot tell.

WITCH: Then I pray you, sir, I prithee tell,

Whether my voice doth please thee?

JEFF: Also, the ears deceive, as know thee well.

WITCH: Then I pray you, sir, I prithee tell,

Whether my kiss doth please?

JEFF: The lips also deceive . . . .

WITCH: Methinks sometimes in truth he loveth me not.

BEAST: Not so, not so, he shall protest:

There is one part of you above all others he desires,

And which he dare not name,

And that is the part above all others he desires to touch,

And yet he dare not.

WITCH: Why then, indeed, he loveth me not.

JEFF: Not so, I do protest, not so.

WITCH: Then I shall ask and you shall answer:
    I pray you prithee tell
    How pleaseth thee my love?

JEFF: Alas, I cannot tell, the heart deceiveth.

WITCH: Then if thou can but say thou cannot tell,
    Methinks thou knowest me not,
    And knowing me not, thou lovest me not,
    And loving me not, thou pleaseth me not,
    And so, farewell!
        Beast and Witch exit into closet.

JEFF: Not so, good maid, I know thee well,
    For thou art the Devil and I am in Hell.

BLACKOUT.

THE FORTY-EIGHTH SCENE

S.M.: [*Off*] Forty-eight—go!
    *Lights up: Actor 1 as Jeff is standing downstage center.
    He is holding the chicken carcass by each wingtip so that
    the legs hang down and the body position is that of a liv-
    ing bird. This scene is done as a monolog directly to the
    audience.*
        *The Actor makes chicken noises and flaps the wings.
    He talks in a funny voice:*

ACTOR 1: "Here I am, just a happy chicken, walking around. . .
    And look—here come the nice people that always feed me!
    Now, that's funny, the nice people have a knife . . . .
    Oh, oh—I think the people are coming to cut off my head!

Oh, no! The people want to cut off my head!
Help! Help! No—get away!
Help! I can't fly! They clipped my wings!
Oh, no! I can't run! I can't get away!
Oh, no! Here it comes!
AHHHHHHHHHHHHHHHHHHHH!........."
  He drops one wingtip and shakes the chicken violently.
Er-laddle-laddle-laddle-laddle-laddle-laddle-laddle...
Er-laddle-laddle-laddle-laddle-laddle-laddle-laddle...
YAH!
  With a great shout, He throws chicken into a corner.
Get away!
Get away from me!
  He crosses to chair, sits in front of TV.
Get away, dead thing.
It's a dead thing!
It's all dead, it's all pink inside and juicy....
It's all like, soft ....
Somebody's going to have to eat it, you know.
Otherwise, you're not supposed to cut the head off.
Somebody better eat it....
But not me, boy, not me. I'm watching TV....
  *Beat. Then suddenly he jumps up and points to the
chicken.*
Get away! Get away from me!
It's all moving around, everything's all moving inside.
But you know what's really gross?
(You're supposed to say: No, what's really gross?)
What's really gross is... [*He mumbles into a cupped hand*]
EWWWWWW! PRETTY GROSS, HUNH?
  And he runs upstairs.
BLACKOUT.

THE FORTY-NINTH SCENE

S.M.: [*Off*] Forty-nine—go!
  Lights up: Actresses 1 & 2 as Witches watch TV
  throughout scene. Actor 1 as Jeff is holding chicken.
JEFF: This is yours, isn't it? Isn't it?
  Isn't it yours?
  It is, isn't it?
  I'm going to put it somewhere. Why don't I?
  Why don't I put it somewhere for you?
  Why don't I just put it somewhere?
  He puts the chicken somewhere.
  How's that?
  Or. . .I could put it over here . . . .
  He puts it somewhere else.
  Or. . .I could put it over there (why don't I?).
  He puts it somewhere else. These changes need not be
  very great.
  Or, wait—I'll put it over here . . . .
  He puts it somewhere else.
  Or, no—wait—I'll put it over there . . . .
  He puts it somewhere else.
  Or, maybe—no, wait I'll put it right over here, like this.
  He puts it somewhere else.
  Or maybe like this?
  You like it like this?
  He puts it somewhere else.
  Or maybe I'll just move it like this, I'll just move it around
  like this over here and like that over there I'll just move
  it all over like this and like that and just move it around
  I'll just move it a little and just a bit more over just a bit

more over just a bit more over just a bit more over...
BLACKOUT.

THE FIFTY-SIXTH SCENE

S.M.: [*Off*] Fifty-six—go!
Lights up: Actor 1 as Jeff is yelling at a Ghost.
JEFF: Get out!
Get away from here!
Get out of here!
Get away from here!
Get out!
Get out!
Get away!
Go away!
Get out!
Get ouuuuuuut!
OUUUUUUUUUUUT!
Jeff becomes increasingly agitated. The Ghost never moves. The scene is cut short by:
BLACKOUT.

THE FIFTIETH SCENE

S.M.: [*Off*] Fifty-go!
Lights up: A Ghost sits watching TV. Actor 1 as Jeff stands against the upstage wall.
JEFF: There was so much...
So many things I wanted to tell you...

And I never could, the words came out all wrong,
They meant different things to you and me. . .
I couldn't express myself:
I'd try to explain something and every time it seemed the
words became distorted in traveling the space between us.
How was it possible that we could become such strangers
When we had started with an understanding that went
    beyond all words,
In which our two blind souls communicated perfectly by
    touch?
I've never known such helpless sadness.
Were we really so completely wrong about each other?
I watched you turn away from me, give up on me,
As everything became corrupted by suspicion,
And when I tried to show you how I loved you with such
    passion
You thought it was only the sex I was after.
And you were right—that was the passion—
But you were wrong to think it wasn't love.
And in your eyes, it was just some guy out for a little
    pie . . . .
Because you were stupid!
Stupid and square and repressed and self-righteous and
fucked up in the head with every god-damn shitty little
    fear. . .
And you said you were going to free yourself?
You said you wanted everything from life?
You said you were going to take it all and grow and be-
    come this great artist?
How? When everything had to be so safe? Without risk?
Without danger?
And you thought I was really going to leave this woman

I have lived with for nine years and who has supported
me and cared for me and loved with me and laughed with
me and grown with me and suffered through this and a
hundred other kinds of bullshit and still loves me? Whom
I will always love?
She is my other self!
And I was to leave her for you? You must be joking!
No, you were right. I was exploiting you.
Because I knew all along you were nothing and I just kept
turning a blind eye to that because the sex was good.
I had no respect for you—I just used you.
And you could see that, and so eventually you rejected me.
Except I did love you. And I still do. I still do.
Except I don't.
Except I do, don't, do, don't, do, don't . . . .

> *Jeff takes sheet off Ghost revealing Actress 1 as Joan.*

Hello, Joan . . . .
BLACKOUT.

THE FIFTY-SEVENTH SCENE

> *Actor 1 screams.*
>
> *Actor 1 screams again.*

ACTOR 1: Help me!

> *Lights up: Actor 1 as Jeff is lying on the floor and*
> *screaming.*

Help me!
Somebody help me!
Somebody please help me!
Help me, help me, help me!. . .
Oh God, help me, help me, help me!. . .
OH—SOME—BO—DY—PLEEEEEEEEEEASE   HELP

ME!

...[etc.]

    Meanwhile, the voices of the other actors are heard off-stage chanting softly:

OTHERS: The demon in me

Is the demon in me!

The demon in me

Is the demon in me!

The demon in me

Is the demon in me!

The demon in me

Is the demon in me!...[etc.]

    Jeff's cries become weaker as the chanting grows louder. Three Ghosts appear, each at a different entrance.

BLACKOUT.

THE SIXTY-SECOND SCENE

S.M.: [*Off*] Sixty-two—go!

    Lights up: Actress 1 as Joan is watching TV. Actor 1 as Jeff appears outside window, rapping on glass.

JEFF: [*Calls*] Joan!...

It's me!...

Let me in!...

Help me!...

Joan, can't you see me?...

Can't you hear me?...

Help!...

Joan!...

I'm...

    Ghosts pull Jeff away.

Joan never reacts.
AAAAAAAAAAAAAAAAH!
I'm going!...
Helllllp!...
  Jeff disappears.
  Beat.
BLACKOUT.

THE SIXTY-FOURTH SCENE

s.m.: [*Off*] Sixty-four—go!
  Lights up: Actress 1 as Joan is watching TV. There is
  a sudden crashing sound offstage.
JOAN: Jeff?...
  Is that you?...
  Hello....
  Sound of someone coming down the stairs. Joan rises
  in alarm.
  Hello?
  Who's there?
  Jeff?
  Who is it?...
  The Beast appears with the knife in his hand and ad-
  vances on Joan. She screams and tries to run away, but
  trips and falls out of sightlines [e.g.: behind chair]. Beast
  then falls upon her and stabs her to death. The effect
  should be as bloody and realistic as possible. Alter-
  natively, Joan could try and barricade herself in the
  closet and be stabbed there. After the murder, the Beast
  exits, and there is a beat. Then:
ACTOR 1: [*Off*] Joan?

Can you come here a minute?
I think I just cut myself.
BLACKOUT.

THE FIFTY-SECOND SCENE

S.M.: [*Off*] Fifty-two—go!
> *Lights do not come up; only TV illuminates scene. A*
> *Beast appears in the entrance to front door, moving back*
> *and forth in a jerky, spasmodic way.*

BEAST: Zip...
Zip zip...
Zip...
Zip zip...
> *A second beast begins walking in a jerky, spasmodic*
> *way out of the closet and back, also muttering:*

BEAST 2: Zip zip zip...
Zip zip...
Zip zip zip...
Zip zip...
> *Eventually, both Beasts move further into the room with*
> *their odd twitching and bending movements. One begins*
> *the following chant to the rhythm established by the other.*
> *Then both join in, at first antiphonally, then in unison.*

BEASTS: Behold the Lightning Man the Lightning Lightning Man
Behold the Power Power of the Power Power
Of the Lightning Man the Lightning Lightning Man
Of Power Power of the Power Power
Of the zip zip zip zip zip zip
Zip zip zip zip zip zip
Power Power zip zip

Power Power zip zip
Lightning Man the Lightning Lightning Man
BEHOLD the Lightning Man the Lightning Lightning Man
Behold the Power Power of the Power Power
See the Lightning Lightning
See the Lightning Lightning
Lightning Man the Power Power
Lightning Power Power
Lightning Man the zip zip
Lightning zip zip zip zip
Power zip zip Power
Power zip zip Power
Power zip zip zip zip
Zip zip zip zip zip zip
Zip zip zip zip zip zip
YAH!!!!!

Beasts freeze on shout.
END OF SCENE.
Beasts exit severally.

THE SIXTY-FIFTH SCENE

Lights do not come up; only TV illuminates scene. Bird-call sounds; closet door opens slowly. A bright light from within falls across the stage. A Beast stands in threshhold with a shoebox held out before it. As the Beast crosses the stage, another identical Beast appears in doorway so that a never-ending procession is set up. Actress 2 speaks from offstage.

ACTRESS 2: [*Off*] If I speak to you now
Of the primitive days

When the creatures before you
Came down to the river
To drink by the moonlight
In numberless numbers,
Will you walk on this earth
In the sunlight
Aware
Of the numberless numbers
Of creatures before you
That walked on this earth
In numberless numbers
In sunlight and perished
In layer on layer
Of earth that was walked on
By creatures that perished
In layer on layer
In numberless numbers
Alone and screaming
As you must do,
As they have done?
Life feeds upon living.
We are all one eating each other.
And the primitive days are coming again.
   *The door closes slowly. The last Beast out stops
midstage.*
END OF SCENE.

THE THIRTY-NINTH SCENE

S.M.: [*Off*] Thirty-nine—go!
   A light goes on at the head of the stairs; otherwise, this

scene is played by the light of the television.
Actor 2 as the Beast is watching TV. Actress 2 as the Witch
enters from upstairs. She speaks in falsetto.

WITCH: Who's come creeping 'round my little house tonight?
   Is there someone at the door? Is he coming inside? Is it
   somebody who's lost and he's not where he's supposed to
   be? Who can it be? Tell me who can it be?

BEAST: It's the wind, little mother, just the cold north wind
   Come blowing 'round your warm little house.

WITCH: No, but somebody's eaten all the food in my cupboard,
   And it can't be the wind because the wind is never hungry.
   And somebody's been walking 'round all up and down
   and everywhere.
   Who can it be? Oh, who can it be?

BEAST: It's a bird, little mother, just a frightened little bird
   Seeking shelter from the stormy winds outside.

WITCH: Oh, I think somebody's lying in my little house tonight,
   And it can't be a bird because a bird can't talk.
   So it must be a man, and a small one by the sound of him:
   Now who can it be? Oh, I wonder who it is?

BEAST: My name is Jack and I've come here to kill you,
   And live in your cottage and eat all your food.

WITCH: Such a proud boast from such a little man!

BEAST: I have a knife!

WITCH: But the blade is too short.

BEAST: I have another knife, my father's knife.

WITCH: But see, the blade is grown so dull.

BEAST: Then kill you I shall with my own bare hands!

WITCH: But they are both so weak and I am powerful:
   For you are in my house and far from home,
   And you have eaten of enchanted food,
   And all of this can disappear at my displeasure,

And then you would be lost again and hungry in the night
And alone in the heart of the cold and pitiless forest.
BEAST: But I have left a trail.
WITCH: Of crumbs, and birds have eaten them.
BEAST: But I have left another trail.
WITCH: Of stones, and the wind has covered them.
Therefore, here shall you stay,
And we in loving lay,
Forever and a day,
And I shall have my way,
Or else I will abandon you!
The Witch cackles, exits towards kitchen.
BLACKOUT.

THE SIXTY-SIXTH SCENE

*Lights up: Actor & Actress 2 as Jeff & Joan are watching TV.
Actor 1 speaks from offstage. Periodically, a Ghost seems
to pass across the window, then across the hallway to
door. This should be done by using two different Ghosts
and the length of time between the Ghost disappearing
from window and appearing in hall should fluctuate.*
ACTOR 1: [*Off*] And I become spirit,
When I knew that I was spirit,
And I became spirit,
When I noticed I was spirit,
And that what I was was noticing,
And that noticing was spirit.
And I became spirit
When I noticed I was thinking,
And that what I was noticing was thinking,

And that what I was was noticing and thinking,
And that noticing and thinking were spirit.
And I became spirit when I heard my name called,
And I knew it was my name,
And that the spirit called me,
And that my name was spirit.
That spirit is spirit
That walks as spirit,
In a world of spirit,
Of light and darkness,
Of inside and outside,
Of one and the other,
And all the same . . . .
For spirit is ever there,
And nothing changes,
And everything changes,
And nothing changes,
And everything changes,
And everything changes,
And nothing changes,
And nothing changes,
And everything changes . . . .
BLACKOUT.

THE FIFTY-EIGHTH SCENE

S.M.: [Off] Fifty-eight—go!
      Lights up: Actress 1 as Joan is watching TV. Actor 1
      makes animal wails offstage, then enters as Beast holding
      the kitchen knife and wailing, stopping by Joan. Beat.
JOAN: Stop it.

Actor 1 will use a funny voice throughout scene.
BEAST: Stop what?
JOAN: You know.
BEAST: No, I don't. Stop what?
JOAN: Stop being weird. I don't like it.
BEAST: Am I being weird. I'm not being weird.
Am I being weird? I'm not being weird.
I don't know what you mean, Joan.
I'm not being weird at all.
Here, I'll show you.(I'll just put this little knife away. . . .)
Beast sits down.
See, I'm just sitting here in this very normal way
In this very normal chair in this very normal room
Looking at this very normal television program,
Just being very normal . . . .
Right?
I mean, I think you're the one who's acting kind of weird,
Joan.
In fact, I think you're being very very very weird indeed.
JOAN: Oh, shut up!
God, I think you're being stupid!
I really hate it when you get this way!
BEAST: Trick or treat!
JOAN: Fuck you!
Joan storms out of the room.
BEAST: (Fuck you too, you rancid sack of horseshit . . . .)
BLACKOUT.

THE FORTY-SECOND SCENE

S.M.: [*Off*] Forty-two—go!

*Lights up: Actress 1 as Joan is watching TV. The shoe-
box is still where it was placed in Scene 51. Actor 1 as
Jeff enters, notices box.*

JEFF: What's this?

JOAN: What's what?

   Jeff picks up box.

JEFF: This.

JOAN: I don't know.

JEFF: It's not yours?

JOAN: No.

JEFF: Hunh, Weird.

JOAN: Why? It's not yours?

JEFF: No. It was just sitting right here.

JOAN: That's weird.

   What's inside it?

JEFF: I don't know.

   This twine is that plastic stuff that's impossible to cut.

JOAN: You want a knife?

   I'll get you a knife.

   They're pretty dull but...

JEFF: Yeah, maybe I better ....

JOAN: Okay.

   Joan exits toward kitchen.

   *While she is gone, Jeff manages to slide off string. He
   opens the box and lets out a cry of fear and disgust, quickly closes box and puts it down and stands away, wiping
   his hands as Joan runs in from kitchen.*

JOAN: What is it?

JEFF: Don't come in here!

JOAN: What?

JEFF: Just get me a plastic trash-bag.

   Do we have any plastic trash-bags?

Quick!

JOAN: All right!

> *Joan exits towards kitchen.*

JEFF: Have you got one?

JOAN: [*Off*] In a minute . . . . All right, I've got one.

JEFF: Just stay where you are.

I want you to hold the bag open at the top and I'm going to bring this thing in there. . .

> *Gingerly picking up box, Jeff walks quickly into kitchen.*

[*Off*] Keep the bag away from your body, out from your body. . .

ACTOR 2: [*From closet*] Let. . .meeee. . .ouuuuuuuut. . . .

BLACKOUT.

THE FIFTY-FIFTH SCENE

S.M.: [*Off*] Fifty-five—go!

> *Lights up: Actor 1 as Jeff stands by the window. Actress 2 is visible outside, smiling.*

JEFF: When will I see you again?

I would give anything to see you again.

I keep thinking of you all the time, at every hour,

Alone and in the company of others.

I keep on seeing your resemblance in the faces of others.

I keep you hidden in my secret thoughts and close to me.

I keep on thinking that I'll see you once again somehow,

I keep on saying so, but I don't believe it:

Never as you were then,

Alive and real in front of me

In a room with a door and a bed and a lock,

Because even then, no matter how I tried to hold you,

I could not keep you . . . .
The doorbell rings.
I couldn't keep you . . . .
Actress 2 disappears by walking backwards as doorbell rings again.
And I despair of seeing you again. . .
Actress 1 as Joan enters from upstairs.
I know—don't worry—I'll get the door.
JOAN: I wasn't thinking about that.
It's way too late and we're all out of candy.
Fuck 'em—we're not home.
Joan hugs Jeff.
You about ready to go to bed?
JEFF: Oh, I can't sleep.
I'm going to have at least another drink,
Watch some more TV—I don't know . . . .
JOAN: Well, let me get it for you.
You don't mind do you?
JEFF: I don't mind.
Joan is exiting towards kitchen.
I love you.
Joan returns, touches his face, kisses him.
JOAN: I love you too.
Joan exits towards kitchen.
BLACKOUT.

THE SIXTY-FIRST SCENE

S.M.: [*Off*] Sixty-one—go!
Lights up: Actress 1 as Joan is watching TV. Actor 2 and Actress 2 call offstage; Joan doesn't react.

ACTOR 2: [*Off*] Joan? We're going. . . .
ACTRESS 2: [*Off*] We're going, Joan . . . .
ACTOR 2: [*Off*] Come on, Joan, we're going. . . .
ACTRESS 2: [*Off*] Come on, Joan. . . .
ACTOR 2: [*Off*] We're going . . . .
ACTRESS 2: [*Off*] Hurry, Joanie, hurry. . . .
ACTOR 2: [*Off*] Come on, we're going. . . .
ACTRESS 2: [*Off*] Joanie!. . .
ACTOR 2: [*Off*] Hurry, Joanie, hurry. . .
ACTRESS 2: [*Off*] Come on Joan. . .
ACTOR 2: [*Off*] Here we go, Joan!. . .
ACTRESS 2: [*Off*] Goodbye!. . .
ACTOR 2: [*Off*] Goodbye! We're going!. . .
ACTRESS 2: [*Off*] Goodbye, Joan!. . .
> *Silence.*
> *Joan rises, changes TV channels, sits again.*
> BLACKOUT.

FIFTY-THIRD SCENE

S.M.: [*Off*] Fifty-three—go!
> *Lights up: Actor & Actress 1 as Jeff & Joan are watch-*
> *ing TV. Actor 2 appears from kitchen as Beast.*
ACTOR 2: Hey, you guys?
> We were just thinking of going to the DQ.
> We were both thinking maybe we'd do that.
> How about it? You want to go?
> You want to go to the DQ?
> You're welcome to come along.
> But. . . we're going—we're—we're going to go—unh—

We're going in five maybe ten minutes.

Maybe fifteen tops she's in there taking a leak or something.

So—you want to go to the DQ, hunh?

You want to go?

Or maybe not.

No problem.

It's just something we thought—we kind of go into it—unh...

Actually it was her idea.

But you don't have to, unh.

If you want us to get you something...

You want us to get you something?

Okay—well—

We'll be—unh—we'll be out there getting ready if you, unh...

You know, if you want....

    Actor 2 exits. Jeff & Joan have not reacted. Beat. Jeff turns to Joan.

JEFF: You want to go?

JOAN: I don't know.

You want to go?

JEFF: There's nothing on....

JOAN: Okay, let's go....

    BLACKOUT.

THE SEVENTIETH SCENE

S.M.: [*Off*] Scene seventy—go!

    Lights up: Barestage; birdcall sounds. A Ghost enters

from closet and crosses to window. The Ghost pulls down the windowshade. On the windowshade are these words:

T H E   E N D

BLACKOUT.

Leave It to Beaver
Is Dead

by
Des McAnuff

© Des McAnuff, 1976, 1979
CAUTION: No performances or readings of this work may be given without express authorization of the author or his agent. For production rights, contact The William Morris Agency.

Leave It to Beaver Is Dead was originally produced at the Theatre Second Floor, Toronto, Canada, in February 1975, with the following cast:

Saverin .... Geza Kovacs

The Lizzard .... Carol Lazare

Dennis .... Philip Craig

Luke .... Larry Davis

Bill Thompson .... J. W. Messinger

Songs By Des McAnuff and Larry Davis
Producer: Bill House
Director and Designer: Paul Bettis

Leave It to Beaver Is Dead opened in New York City on March 21, 1979, at the New York Shakespeare Festival's Public Theatre, Joseph Papp, Producer. The production was directed by the author, with the following cast:

Saverin .... Mandy Patinkin

The Lizzard .... Diane Wiest

Dennis .... Saul Rubinek

Luke .... Brent Spiner

Bill Thompson .... Maury Chaikin

Set Designer: Heidi Landesman
Costumes: Jennifer Von Mayrhauser
Lighting: Victor En Yu Tan
Stage Managers: Sherman Warner and Peter Dowling

For Ken and Andrew
With Love and Thanks to Paul

PART I

(The Space: The laboratory and living quarters of an organization called "The Show." Brown and warm! A large floor area covered and cluttered with articles, implements and objects that relate directly or loosely to "The Show"; many doors, one leading to a washroom, some eventually leading to the street. Beds, filing cabinets, hammocks, a tent, a sand box, a primitive ladder, a barber's chair, a wall clock, colourful cushions and assorted pieces of useful kitsch, Christmas tree lights, rare exotic posters, a large blackboard, stacks of Coca-Cola bottles emptied, stacks of Coca-Cola bottles full, huge tropical plants, a dark room curtained off, a stereo system, the odd remnants of a by-gone drug clinic, a few business phones, cold pool hall hanging lights, warm reading lamps and hot Chinese lanterns may be found in the space. The room is a classic Nineteen Seventies' wonderworld with practical and popular items from early rock-and-roll to date. It is a contemporary laboratory serving the functions of the organization as well as a museum of the Fifties and Sixties complete with hub caps, juke box, malt shop stools, water pipes and traces of glitter. Saverin, Lizzard and Luke, the hosts of "The Show" have full access to the multiple lights and sounds in the space. The Scene: The audience is invited into the underworld by Lizzard and Saverin as guests of "The Show." As the guests enter, Saverin and Lizzard make last minute preparations for their main guest of honour, Dennis, by changing records, adjusting the lights to dim, changing clothes, arranging details, and shaving Lizzard's legs with a straight razor. Lizzard clicks on and off a cassette recording of Dennis talking. Saverin foams her legs and draws the blade of a straight razor over her calves with graceful

*expertise. There remains a confusion of noises until Saverin
switches off the stereo. Lizzard turns back to the beginning
of the of the tape of Dennis. Saverin resumes shaving her
legs. They listen.)*
DENNIS: [*on tape*] This is Dennis. Dennis. J. The trusty leader.
Are you all listening to me? Luke? Saverin? Whoever's
left? Hope the tape's in the right hands. Three a.m. here.
I'm sitting in my room eating grapefruit. Hello grapefruit!
O.K. This is a message to the Front. It has to be tape-
time because. . . because our lines seem to have gotten
crossed somewhere and I wasn't getting through. I
thought you'd find this hard to resist. So. Hello. What
happened, do you think? "Don't send me no more letters,
No?" Eh, Saverin or what? No reply? Why should I write
dead letters on top of everything else? Good evening, here
is the news. The exchange program is stupid. Fucking
Canada. I should never have transferred up here. It's suicide. The University of Guelph is Desolation Row under
cover and I am crying in the wilderness, kids. I'm coming
back. Early. . . earlier than. . . . I'm coming back, that's
the message. Don't have strokes. Guelph and pre-med.
Pre-med is really the "forget number" of all time. Two
years are enough. I've almost choked on them. Two
years—a taste. Guts, gore, grind. I can't hack it. One long
dissection. The frog and onwards and upwards and in-
wards. It's gotten so bad lately that I almost. . . I almost
tried to. . . I almost tried to fuck myself. And Guelph. I
had a date tonight. It was disastrous. Pool halls, malt
shops, bowling alleys, shit kickers, no decent women so
forget it. To speak truth, our old mission the drug clinic
is pulling me home. Return of the runaway. Del Shannon.
And I'm glad you're there. . . if you still are. You know,

I only heard about the change of address because I
bumped into Harold Leamon's sister here, and she'd heard
something weird from Harold. Are you going under-
ground? Further down the road seems like high intrigue
to me. Deep downtown. I'm really eager. Can you adjust
to fit? That's it, mystery men. I'll be arriving at 8:30 at
the station on the 13th. I'll come over right away and
give you a good hard talking to. Seriously, all is forgiven
after Guelph and pre-med. Love you anyway. I've got. . .
we've got to get it all together. . . again. Children, goodnight. I'll beat you in the morning. This is "Dennis J."
signing off. Later.

> *The tape clicks off.*

LIZZARD: Tense!

SAVERIN: Tense!

LIZZARD: Choice.

SAVERIN: O.K.

LIZZARD: Pre-med. Post med.

SAVERIN: Whiskers. Bend back. I missed some whiskers. [*He
resumes shaving.*]

LIZZARD: We'll see how far it goes. Maybe a party at the end
of the show. Maybe.

SAVERIN: I sense a marathon coming on. Maybe.

LIZZARD: Probably tomorrow for the party.

SAVERIN: To be optimistic.

> *A silence. He organizes; she thinks.*

LIZZARD: Flash! I think I've got an idea for a bit. I want to
make a deal with the folks upstairs. The pet department.
It's a belated Christmas gift as part of the reception. I
hate to bring up the evening's black and blues dues, Saverin, but I'm coming out in search of funds.

SAVERIN: Later!

LIZZARD: Sorry son. I'm out. It's a necessity.

SAVERIN: I'm begging 'cause of the rush.

LIZZARD: It's a last minute effect.

SAVERIN: Is it good?

LIZZARD: Very.

SAVERIN: Expensive?

LIZZARD: Seventy-five and it's alive.

SAVERIN: Take seventy-five from petty cash but let my high pri job finish itself first, please.

LIZZARD: Plus twenty-five.

SAVERIN: O.K. One even.

LIZZARD: One even, plush twenty-five.

SAVERIN: What happened to seventy-five?

LIZZARD: I'll take one twenty-five to cover my fee plus accessories.

SAVERIN: Some number for the old leader of the pack.

LIZZARD: Nothing's too good for the founding father.

SAVERIN: That's right. Some number indeed.

LIZZARD: [*She takes the money from an envelope and puts the envelope in a till*] Want a hint?

SAVERIN: Do you want me surprised?

LIZZARD: I want Dennis to be surprised.

SAVERIN: Well.

LIZZARD: I don't want you in a shocker, do I? If I alienate you, I'll end up alone with him.

SAVERIN: The gift.

LIZZARD: I am buying a yellow parakeet for Dennis. Alive!

SAVERIN: A little heavy.

LIZZARD: A budgie.

He makes a finishing stroke.

SAVERIN: A yellow budgie.

LIZZARD: Is my hair freaky?

SAVERIN: Muss it. We want your ten cent ravaged look. Pre-conceptions.

LIZZARD: If you were him could you recognize the eyes.

SAVERIN: In the whitest of light. That's the idea, isn't it?

LIZZARD: Provides heavy duty contrast. "Who is this creature?" Fantasy land. I'll change my name every other round. What do you think, Saverin? Sandy "Skip" Henderson, Doctor Kathryn Kildare. Prom Queen Pam.

SAVERIN: Polythene Pom Pom Pam. Interesting. Take your "B"vitamins.

LIZZARD: Maybe he'll be very late. It's fashionable to be very late. Leave it to Dennis.

SAVERIN: I nicked your calf.

LIZZARD: O.K.

SAVERIN: Dust. Tea. Coke. Butts. The tube. Leg hair. Costumes. Incense.

LIZZARD: I'm a bleeder, buddy. I need a Band-Aid.

SAVERIN: Fuck the Band-Aid. Coagulate.

LIZZARD: If we're lucky he might notice the gash.

SAVERIN: Oh Ho!

LIZZARD: Oh Ho!

SAVERIN: Sunglasses. Hat and yardstick. Razor.

LIZZARD: Ah! Do we hide all sharp objects? No. We can't.

SAVERIN: Not with Dennis.

LIZZARD: He'd miss the point of the show.

SAVERIN: Sharp.

LIZZARD: And so the danger course is pursued.

SAVERIN: We call it taking a chance on having an effect. On your toes.

LIZZARD: Best friends bring high stakes. Breathe deep. Let's get scared.

SAVERIN: Nothing cleans like a little honest fear.

LIZZARD: But even escape routes must be considered, Saverin.
All options must be explored for the love of Dennis J.
Last chance to abort mission "Re-entry." Leave a sign on
the door. Just tack a sign on the door and skip away.

SAVERIN: I don't think so.

LIZZARD: "Welcome home from your journey, Dennis."

SAVERIN: Check the details. You're looking very manufactured.
[Gives her a compact]

LIZZARD: "We folded your drug clinic. Sorry sweetie. Love
Saverin."

SAVERIN: *[fills two wine glasses with Coke]* Incense. No candles
but a snort of incense just as he does the big entrance.

LIZZARD: A sign would be heady. Then he wouldn't punch your
face in like in eleventh grade behind the stadium. Cheer
up, boy.

SAVERIN: The tapes. The discs. The gun.

LIZZARD: Dennis loved his doper's clinic. Oh, oh.

SAVERIN: We has a big gig to make, ma'am. Get it up.

LIZZARD: Thump out. Time for you to take your lumps.
Danger field.

SAVERIN: I'll get the Handy Andy.

LIZZARD: Saverin. The point is—keep it down.

SAVERIN: Right. In the meantime, let's get it moving.
Luke comes in from the street.
Luko!
*Luke pushes a shopping cart filled with brown paper
bags and a table-top baseball game. His hair is cropped.
He is dressed in a jogging suit with yellow sunglasses to
brighten his activity on the street.*

LUKE: Presto.

LIZZARD: *[moving to a shaving mirror and smiling at Luke]*
For starters I need a dinky mole on the cheekbone.

SAVERIN: How will the space grab his ass?

LUKE: Brown!

[*A silence. They look at each other*] Warm and homey. It'll take him thirty seconds to start tidying up.

SAVERIN: What you got, Luke?

LUKE: Gifts from Terry and the Afghans. Been visiting.

LIZZARD: Clear the slate?

LUKE: No interruptions. It's a free night for Dennis J. But I've got an option pending.

SAVERIN: And so?

LUKE: Terry wants to come up in the wee wee hours and lay some entertainment on the post evening session. The Afghans want to bring some friends and have a High Hockey Mass. I reminded Terry of our exorbitant rates, but he placed one hundred ones in my pocket as a down payment. I told him we were expecting our old leader Dennis back from the fog, but. . .

LIZZARD: Don't move too fast with Dennis J.

LUKE: They just want some jungle snapshots of themselves playing rock and rope tricks with you and the Lizzard. The dawn patrol. A party for Dennis would be an easy gig.

LIZZARD: Providing it doesn't turn into a wake.

LUKE: What do you think?

SAVERIN: Later, Maybe. Interruptions are red, red, red. Patience, all parties. Keep control of the doors and phones.

LIZZARD: We need to be alone tonight with our jock in the box.

LUKE: O.K. I'll postpone Terry and the Afghans, but. . . we'll keep the front, my colleagues. After Dennis's marathon, maybe we can drop Terry on his head. A little tea. You can boogie. Lizzard can address the crowd. Terry loves to meet new faces.

SAVERIN: The question is, does Dennis?

LIZZARD: We should keep our Terrys and the like well hidden from beginners.

SAVERIN: Expectations! Expectations!

LUKE: Dennis leads. We provide. Dennis reacts. We respond. We dunk him in good loving because aside from old times we can use his knowledge. He may have forgotten that he helped plant the seed as I'm sure the medicine dues at Guelph are like mind sludge. We'll just gently remind him so we can all enjoy the show. He's wise to our new move deep down inside. Dennis left us before he got left behind. He'll catch up. We welcome the good student home from night school. Watch Dennis go from the dean of the grant application to the prince of profit.

LIZZARD: Easy. Don't get tricked into explanations. The object is not to talk the talk but to walk the walk.

SAVERIN: Right, right, Dennis wins all the arguments. I love him. There he is at center field still playing all star team captain of a suburban clinic for drug addicts. Dennis, Dennis.

LUKE: He's some slugger.

LIZZARD: Tonight he's just the patient.

LUKE: He'll go for the bomb.

LIZZARD: When he passes, he'll serve as apprentice because Dennis is an asset and we're into expansion. We love him. But slow and easy. Save him first. Listen for the cracks underneath the F.M. voice. No rushing. Let baby Dennis step back slowly, one layer at a time, one year at a time. Don't let him talk you into believing that he can graduate early. Past relations bring deviations.

SAVERIN: We don't want him to become some kind of peripheral character.

LIZZARD: And we don't want him papering the walls with his suicide notes.

LUKE: Right.

SAVERIN: Right. Be careful children.

LUKE: He'll hang on, old friendly.

LIZZARD: Just another customer.

LUKE: Just another guest on the farm.

LIZZARD: But very welcome. Starters?

SAVERIN: The show should open without any set bits.

LUKE: Strictly off the cuff, nothing up the sleeve.

LIZZARD: I'll need room to move tonight.

SAVERIN: He'll love you heavily.

LIZZARD: We'll keep his head turning.

LUKE: We'll cook.

SAVERIN: Time is pressing.

LIZZARD: I'm changing gears. It's a power shift. Sweet dreams but stay awake.

SAVERIN: Luke you ride shotgun for me undercover.

LUKE: O.K. And I'll phone Terry. We can have the party planned as a possible for Dennis if we make it that far.

SAVERIN: Maybe. Let's boot.

LUKE: I'll come out when I feel the urge. You provide the pounce. [*He leaves.*]

SAVERIN: I should keep notes.

LIZZARD: I'll watch you, Saverin. I won't let you drift.

SAVERIN: To your stations. Show starts at nine bells on the button.

LUKE: [*He comes back*] Wham! He's out there waiting! He's just waiting and looking. Ready, ready.

SAVERIN: What time is it? [*Saverin turns off almost all of the lights and stands in a dark corner. Lizzard scrambles to the entrance of the tent.*]

LIZZARD: It's showtime.

LUKE: [*from the darkroom*] Bon voyage!

SAVERIN: Fucking Accutron.

LIZZARD: Keep it down.

SAVERIN: O.K.! When I call "Curtain," it's silence. He'll stomp in within the minute.

LIZZARD: He's sure to sneeze at the dusty dirties.

SAVERIN: Thirty seconds.

LIZZARD: Hey. More quotations. I found the postcard with the Mountie from young Dennis J.

SAVERIN: He's out there waiting. What's he doing out there?

LIZZARD: [*in and out of the tent. She explores.*] I found my M and M's. Far out. Hot line. The lady finds her M and M's.

SAVERIN: What's he waiting for? It's crazy.

LIZZARD: Keep it down!

SAVERIN: I tell Dennis we buried the clinic. You pop out. Two words. First word.

LIZZARD: You.

SAVERIN: Second word.

LIZZARD: Dead.

SAVERIN: Congratulations.

LIZZARD: The body surfaces and mother starts practising her mute...

SAVERIN: [*calls numbers spasmodically*] 12, 11, 10, 9, 8, 7, 6, 5, 4,

LIZZARD: Stiff.

SAVERIN: 3, 2, 1.
Curtain!

LIZZARD: Blast off!

Pause.

SAVERIN: What's he doing out there?

LIZZARD: He's writing you a suicide note. Keep it down.

SAVERIN: Where the fuck are you, Dennis?

LIZZARD: Guelph's in another time zone. No speeding. Keep it down.

SAVERIN: Dennis J. Doctor D. Would the crew please hold their remote stations.

Telephone rings.

Fuck!

LIZZARD: Keep it down, Saverin. Seriously.

SAVERIN: [*on phone*] "The Show." Which poodle?

LIZZARD: Let Dennis talk to the Poodle Lady. That would turn his head around.

SAVERIN: [*on phone*] The poodle looks cuddly. Good enough to eat. I'm sorry, Madam... I can't talk. [*Saverin slams the phone down. Lizzard quietly cues up the tape from the tent. Saverin returns to his position in the darkness.*]

DENNIS: [*his voice, out of sight, knocking*] Saverin. Saverin? ... Saverin!

SAVERIN: [*very quietly*] Paging Doctor D. Doctor D. Dennis, Den-nis.

DENNIS: [*Not hearing him, out of sight, Dennis slams a door.*] Saverin?

He can be heard walking cautiously, then boldly.

Saverin!

SAVERIN: [*whisper*] Come on, Doctor. Dennis J. Doctor D.

DENNIS: Saverin!

Dennis walks into sight past Saverin. He carries a tote bag. Saverin flicks on a photographic light which glares into the eyes of Dennis. Dennis blinks. Saverin emerges from behind the light with the two wine glasses filled with Coke and a cane. He hands one glass to Dennis and twirls the cane. Dennis smiles, sniffs the Coke and tastes.

Fine bouquet. Good year. Ten ounce can. Opened between eight and eight fifteen.

SAVERIN: Twenty-six ounce bottle. Opened at seven thirty. [*A pause*] Yesterday. [*A silence*]

DENNIS: Well, we have flat Coke.

SAVERIN: Flat, was it?

DENNIS: Flat cola. Yes. No bubbly carbonation.

SAVERIN: Flat indeed.

DENNIS: Certainly was flat.

SAVERIN: On the other hand I'm sorry if it was, how shall I say?

DENNIS: Flat?

SAVERIN: Flat.

DENNIS: Don't mention it.

SAVERIN: I wouldn't dare.

> *A pause.*

DENNIS: Well hello, Mrs. Wilson.

SAVERIN: It's Dennis-the-Menace. Are you late?

DENNIS: Surfing on the subway.

SAVERIN: Subway surfing?

DENNIS: Has Luke made it to South Ferry?

SAVERIN: No hands?

DENNIS: No appendages. I just fucking floated, dear.

SAVERIN: Subway surfing?

DENNIS: Has luke made it to South Ferry?

SAVERIN: We don't do it anymore. [*Saverin tours Dennis around the space. Dennis explores in the dim light straining to see*]

DENNIS: What? You went and got grownup Saverin. Shame. You soft like pig, huh?

SAVERIN: How's your mother?

DENNIS: Gorgeous. How's your mother?

SAVERIN: Gorgeous.

DENNIS: Too bad they're married.

SAVERIN: How are the tits on your old mom?

DENNIS: Nicest in the whole world.

SAVERIN: Have you been out home to see her yet?

DENNIS: I surfed straight here from the station.

SAVERIN: It is said that Mom's teats get old.

DENNIS: I got a message from her telling me to forget visiting. She's taking off on old Burt. Finally. Seems she got herself a young shiner with some blue chip stocks. They're off to Miami. Dear Mom. I think she got bored. She wants to put those old teats to good use. Burt's cracking up on his own, as soon as she was gone, splash, right into the toilet. Poor Burt!

SAVERIN: Lucky Mom!

DENNIS: So much for my free room in the split level. I'll have to crash out here with you. I'll have to. After we clean up. What's with all this mess, Saverin?

SAVERIN: Hey! What brand do I smoke?

DENNIS: Camel with a filter.

SAVERIN: Have one without, Dennis. J.

DENNIS: Pretty strong, son.

SAVERIN: I smoke them all the time, Doc.

DENNIS: Thanks for all the letters, telegrams, candygrams, greeting cards and long distance calls, shithead.

SAVERIN: Have a Camel, Dennis. J.

DENNIS: I still smoke menthol. No, sincerely, I want you to know that I'm touched.

SAVERIN: My fingers are too fat for dialing now, you see? Cold and numb. I've forgotten how to read or write. I thought you might use your university smarts to help grease up my head.

DENNIS: I write you at camp for eighty-seven years and you

don't send me as much as a fucking postcard.

SAVERIN: Mind if I smoke? Well. You know.

DENNIS: You got my tape.

SAVERIN: We studied it carefully.

DENNIS: You're kidding.

SAVERIN: No. *[A silence]*

DENNIS: How lofty, Saverin. Who had the space before you?

SAVERIN: Various persons. Various.

DENNIS: Why didn't they take their garbage with them?

SAVERIN: Ah. We thought they had.

DENNIS: You could use some organization, maybe.

SAVERIN: I saved all your letters.

DENNIS: Really.

   The telephone rings.

SAVERIN: Who knows you're here?

   It stops after one ring. A pause.

DENNIS: Wrong number.

SAVERIN: Ya.

DENNIS: Does Doctor Bromley still drop by?

SAVERIN: Along with several others from time to time. There's no shortage of resource people.

DENNIS: You told him about. . . that I was coming back.

SAVERIN: He seemed interested.

DENNIS: I like it [*the room*].

SAVERIN: You like it?

DENNIS: I like it.

SAVERIN: He likes it.

DENNIS: When did you move?

SAVERIN: About a week. Two weeks. Three weeks. It's been about, let me think.

DENNIS: A month.

SAVERIN: A month. Ya. And a week. Maybe longer. How was

Guelph?

DENNIS: Fucking awful. *[Takes off his coat, tries to get comfortable]*

SAVERIN: Be specific.

DENNIS: It didn't make it with me, what do you want? The faculty would probably say I couldn't cut the...ah, it's bullshit. I copped out with strict intentions, so I'm not your classic stray dog drop-out. I picked up some valuables. Maybe, now, we'll know what the fuck we're doing. At the very least I learned how to connect with pharmacists for looser scripts. We'll start sidestepping some of the conservative Rexall paranoia crap.

Pause.

I didn't think I'd be back so soon.

SAVERIN: My God. Those hands. My son the doctor. And he was such a little cuddly fat boy. Only yesterday. I think. Or maybe longer. Ya. Wednesday he was fat. Thursday, Friday. Today he's on his way to sawing up bodies.

DENNIS: Too bad there's no closet space, that's a drag. But you moved all by yourself. So "Operation Deep Downtown."

SAVERIN: Return to "Leave It To Beaver" where we find Beaver left as an ulcerous stomach.

DENNIS: It's a better space than 291, isn't it? We won't miss the old plaza.

SAVERIN: Starring the late Hugh Beaumont, Barbara Billingsley, Tony Dow.

DENNIS: And Jerry Mathers as the Beaver. Speeders are multiplying around the town. That's what I hear. Are you busy?

SAVERIN: Very busy. He's dead, did you know?

DENNIS: My hands are dirty.

SAVERIN: O.D.'d on his own ambition.

DENNIS: In here?

Saverin points him toward the washroom. He goes.

SAVERIN: Hey. [*A pause. Dennis turns*]
It's good to see you.

DENNIS: Busy boys again. [*Goes into washroom*]

SAVERIN: Lots of gossip on which to catch up over a bottle of catsup. My son the medicine man. The last of the Mohicans.

> *Saverin takes up a new position behind a few plants and a bird cage, out of the way. Dennis returns, hands dripping, not seeing Saverin.*

DENNIS: Saverin! Sav? You got a — [*A towel lands at Dennis's feet*]
So. What's with the empty bird cage?

SAVERIN: The budgie died.

DENNIS: I'm sorry.

SAVERIN: Ya. Well. You know. He was old.

DENNIS: Who found the corpse?

SAVERIN: I did. I've got him right here on the rocks.

DENNIS: What?

> *Saverin takes a dead parakeet from a water jug packed with ice.*

SAVERIN: We were away for the weekend. I found the corpse on a Monday. He starved to death. I got all teary when I found him, but that was phoney wasn't it? I mean if I had cared, I would have fed him.

DENNIS: Is that the same parakeet? Didn't your uncle give it to you?

SAVERIN: I don't remember.

DENNIS: You should dispose of it, don't you think? I mean, really. You should get rid of the thing.

SAVERIN: We need it until we get a replacement. It was very popular.

DENNIS: You should get the cage out of here. It's depressing as hell. There's feathers all over the place. God, Saverin you haven't even emptied the shit tray. What was his name?

SAVERIN: I don't know. I don't think we had a name for him. Actually that's a fib. Lately we've been calling him Dennis. [*He tosses the dead bird to Dennis*]

DENNIS: [*fumbles and tries to remain in control*] You spoofing me, Sarge?

SAVERIN: Needed a monitor to clean the chalk brushes, empty the garbage, feed the bird.

DENNIS: Father's been away on business. . . [*He tries to put the bird down casually.*]

SAVERIN: Could you have brought the budgie back to life?

DENNIS: [*awkwardly*] No time. Been active. Jacking off through Inorganic Chemistry. Watching the dregs of the frats hang moons from the residence windows. Full moons. Half moons. Jazzing with the nurses. Great women, really. Ouch. Been schooling dear. I feel dirty. I need a shave.

SAVERIN: [*sings*] The leader of the pack. *[Quietly mumbles]* Met him at the candy store. Turned around, winked at me. Get the picture? Yes, we see.

DENNIS: You shouldn't give a speeder valium. Did you know?

SAVERIN: Really?

DENNIS: It's dangerous. We could have fucked up a lot of people.

SAVERIN: The spoils. We were dancing with the spoils. That's all. Dancing, so free with Dr. D. I got a haircut.

A pause. Dennis goes back into the washroom. The toilet flushes.

DENNIS: God, it's dusty. Don't you dust? We're going to have to catch up for your lost month. You obviously haven't been sweating your ass. We'll rent a Hoover and borrow a van. We'll have to clear the space completely. There's barely room for the essentials the way it's set up. I don't see the oxygen, what, did you pawn it, babe? The junkie decor is deadly. It wants editing. If I was going over the top the atmosphere in here would soak up my mind. Hardly calming. Not too healthy, lad. You'll do in some young garbage head with shock from the birdcage. Very bad taste, Saverin. Hallucinations of great angry birds.

SAVERIN: [mumbles] We folded the clinic in January, January, January.

We folded the clinic in January. Hell low Den.

Dennis comes out of the washroom and looks at Saverin.

DENNIS: Whose razor? What did you say?

SAVERIN: [mumbles] We folded the clinic in January, January, January. We folded the clinic in January. And introducing.

DENNIS: What? Saverin, what? What is this? What?

A light comes on in front of the tent. Lizzard emerges. She is dressed like a Goddess. She wears the cassette tape recorder slung over her shoulder. Music comes from the machine. She strums it like a guitar. Dennis continues to ask, "What?"

LIZZARD: [sings over the recorded music]
"Easy teasie, give bare back a smack.
Got some school boys to lay down a track.
The head gets busted just give it a crack.
Say soothe me, smoothie, I'm here to relax.
Imagination, your personal delights
Fears, tears, frights.
Think fast. It's got to last."
The tape clicks off. She speaks.

Very merry Christmas, Dennis! A bit belated but very merry.

DENNIS: Hello, Loretta. *[A pause]*
Loretta?

SAVERIN: Dennis, I'd like you to meet Lizzard.

LIZZARD: Who's Loretta?

SAVERIN: An old patient of ours. This is Lizzard.

DENNIS: Hello, Loretta.

LIZZARD: *[picks up the straight razor]* I don't know "Loretta." Like a shave, mister? You asked for a shave and a wash. Why everybody's doing it. Hair or bare? Bare for you, Dennis.

DENNIS: Tra la la.

LIZZARD: Especially for ankle men. And track and field men. The use of hair on modern man is completely fucked anyway. You don't need to be an ape. Change your image. *[Goes to shave his chest and he goes along with it with a nervous giggle.]*

DENNIS: You shouldn't have gone to so much bubble.
  They gently seat him on the couch and bare his chest by opening his shirt.

LIZZARD: You're still not allowed to hit girls. Don't fight it, Dennis. I've been shaved clean for a year. I'll bet you'd look like a pin-up.

DENNIS: Get away from me.

LIZZARD: Just half way.

DENNIS: You're welcome.

LIZZARD: It scrapes, doesn't hurt. *[Cuts him]*

DENNIS: Ow!

LIZZARD: So much for Dennis the Maso.

DENNIS: You cut me. What was that? You cut my chest.
  He breathes heavily.

DENNIS: It's enough to kill you, Saverin. I'm splitting my tummy.

A silence. Dennis tries to laugh.

LIZZARD: My name is Lizzard. Could I have a talk with you? I'm from "The Show." My friends and I could really get off on spending some time with you. Hard to believe? Maybe you're missing something. You might not cop this right away, but there's no need to feel modest. You've just got to lie low, make your choices, and let it happen.

DENNIS: Very nice, Loretta. I'd love to play but I'm tied up right now.

LIZZARD: My name is Lizzard. Could I have a talk with you?

SAVERIN: I was afraid to write to you, Dennis J., old buddy, old chum.

DENNIS: Well. Nice reception.

SAVERIN: We folded the clinic in January, January, Jan. . .

DENNIS: [*breaks his cool*] It's not yours to fold!

SAVERIN: [*quietly*] It's done. [*A silence*]

LIZZARD: [*kindly*] Quite a startler! Come on Dennis J. Put pride aside and think on it. I don't expect you to articulate your admiration right away. Keep it on the inside, naturally. No rushing.

DENNIS: Oh yes. You've come a long way, Lor —

LIZZARD: Who's Loretta?

A pause.

DENNIS: Is this a joke?

LIZZARD: I'm Lizzard.

DENNIS: Is this a joke? Is it?

SAVERIN: No!

LIZZARD: No!

DENNIS: It's a joke!

Dennis walks away. Stops. Looks back.

LIZZARD: It's time to ante-up. We should see how much you've got at stake.

Lizzard goes through Dennis's belongings, carefully choosing articles of clothing and personal products.

DENNIS: I really don't need you to do that.

SAVERIN: Does it bother you, Dennis?

DENNIS: It doesn't bother me, Saverin. Oh no.

SAVERIN: You're not enjoying the show.

DENNIS: Trains make me nervous. Surprises make me hysterical.

SAVERIN: Let's be very gentle.

DENNIS: No, you don't seem to be understanding what I'm saying to you. I'm here. I came home to work on the drug clinic. The one that I raised the old funds for, sweetheart.

SAVERIN: It's been replaced.

DENNIS: That corner. Along that wall. Or by the door. Where should we put the oxygen?

SAVERIN: The clinic's gone bye-bye.

DENNIS: Fuck you.

SAVERIN: Don't be hasty.

DENNIS: Nothing has been resolved.

SAVERIN: Mister Clinic was officially declared dead a year ago last January, Doctor.

DENNIS: I raised the money.

SAVERIN: Welcome back.

DENNIS: Thanks. Would you mind moving over? I'm expecting some druggies.

SAVERIN: Hey, Hey, Hey. Right this way. We've got something for everyone. Mom, Dad and the whole gang. You don't have to be a doper. There's hope and fun for everyone —

DENNIS: So?

SAVERIN: So it's better than a clinic.

DENNIS: What?

SAVERIN: Take your time. No rushing. I've got the show for you.

DENNIS: I think I'm going to punch you in the stomach.

SAVERIN: Play slapsies.

DENNIS: Have you been goofing?

SAVERIN: You don't have to be cocky, Dennis, really. You've come to the right place. Don't misunderstand.

DENNIS: What's this for?

SAVERIN: It's for your benefit. Not mine. For you.

DENNIS: Yes?

SAVERIN: I am the ghost of Christmas past. Look around, just look around.

DENNIS: I'm looking. O.K?

SAVERIN: You just look right on past the shapes, the checks and the capes and the canes and the purple jerk-offs. You look into the faces. Like somebody carved them all from potatoes. They're not the same faces that walked by in years gone past.

DENNIS: So you snapped your fingers and folded the clinic. I get it? Mr. Super Session, Joe Dimaggio!

SAVERIN: They're muted, Dennis. They're all gummed up. They're looking back at...

DENNIS: I don't know what to say to you. Is that what you want?

SAVERIN: Listen! They're looking for things they weren't looking for in years gone past. Didn't know they were there.

DENNIS: Like what?

SAVERIN: You name the brand. The faces are all full of Coke and popcorn and Polanski and Pasolini and strip joints and tub rubs and Panama red.

DENNIS: That's a very good sound. Meaning what?

SAVERIN: And clinics. They're all full of clinics. Up to their eyeballs with clinics. All thoroughly medicated, Dennis.

DENNIS: Is that right? What the fuck is going on?

SAVERIN: Going down. That's a good question. I think we were a little too late, you know? It would have been good but we're back to the carnival. The institutions didn't do it. We're out on the street. We're working the midway again.

DENNIS: You're running a ferris wheel. A side show. A wax museum?

SAVERIN: You name the brand, Dennis. That's the idea.

DENNIS: You're unhappy.

SAVERIN: You haven't been here for awhile. We got bogged out. I'm happy.

DENNIS: You're happy?

SAVERIN: Ya. I am, aren't I? I'm happy. You might have been too, if you had stayed. How was Guelph? You happy?

DENNIS: Just answer the questions.

SAVERIN: Yes, your honour. The directions have all changed. Look out there. Your clinic would get the shit kicked out of it. It'd be an old crippled lady.

A pause.

DENNIS: Could I see the books, babe?

SAVERIN: You want money. Money we got. Eh? You want to eat nice, 'spensive tastes.

DENNIS: I want to see the books, partner.

SAVERIN: They're incomplete. Play slapsies?

DENNIS: Recite them to me. I want to talk about money.

SAVERIN: *[with a lighter]* O.K. Would you like a light? And a Camel dead end? I got this given to me. Very nice. Gold plated. It's one of a set. There's a hundred in a set. Lizzard has ninety-nine. One of our clients in the department store business. He's a real charmer. He's got some nasty habits on the side. He calls me son. Reminds me of Mr. Anderson. He's an amateur sculptor. . . and a finger painter.

DENNIS: Alright.

[*Trying to take control*]

I had a fantasy on the train. What a coincidence. I was
watching this speck on the window, really boring, thinking about us working in a candy store selling black balls
and ju-jubes and caramels to all the jocks and jets. I was
thinking of how much money you could make by starting a real "junk movement." An old fashioned candy
store, you see. I import the bizarre from the East. Cin-
namon-coated Lebanese fruities with the government
stamp still visible. Lots of white sweet powders wrapped
in cellophane. It's the logical extension of the glucose defi-
ciency in your average home-spun speeder's liver. The
Greeks used to call the liver the "seed of the soul," a
typical symptom of liver disease being acute depression.
The crash, you understand, dear. Speed eats up glucose.
So you get rid of the crash by getting hooked on teenage
acne junk. "It's relief, man." So you line the speeders up
and screw ten dollars for a grab bag out of them. Now
the speeders get tummy aches. And I branch off and open
next door with a Candy Clinic to get them off the glucose
which is ruining their bodies and complexions. Cavities
are soaring. I have Candy Freak sessions and talk downs.
They help each other kick their fifty dollar a day sweet
tooth. Plenty of free coffee, plenty of company, commu-
nity service projects, therapy, dental care and so on.
Beside the Candy Clinic you branch off by opening a
Health Food Shop to get every loser back on the road
to a cleaned out body. The same number. Three stages!
Now, as each store wears out its welcome, we play dom-
inoes so that the Candy Store then becomes a Muscle De-
velopment Studio. Then the Candy Clinic becomes an

Art School. Eventually the Health Food Shop changes
into a fucking spiritualist cult. So we remain functional
for the rest of our lives with an endless streak of once
upon a time addicts going from one store to the second
to the third and back to the first. Finally, of course, when
we open a Senior Citizen's Club,Luke turns into a morti-
cian and eats all the profits. But. Just as we got the first
ex-speeder buried this chain boy sits down beside me and
bounces until the whole seat starts shaking. He wants to
look out the window and I take my eyes off the speck.
When he turned up his sleeve I caught a glimpse of the
mess. There were these big black snakes rolling up and
down his arm, enough snakes to make my veins start to
itch. So too bad for you and my fantasy because the train
made it to the station and Dennis is home again.
> *A pause.*
SAVERIN: Amazing.
LIZZARD: Astounding.
> *Lizzard walks off with Dennis's belongings.*
SAVERIN: A warning. There are more than many mindless ma-
nias in the naked city. When the guests start to request
survival courses for which no instructions exist, either
take them into the gloom, Igor, or turn your face to the
wall. They are not asking for methadone nor pills, nor
points. But they've each put in at least ten thousand hours
at the tube. Ten thousand hours is quite a fix. Time for
a little fine tuning. So pay attention, provide looking
glasses, avoid miracle methods, offer workshops where
the only examples to be found come to life in the mirrors. That's the risk factor. That's where the real show
will go on. No brain scanners, no bio-feedback, no
tranqs. It can no longer be considered a science and it's

certainly not an art. But you don't kid that it's free. There's altogether too much shamming going on around and soon snooping into the grant structure begins on a federal level. And they aren't interested in what you offer but what you take. So you'd better build a new house where the patients turn into customers, where the customers become guests and the guests patrons and the patrons clients and the rate client a heavenly host. We are talking about sincerity here and what exactly do you have to gain young man because it'd better be green and growing or forget it, bogus, bogus, we don't trust you, no way, no how, so application dismissed, you're not getting relief 'cause this is not the depression. Profit is the problem, gentlemen. Who really gives a fuck about baby seals. Dennis J?

DENNIS: Is this a prepared speech? Because if it is you realize that it's total bullshit. If there's one thing I've learned to do in the last two years it's to ask questions. I don't need another fucking lecture.

LIZZARD: [*from the washroom, the flushing sound of toilet*] Saverin! The toilet's overflowing. It's going to gush on the floor, Saverin.

SAVERIN: Wriggle the thingy!

LIZZARD: [*from the washroom*] It's serious business. And time for a change.

SAVERIN: Gotta go, Den. Sor-ry. Hate to./ Boo Hoo.

Saverin goes into the washroom. Lizzard comes out wearing Dennis's clothes.

LIZZARD: How can anyone get any work done with a temperamental toilet.

[Quietly to Saverin] Everything hunky?

SAVERIN: [*from washroom*] Until this.

LIZZARD: Well, that's alright. Use it.

SAVERIN: [*from washroom*] A little music?

LIZZARD: Maybe. How about music, Dennis; you like?

DENNIS: Keep talking, Saverin.

LIZZARD: You look really good, Dennis J.

DENNIS: Thanks. You look a bit crazy, do you mind me saying?

LIZZARD: Not crazy. Can I play you some favourite cuts from . . . Well. What would you like to hear? Something from old times.

DENNIS: Nothing.

LIZZARD: Big Brother and the Holding Company? It's your album.

DENNIS: Alright. O.K.? O.K. . . That's alright.

LIZZARD: [*She produces a broken record.*] Bad choice.

DENNIS: [*just bursting*] Hey! What is the problem? I'm sure we're having a good time, but really.

    A pause.

Are you off?

LIZZARD: Don't talk to me like you know me, Dennis J. That would be just too fast. Relax!

DENNIS: Are you off?

LIZZARD: Off what?

    She plays a Fifties disc on the juke box. They shout above the racket.

DENNIS: Are you off? Tell me the truth.

LIZZARD: That's got nothing to do with the show.

DENNIS: Are you off the shit?

LIZZARD: Watch me, Dennis. See how much I'm on.

SAVERIN: [*in the washroom; plays with the lever, water overflows*] Get the plunger.

LIZZARD: What plunger?

SAVERIN: [*from washroom*] Something. A coathanger. Anything. Dennis?

LIZZARD: You'll like it here, Dennis J...

DENNIS: Oh, lovely. I'm captivated, you know.

SAVERIN: [*from washroom*] Dennis, will you help me?

DENNIS: I don't know anything about toilets.

LIZZARD: Hey. We're going to be partners, Dennis J...Isn't
that an opportunity knock? You and I. Partners.

DENNIS: Are we?

LIZZARD: After you chart your course.

DENNIS: Well, I'm not much on crash courses.

LIZZARD: How are you on crash landings?

DENNIS: So what do you do with our Saverin?

LIZZARD: We create opportunities.

SAVERIN: [*from washroom*] What've you got in here?

DENNIS: Opportunities for what?

LIZZARD: I wish it was easy, Dennis. I don't carry a recipe.
You name the brand.

SAVERIN: [*from washroom*] I think it's fixed. [*Water gurgles*]

DENNIS: How'd the album get broken?

SAVERIN: Shit!

[*The telephone starts ringing*] Just hold it please. Something's caught. I can't get my arm . . . in. . . Dennis, come
in here.

LIZZARD: [*on phone*] The show.

DENNIS: Where are the rest of my albums?

LIZZARD: Somebody wants to talk to Dennis J. . .

Lizzard starts to hand the phone to Dennis.

DENNIS: Me? Oh, wonderful.

SAVERIN: No! [*Comes from washroom and takes phone*] This
is Saverin, we'll work it out, I promise. [*Hangs up*] You're
a riot. A riot. Wrong call.

DENNIS: What was that?

SAVERIN: Just a gag. *[Goes back into washroom]*

DENNIS: You're all tricksy tonight. Mmmm? The good ole funster.

LIZZARD: He wanted to talk to him, Saverin.

SAVERIN: *[comes out]* Now look! Somebody's chucked something into the toilet. *[Back into the washroom]*

DENNIS: *[falling apart]* From all I can tell you've turned into a great argument for compulsory military service. You're in a complete mess here. You're screaming for the most basic discipline and I know the guy to give it to you. What am I, third in command, now? Guess what. I can make trouble for you, kids. With three quick phone calls I can get half your funding cut off. Four. Four quick phone calls.

LIZZARD: I don't think you understand, Dennis.

DENNIS: I'll fight to the death.

LIZZARD: I believe you.

SAVERIN: Dennis, would you please come in here and help?

DENNIS: What is this a cat house? It's a cat house, right?

LIZZARD: Just keep those guesses pouring in. They may be off the mark, but are they revealing!

The phone rings. Dennis grabs the receiver.

DENNIS: *[on phone]* Hello! Yes.

Saverin rushes out and watches.

Look. What do you want exactly? I don't know anything about... What do you get from these people? *[Dennis listens for three seconds and slams down the receiver]* Saverin?

SAVERIN: Dennis?

DENNIS: This is gross. Would you like me to leave? Come back later when you're free?

SAVERIN: You can't leave, can you?

> *A silence*

Just play patience. [*Backs into washroom*]

DENNIS: That sounded like Terry. Or Luke.

DENNIS: Who was that? Did you plan that call? Did you plan this?

> *Saverin comes out of the washroom with a dead budgie. Dennis looks.*

SAVERIN: It isn't very funny. You know? It was here for a reason. It isn't very funny.

DENNIS: I see.

> *He sulks.*

SAVERIN: No, you don't see.

DENNIS: You let him die. Not me. You. I just did the decent thing for the bird. It was disgusting. I got rid of it, what do you want? You don't leave dead things around, it's disrespectful. You kept it here for me, Saverin, to fuck me around. You like turning my stomach? You know how I feel about, you know. . .

SAVERIN: It isn't important that I've had him for five years. It isn't important that I've nursed him through colds. It isn't important that he kept me company?

DENNIS: I just did the decent thing for the bird.

LIZZARD: Dead, dead, dead, Dennis. Decent doesn't enter into it. Please try to be more careful as you wear on, my pretty. Don't ignore our property and our rights. Come to think of it, you've got awfully strong feelings about what is wanted and what is waste. Consider the budgie banger. What is vital to the budgie banger is vital to us. Some of our gear comes from specific requests. The budgie body would have been missed due to your thoughtlessness.

DENNIS: It was dead.

LIZZARD: It's O.K. this time. You've just made a mistake. I won't ask you to wipe the floor. But if you trip over anything else that's dead, give us a break, don't flush it.

DENNIS: You shouldn't have —

LIZZARD: Forget it. It's O.K. No harm done.

A pause.

Wow!

SAVERIN: Can I get you something, Dennis? A Coke.

Lizzard seems to leave. She remains within earshot.

DENNIS: I thought I was doing you a favour. I guess you don't think so.

SAVERIN: Hey, that's alright.

DENNIS: Beautiful. Just gorgeous. So tell me.

SAVERIN: In your case Doctor, the prescription is not a description.

DENNIS: So? Tell me.

SAVERIN: Remember when you used to pick me up in the— Impala with —?

DENNIS: No. Tell me. I'm interested.

SAVERIN: [*sings*] You got to tell me you're coming back to me, you gotta tell me you're coming back —

DENNIS: Gorgeous. You close the clinic and —

SAVERIN: Hey, What was my locker combo?

DENNIS: You think you can twist your way —

SAVERIN: What was my locker combo? What was my locker combo?

DENNIS: Forty-three, thirty—I forget. O.K.?

SAVERIN: It's been a long time. Aren't you excited?

DENNIS: You're fucked up.

SAVERIN: I know you're a pervert. You became a pervert in Guelph.

DENNIS: Go on!

SAVERIN: I'm showing you. Be excited.

DENNIS: O.K. . . I'm fine. I'm waiting with baited breath, dear.
I'll be happy to change the goddamn subject. Agreed?

SAVERIN: You don't know what the subject is.

DENNIS: Isn't that the subject?

SAVERIN: Right. Very fast.

DENNIS: O.K. How's old Luke?

SAVERIN: Active. Attentive.

DENNIS: How's the filming coming?

SAVERIN: He isn't doing it anymore.

DENNIS: No?

SAVERIN: He's into stills. . . ya, and he's good. He's making
money.

DENNIS: Stills?

SAVERIN: He's really good.

DENNIS: Portraits, or what?

SAVERIN: [*Turns on a tape recorder. Old Rock and Roll*] Commercial. Very commercial. For a while he was doing fake
accidents and sending them to the Enquirer. He got six
printed. Lizzard and I posed for him, smeared chicken
blood all over each other. He did car crashes, you know,
train wrecks and one beauty suicide.

DENNIS: I don't want to hear about it.

SAVERIN: Then he got into the pornies. As a matter of fact I
heard him called "Porny Luke" a number of times. But
he was really into accidents. Then about a year ago he
left everything behind and started to get serious.

DENNIS: I knew he'd screw up. He just did too much dope,
much too much.

*Luke enters from the darkroom. He wears aviation
coveralls. He has a camera around his neck and carries
a basketball behind his back. And a yo-yo.*

LUKE: Dennis J. Dennis?

DENNIS: How do you do?

Luke laughs. Dennis laughs. It is eerie.

LUKE: Hel-lo Dennis.

A pause. Saverin and Lizzard lay back.

DENNIS: Luke. Howdy Luke. I was just asking about old Luke. I wouldn't recognize you normally.

LUKE: Oh, I've been gathering up the crumbs, champ. Did you play much ball up in higher learning?

DENNIS: Not much. I was considered bush league.

LUKE: Ya? What's been happening?

DENNIS: Nothing.

LUKE: What's been happening?

DENNIS: Nothing. Have you been here all along?

LUKE: Well, we didn't want to confound you with numbers. How's the show? Are your toenails still growing?

DENNIS: What?

LUKE: You've been studying. You know about corpses, now. Toenails and hair growth after — [*gestures throat cutting*]

DENNIS: I'm amazed. I guess you've been hearing. I'm amazed at the detail. Amazed, not pleased.

LUKE: Smile for me, Dennis.

DENNIS: How's my old friend, Saverin?

LUKE: He got a job coaching. He premiered as a stand-in. He's doing wonders.

DENNIS: I'd really like to see him.

LUKE: Have you had access to a T.V. tube?

DENNIS: Yes.

LUKE: Stereo?

DENNIS: Yes.

LUKE: A laboratory? A gymnasium? How about loads of journals and books and stuff?

DENNIS: Yes.

LUKE: Good. May all come in nifty. *Throws the ball at Dennis. Dennis drops it.*

Oh, oh.

Dennis picks up the ball and heaves it at Luke. They chuckle.

DENNIS: How's your lady?

LUKE: Milady? Milady, which?

DENNIS: How's Allison been keeping. Slim and trim?

LUKE: She's come and gone boobie. What a strange phrase chooser. Milady. She's off to Colombia in search of flowers. If she comes, she goes. But we've been seeing her young brother, the blonde Terry.

DENNIS: The horror show freak.

Saverin comes in closer.

LUKE: He was asking about your career in mending accident victims. I told him I'd be sure to get you to drop by with some information as a friend of a friend.

DENNIS: Forget it! I'd like to see some of your pictures. No, I wouldn't.

LUKE: We should check with Saverin. Saverin?

SAVERIN: Dennis?

DENNIS: Forget it. O.K. Who gives the massage?

LUKE: Name the brand. Want to make some calls?

DENNIS: Do you give banquets?

A pause. Dennis laughs.

LUKE: What are your feelings, Saverin, about group suppers?

SAVERIN: Yes.

LUKE: Yes, we do, for parties of ten. Low key and quiet without damage or muss. Just bring nine friends.

DENNIS: Sleazing?

LUKE: Meet new friends but keep the old. One is silver and

the other is gold. Does that shock you?

DENNIS: Do you keep a guest list that I could ponder?

LUKE: We saved your check-in book. But it's obsolete. We've got a lot more WASP names now. We get support from the local parish. The Episcopalian Church Women and Reverend Poole. Did you ever really get down with Reverend Poole? Oh you knew him but... Reverend Poole... really progressive.

DENNIS: [*picks up the football and starts playing frantic catch with the boys*] I got a letter from the big city. It said "Dear Dennis" followed by three blank pages and "Love Luke" with a P.S. and another blank page.

LUKE: You're welcome. I shaved my moustache. Did you notice? Clean shave and a clean smile. I heard you were coming.

A pause.

DENNIS: Oh, and you look lovely Luke. What's going down?

They group around him. Hugs, kisses.

SAVERIN: Welcome home, Dennis.

LIZZARD: Welcome, Dennis J.

LUKE: Welcome home, Dennis.

SAVERIN: We're in equal cahoots... cheerful partners. "The Show."

LUKE: You're playing catch-up but don't be upset boobie.

DENNIS: Maybe we should call a project meeting.

LIZZARD: A project meeting.

They prepare a kind of meeting.

LUKE: A project meeting.

SAVERIN: A project meeting.

Saverin and Luke fight for the same chair.

LIZZARD: Boys!

SAVERIN: Dennis?

They all turn to him.

DENNIS: [*enraged*] Hey. I've got an idea. Why don't we start
a fuck it?

LUKE: He's put off a bit I think, aren't you?

DENNIS: Fuck it.

LUKE: [*with camera*] I'll do the second verse. Rock the baby.
If you're only ready to pose, Dennis, that's fine, that can
be part of the package, take your time. But I can only
hypnotize the willing. I have to lay back until you seduce
yourself into poses. I can see potentials in you, boobie.
I've made a discovery. There's no point in slipping past
our own talents. You can't expect me to get into a straight
baby taking number. Me with my nose for sniffing unob-
vious sexuality with my friend the camera. No yearbook
photos for this kid. I've got ten years of rock and roll
wizards and profits to work off. Alright, good, close your
eyes, keep those lids shut tight. Closed peepers through
a blue tinted lens could be turned into a drowning victim or even an O.D. for dead body freaks. Now that's
an under privileged group that should hear about us, Dennis really. If we won't deal with them who will? What
if they order their family portraits chicken bloodied? It's
only catsup, Dennis. And catsup is better than the real
thing. Who's to say what needs we satisfy, what atrocities
we prevent? There's only one thing Dennis. I'm a sidekick
no more. That's a gas. Everybody's a center shot, no more
sidekicks. It's too dangerous. The new organization is
called The Show. There are no more drugs. There are
no more leaders. But, every night there's at least one star.
Tonight, Dennis, you're that star. People come to the
show to play out their problems. Sometimes they pay
money, Dennis, but we always pay attention. If you want

to know what we do—just reach out. It's your journey. You determine the course of the trip. We've read your letters, boobie, and we're afraid you're coming very close to letting go of the branch, so hold it. Hold it. I think you're going to like this picture.[*Takes a photo*] That was a past presidential portrait, Dennis. We appreciate the pre-med trouble you've gone to, new boobie. But how's about starting again? But that was O.K., boobie. That was perfect, perfect. Fever, Dennis. Fever.

DENNIS: Fever what?

LUKE: You remember. In the morning?

DENNIS: Fever?

SAVERIN: Fever.

LUKE: Yabayabayaba. All thru' the night. You remember?

DENNIS: No, why, should I?

LUKE: Come on, the McCoy's with those gloopy voices. "You a give a me a fever." You dance like you're dead, all stiff and stricken.

DENNIS: I don't move my ass for anyone; never did.

LUKE: Just like a zombie. Fever.

DENNIS: Luke. I can see through the windshield. Hi Luke. See me? No matter how hard you try at living the life of Riley I'll still be able to see little Luke the yellow jacket lush.

Don't be pretentious, chum, I remember pulling the point out of you on the kitchen floor. You're going to help me crack my mould? You know what to expect then, Luke. Once and always a sidekick. Entire movements have collapsed because of sidekicks thinking they could run the show. We know that I'm still the master of the games and we know that you're still the sidekick, so be alert, Luke, because wherever I'm going it's likely you're coming along.

A long silence. Dennis is frozen. Luke and Saverin
watch Dennis. Dennis turns away and lights a cigarette.
He tries to busy himself. Lizzard is in the tent. The silence
continues. Luke and Saverin keep watching.

DENNIS: Where is she? Loretta?

LUKE: What, Dennis?

DENNIS: [*into locker room lightness, but he is spooked*] The
girl. Who is she really?

LUKE: She's our Lizzard lady, boobie. Would you like to be
properly introduced?

DENNIS: How did she worm in? What's her function?

LUKE: She's very, very good.

DENNIS: At what? She was just a druggie, a smack out. What's
she good at?

LUKE: You name the brand.

DENNIS: Oh ya? Can I burn my fingers? Come on. What's her
number?

SAVERIN: You'd better be careful, young man, because this is
no Veronica, Archie. We're talking about a supernova.
She'll peel your scalp back, tear your jock off and make
you enjoy it. It's fright night.

DENNIS: You always did like stray dogs and birds with broken
wings. What's her gift?

SAVERIN: Palmistry. The ultimate interviewer. The gleaner.
The Queen of Spades. The keeper of the records. The gift
of life. Violins in the background, the school orchestra,
way in the background.

DENNIS: Why Lizzard?

SAVERIN: I'm not sure. It's not a name that gets confused with
the pink and the cuddly.

DENNIS: Really?

SAVERIN: Really.

DENNIS: A banana lady.

SAVERIN: Chiquita, really.

DENNIS: Really.

SAVERIN: She's a hitmaker with a bullet. Solid gold.

DENNIS: I don't believe you.

SAVERIN: That's your drawback. But we can work it out. Dennis J. for Jughead.

DENNIS: O.K. I'll take my chances. Let's have some fucking fun.

SAVERIN: You've been warned. She goes close to the edge. Don't stub your toe-toe and trip out.

DENNIS: I'll take my chances.

SAVERIN: That a boy. The customer's always right. Name the brand.

DENNIS: I'm not fussy.

SAVERIN: Name the brand, sir. Give me a brand.

DENNIS: Alright. O.K. Sure. Give me a scene that relates to me. Me in the flesh. Anything. You know me. I'm at your disposal. Good old Dennis. Me. That's the brand.

LIZZARD: Hello boys. Having a good time? [*She appears from the tent as a contemporary gypsy.*]

DENNIS: Hi there, Loretta.

LIZZARD: Who is this?

SAVERIN: Be careful, Dennis. We were having a discussion, Ma'am.

LIZZARD: Well that's enough of that. Who have we got here? Do I know you?

SAVERIN: The good doctor, remember?

LIZZARD: Hmmmm.

SAVERIN: Sorry. He's all we've got.

LIZZARD: He's all I've got. Good evening, doctor.

DENNIS: Hi, nurse. If you want me, it's alright, it's alright . . .

SAVERIN: Play patient, kid. Clean up your act. [*He grooms Dennis*]

LUKE: It's "Show Time."

> *Luke and Saverin take Dennis to the entrance of the tent.*

DENNIS: How do you do? What do you do?

> *Extends hand for handshake; Lizzard holds and examines.*

LIZZARD: A good hand for healing. Maybe.

DENNIS: Why, Loretta.

LIZZARD: Take a seat, please sir. Be comfortable.

DENNIS: Alright. Sure.

LIZZARD: You have that hand ready at all times, for any emergency, don't you? Be easy. Relax.

DENNIS: I'm relaxed. Anything I can do?

LIZZARD: Just keep those fingers out of the fire. Hello.

DENNIS: Good evening, miss.

LIZZARD: Just a few questions for our files. Some added information, you understand. There are a few gaps in the picture.

DENNIS: O.K.

LIZZARD: What is your name, sir?

DENNIS: Dennis.

LIZZARD: Sex?

DENNIS: Masculine.

LIZZARD: Nicknames?

DENNIS: Not any more, dear.

LIZZARD: Address?

DENNIS: Well—I used to live. . . well —

LIZZARD: Be brief, please!

DENNIS: Here, I guess.

LIZZARD: Here? Alright. Occupation?

DENNIS: I was head of a—well, I studied medicine for a while, but —

LIZZARD: One word answers, if you please, sir.

DENNIS: Organizer. Leader.

LIZZARD: O.K. Religion?

DENNIS: Atheist?

LIZZARD: Atheist?

DENNIS: Yes, well —

LIZZARD: Thief?

DENNIS: What?

LIZZARD: Have you ever stolen?

DENNIS: Yes.

LIZZARD: What have you stolen?

DENNIS: Money. Not very much. When I was a kid.

LIZZARD: One word. Have you ever participated in a perverse sexual act?

DENNIS: No.

LUKE: Come on... Playing doctor with them young girls?

SAVERIN: And boys?

LIZZARD: Do you have homosexual fantasies?

DENNIS: No.

LIZZARD: Alright. Do you masturbate frequently, young man?

DENNIS: Hey. Not anymore. No. No need —

LIZZARD: O.K. son. One word. Has everything you've told me been the truth entirely?

DENNIS: Yes, it has. Sure. Yes.

LIZZARD: Purpose?

DENNIS: What? Oh. Yes. Success. No. Happiness.

SAVERIN: Dear, dear. My goodness gracious.

LIZZARD: Lose.

DENNIS: Date.

LIZZARD: Date.

DENNIS: Napkin.

LIZZARD: Are you familiar with the expression "Scratch a jock and you'll find a queen"?

DENNIS: This is bullshit.

SAVERIN: Dear, dear, my goodness gracious.

LIZZARD: What are your fears?

DENNIS: Ah...

LIZZARD: Fears.

SAVERIN: Fears.

LUKE: Fears?

DENNIS: I guess—I don't know —

LIZZARD: Love?

DENNIS: Friends.

SAVERIN: Got many?

DENNIS: A few.

LIZZARD: Girlfriends?

DENNIS: Many.

LIZZARD: Fears?

SAVERIN: Fears.

DENNIS: I really can't...I don't know, ah...

LIZZARD: Date, sweetheart?

DENNIS: What? Friday.

LIZZARD: Music?

DENNIS: Rock.

LIZZARD: Stone?

DENNIS: Heart.

LIZZARD: Knife?

DENNIS: Cunt—cut.

LIZZARD: Cut?

DENNIS: Red.

LIZZARD: Date.

DENNIS: Meat.

LIZZARD: Body.
DENNIS: Cream.
LIZZARD: Girl?
DENNIS: Boy.
LIZZARD: Red.
DENNIS: Soft.
LIZZARD: Soft.
DENNIS: Limp.
LIZZARD: Fears.
DENNIS: No.
LIZZARD: Dope?
DENNIS: Help.
LIZZARD: Degrees?
DENNIS: Eat. No. Lecture, bullshit. No —
LIZZARD: Fears?
DENNIS: Mess, mess.
LIZZARD: Ambition?
DENNIS: Hard,—ah—
LIZZARD: Beach?
DENNIS: Boys.
LIZZARD: Blue?
DENNIS: Boy, no, beard, — jeans.
LIZZARD: Fears?
DENNIS: Suck.
LIZZARD: Hole.
DENNIS: Dip. Deep. Dinner.
LIZZARD: Knife.
DENNIS: Cut. Stab.
     Luke places a knife in front of Dennis.
LIZZARD: Life?
DENNIS: What? Stroke.
LIZZARD: Doctor.

DENNIS: Ah. Wound. White. Soft.

LIZZARD: Budgie.

DENNIS: What? Dead. Soft.

LIZZARD: White. Stroke. Smack. Dust.

DENNIS: What?

> *He picks up the knife.*

LIZZARD: Soft. Heart. Rock. Guts, gore, grind.

DENNIS: What is this? What?

LIZZARD: [*almost speaking in tongues*] Cut. Suck. Jeans. Mess. Red. Snap. Cut. Give me your hand. Doctor. Wound. Give me your hand.

> *He does.*

Sponge. Eat. At the table. Knife. And fork. Now. Dinner. Date. Friday. Dinner date. Yes. I've got it, doctor. Why, doctor, I'd love to. I'll see you after the lecture.

> *Lizzard leans over and kisses him.*

DENNIS: What lecture?

LIZZARD: I've got it. It's coming. It's O.K. It's coming. A white cloth on the table. Does that mean anything to you. . . white with some red. Table napkins. Meat. Knife. Cloth. There's a white room. Cream sir? With your meat? Red meat.

> *Lizzard sets up the scene for Dennis, involving a white cloth, a table and appropriate utensils.*

DENNIS: [*terrified*] What meat? What kind of meat.

> *The table is set.*

LIZZARD: No. You meet. It's a date—for a Friday dinner. A lecture, on white bodies with a sharp, ah. . . knife and fork. A girl, yes, a girl at the table, on the table. Cut there. Cut the meat—something—very hard, there, no very soft, soft —

DENNIS: What's that? What is it? How do you know that?

LIZZARD: Don't go. What will everyone think? You're soft,
you're going white. Here's the meat. Don't go, doctor.
Dennis. Baby Dennis. Watch the cut. Come on now, it's
coming. Don't go. Red. It's coming, Doctor.

DENNIS: Red what? Look, ahhh, I can't, it isn't —

LIZZARD: Alright, it is coming, don't go, baby—baby, don't go.

DENNIS: What are you? What are you trying to do? What are
you doing?

LIZZARD: [*in a fever*] Something's stuck, there's something cut
here. It's gone bad, hasn't it? Red stuff, cream stuff, limp
stuff, falling, coming, dead, dead, dead. On the table.
It's blood on the table. That girl across the white room. . .
oh-oh. . . pissed right off, poor Dennis, on the floor, lying
there. Oh get the jeans right off, get them off, get off.
Get off! Late for a date. Something got broken. You're
soft. We aren't making it. The dinner date is ruined, the
operation is a failure. The cut has been made. The slit
is there. The crack is there. Cracked right up.
   A pause.
Dennis J. fainted. He's so soft.

DENNIS: Alright. O.K. You don't know that. Fuck off fuck
right off just fuck right off alright O.K? Fuck off, O.K?
Just fuck off.
   Dennis dangerously rises with the knife mumbling.

SAVERIN: [*on edge*] It's O.K. It's alright.

LUKE: [*on edge*] It's O.K. Dennis. It's perfect. It's perfect.

SAVERIN: It's alright, Dennis.

LIZZARD: Dennis. No tricks. There are no tricks. So don't fight
it.
   Dennis stands there limply with the knife.
Numbers aren't done for fun and games. It's real, isn't
it? It's for real. We're not playing games for fun and

games. Trust me. You're really doing fine. Just don't back
off the way you do. You'll disappear over the edge. Let
it happen. Relax, captain. We really want you to stay.
We know you, Dennis J., we really do. It's alright.
Wham, bam, thank you man.

DENNIS: I know you. I went to school with you. I could look
up your phone number. You played the girl in "Bye-bye
Birdie" at school. You're Lo —
    She kisses him on the mouth.

LIZZARD: I'm Lizzard.

DENNIS: Pleased to meet you, Lizzard.

LIZZARD: Yep. Same here. I'd like to hear someone sing some
oldies but goodies...
    *Lizzard slides away. Luke follows her watching Dennis
    as he goes.*

SAVERIN: [*a silence, he hums*] Mmmm...mmmm...mmmm
...mmmm...
    [*sings*] and there's going to be trouble, hey la, hey la, my
boyfriend's back. Mmmm......mmm...he's kinda big
and he's awful straw-ong, hey la, hey la, my boyfriend's
back. Yes my mmmmmmm.
    [*Speaks*] The Love Striparama All Nude Show!
    The room is quiet.

DENNIS: What?

SAVERIN: The Love Striparama All Nude Show. That's what
the sign says across the street.

DENNIS: You are so wrong. The Hungarian Bakery's across
the street.

SAVERIN: No, beside that.

DENNIS: Grievdorf's Tavern. I remember Grievdorf's, so fuck
off!

SAVERIN: Uh-uh.

DENNIS: I remember Grievdorf's Tavern. It's the shits.

SAVERIN: No. It's gone. Since about May.

DENNIS: May?

SAVERIN: The... Love... Strip...a...ram... a...
All...Knew...d... Show. It doesn't work. The words
don't fit together. Love and ram. Strip and knew and
show.

DENNIS: Well, what can I tell you? They're a substitute for
the sexually unbalanced. It's a necessary institution just
like dentistry, or, oh...med...
He stops. Saverin smiles.
Unless of course, they brought back the lash. That would
be the cure-all-arama. The lash. Twenty strong strokes
on a first offense for anything nastier than drunk driving. Save a lot of expense on the old jail; the public rip.
Fuck liberalism. The lash. You wouldn't get the same slip
from any offenders or they'd get twenty-two and then
twenty-four. It's the ultimate deterrent. The lash. That's
what ought to be done. That would straighten all. Mur-
derers hanged and rapists whipped in front of crowds.
*Dennis furiously picks up his coat and gloves. He walks
quickly toward the street entrance. He stops with his hand
on the knob. Lizzard and Luke come to watch him. After
an uncomfortable pause.*

SAVERIN: What happened way up there in Guelph?

DENNIS: [*Turns. He takes off his coat slowly and drops it on
the floor. He walks back to Saverin. He picks up the dead
budgie and sits on a cushion.*]
A silence.

SAVERIN: Do you ever think about Shirley-Ann Foebee? She
was in Mr. Anderson's homeroom in ninth grade.

DENNIS: We had Anderson in tenth.

SAVERIN: You don't think about her, do you? She left. Everybody whispered about why she wasn't coming back. Except you. You wouldn't talk about her. She missed the last two months. Anderbum just went on and finished out the year, getting chalk all over his plaid jacket, and we just kept playing "The Platters Greatest Hits" over and over.

DENNIS: I suppose she had leukemia or something.

SAVERIN: Next thing you know it was summer. You think they forgot to tell us, or what? You wouldn't talk about her, remember?

DENNIS: It's irrelevant.

SAVERIN: It didn't matter after that. We just forgot. Came back to school and you won that thing in track, didn't you?

DENNIS: You were close, Saverin. Number two tries harder. I feel awful.

   Lizzard and Luke move in warmly.

SAVERIN: I don't think you've been the same since that big kid poured coke all over your head, in front of the girls in the cafeteria.

LIZZARD: Tense.

SAVERIN: And now, who gives a shit about Shirley-Ann Foebee?

LUKE: Fever, Dennis.

LIZZARD: Where'd you put my M and M's?

SAVERIN: You ate your M and M's.

LUKE: [*hides the Smarties*] No. I ate them M and M's. I ate them M and M's all.

LIZZARD: Prick.

DENNIS: I'm going to stay, Saverin. I want to know how you do it. But give me a break. Some tea? Tea, eh? Put on some music. Ya. Give me a break. Ten minutes.

Tea is made, music is put on, Lizzard writes on the blackboard "Take a break," and everyone has a break.

END OF PART I

PART II

After the break, drinking tea, Lizzard, Saverin, Luke and Dennis casually group together. The music is turned off. Dennis and Saverin earnestly sit down to a game of speed chess. Dennis sets the clocks at two minutes each. They proceed to play a twenty four move game in under ninety seconds. Saverin turns the game into checkers and Dennis wipes all the pieces off the board.

DENNIS: Checkmate.

LUKE: So what have you been up to, all these days, Dennis? To be genuine.

DENNIS: Nothing.

SAVERIN: Nothing?

LUKE: How's old Riverside Floral Clock Park?

DENNIS: How do you know about that?

LUKE: Round, round, get around, Guelph.

DENNIS: Oh yes? Dopers hang out there now. We've tried to set up an "on campus" centre but the —

LIZZARD: [*to Luke*] You can just go buy me some more M and M's, kiddo bum.

DENNIS: [*realizing that it doesn't apply*] What the fuck am I saying?

LUKE: We all thought you'd go back to Camp Kaidjuwakoonut

for the winter break.

DENNIS: Camp Kichicon.

SAVERIN: The camp for young freakies.

LUKE: Well, what is this then? What is this, Saverin? No point in tripping all the way north when we have a camp right here. Camp Catsup.

DENNIS: I had a job. They had a job for me. I came here. I told them to fuck off.

LUKE: You give me fever. Fever in the morning.

DENNIS: Do you still have Harold Leaman's address? I'm going to find Harold, man.

SAVERIN: Harold Leaman's teeth fell out from too much point. He shot his talent. He got into jamming heavily. He eroded, man.

Saverin and Dennis go into mock locker-room rock jargon.

DENNIS: He's good, man. He kicked it off, didn't he?

SAVERIN: He was good, man.

DENNIS: I called his sister. She told me he was fine; she figured that we'd helped the boy.

SAVERIN: Oh well.

DENNIS: She told me he made it to the acid rock reunion at the Garden backing up Steppenwolf. Oh, dear. Steppenwolf for sure.

SAVERIN: Did she give you the old Leaman twinkle as she shot the breeze?

DENNIS: Steppenwolf for sure. Remember? We signed old Harold's Adidas.

SAVERIN: No teeth.

DENNIS: I kept saying "hullaballoo" every time I felt like saying "bullshit." She thought I believed her. Leaman's fast, but not Steppenwolf. That was a great band. But I do believe Harold kicked.

SAVERIN: [*deadly serious*] Bargain Harold's teeth came out, Dennis.

DENNIS: [*ignoring him*] You got any Steppenwolf? For the old days?

SAVERIN: Not a chance. Steppenwolf.

LIZZARD: Steppenwolf?

LUKE: Really milky.

DENNIS: What's wrong with —

LIZZARD: Steppenwolf. Wow, come on, now.

DENNIS: I just thought that —

SAVERIN: Not a chance. Steppenwolf.

DENNIS: What's wrong with that?

    A pause.

Alright, I don't care.

SAVERIN: [*sings. Luke joins in for a short duet*] "Well, you don't know what we can see. Why don't you tell your dreams to me! Fantasy will set you free!"

DENNIS: O.K. Doesn't fit anymore. I understand. I get it. [*Dennis picks up a toy holster and gun. Slight panic. Lizzard and Luke move out of range*]

SAVERIN: Don't point it at me.

    Pause.

You're getting old, Jessie.

DENNIS: [*He wants to play the game*] So are you.

SAVERIN: Just old enough to know I'm getting old.

DENNIS: I can still lick ya, Wyatt. Ain't nobody faster than the brothers. Least wise not the likes of you.

SAVERIN: Harold Leaman was faster.

DENNIS: No he wasn't.

SAVERIN: You ain't never going to change, Jessie. Put the gun down while there's time.

DENNIS: Got the finger greased, son?

LUKE: How's it going, Jessie?

DENNIS: Nice try, boys, but no tricks. Never looked over my
shoulder before.

Saverin tries to take the gun. Dennis refuses.

SAVERIN: Then you're too smart for me, Jessie. But you're getting rusty, old timer.

DENNIS: You think that tin badge'll help you now?

SAVERIN: They're going to lynch you, buddy. I might as well
save them the trouble.[*With his finger, aims at Dennis,
point blank range*]
Bang.

DENNIS: Missed.

SAVERIN: I got you.

DENNIS: Not even a graze.

SAVERIN: Can't you lose once in a while? Right in the forehead,
shithead.

DENNIS: No way. Bang.

*Lizzard turns off the lights. Total darkness. She follows
Dennis with the beam of a flashlight.*
Wyatt?

SAVERIN: [*moving in the darkness*] I hear old Dale Evans is
knocked up again. You wouldn't know anything about
that, would you, Jess?

DENNIS: Bad mouth. I'm going to kill you for sure, son.

A pause.

SAVERIN: Jessie?

DENNIS: Wyatt?

SAVERIN: You shoulda hung 'em up long ago. Steppenwolf.
Christ!

DENNIS: Bang, Bang, Bang. You're hit Wyatt.

SAVERIN: In the leg, you old geezer. Won't hurt my

shooting. . . none.

DENNIS: Bang!

SAVERIN: Missed me.

DENNIS: Bang.

SAVERIN: Your hand's trembling, Jess.

DENNIS: Bang.

SAVERIN: The old 44's only got six. Too bad for you, Jessie.
   The lights flash up. Luke and Saverin grab Dennis.
   Things get rough.

DENNIS: Give me a chance, kid.

SAVERIN: [takes the gun] This is it, old timer.

DENNIS: I'm begging you, Wyatt.

SAVERIN: The times are changing. People got a whole new way
   of looking on things.

LUKE: [to Saverin] Don't worry about stains on the carpet.
   Don't worry about splatters on the wall.

DENNIS: [struggling] I'm pleading with you kid.
   Luke holds Dennis in a full Nelson on the floor.

SAVERIN: The former styles just don't make it anymore.

LUKE: The gun's loaded.

DENNIS: Don't let him do it, Chester.

LUKE: I'm Luke. The gun's loaded, boobie.

SAVERIN: We got to reform you. . . Jessie.
   Dennis is on his knees. Saverin holds the gun to his
   temple.

LUKE: You're going to get it, Dennis.

SAVERIN: Too set in your ways. That's the trouble. You don't
   keep up on what's happening.

LUKE: It's loaded, boobie.

DENNIS: Funny stuff.

SAVERIN: You listening, Jessie?

DENNIS: Can't hear you too well. I'm going deaf.

SAVERIN: You're a lost cause, old fella. But if I don't get you, somebody else will for sure.

LUKE: Bye Dennis.

SAVERIN: I sure wish you'd give it a try.

DENNIS: Can't hear you.

SAVERIN: You can't bullshit forever.

DENNIS: That's enough.

LUKE: Brand him.

DENNIS: Fuck off.

SAVERIN: Don't try anything, Jessie, I mean it. This country's had enough of you and your gang.

DENNIS: [*violent struggling*] Take it easy.

LUKE: The gun's loaded.

DENNIS: Christ, will you —

SAVERIN: There's been enough blood spilled already with your pranks. Hopalong Cassidy, Billy the Kid.

LUKE: Mat Dillon, Bat Masterson, on the sheets.

SAVERIN: Big Gene Autrey.

LUKE: Cisco Kid, Doc Holliday, Mr. Anderson.

SAVERIN: Frank James. Your brother Frank, the transie. Your old Burt. Doc Bromley. The Reverend Poole.

DENNIS: That's it. O.K. Luke. Let go.

LIZZARD: Alyson Baker. Loretta Lang.

SAVERIN: Shirley-Ann Foebee. Harold Leaman.

DENNIS: Can't hear you, Jessie. Wyatt. I mean you, Wyatt.

LUKE: Harold Leaman. Harold Leaman.

DENNIS: Fuck off.

SAVERIN: You're all washed up.

> *They move away from him, gurgling. A silence. Dennis rises. Saverin turns to him with one fist clenched and one fist holding the gun. He opens the clenched fist and shows Dennis six bullets which he's apparently taken from the*

gun. He drops them on the floor.

SAVERIN: [*seriously*] Bang!

> *Dennis stares. He laughs hysterically and staggers about.*

DENNIS: [*to Luke*] Bang! Why don't we start a fuck it?

LUKE: Dennis.

> *Slaps him. Dennis stops laughing and listens bewildered. Luke is cool and kind.*

Please, boobie. I know what facing the spoils for that first flash can be, but don't lose it. Please. If you want to demonstrate a particular talent that involves "The Show," well then, by all means demonstrate. But Dennis. . . don't just dictate. Don't assume you know. There are secrets around here. One morning many months ago, I awoke and found a note nailed to my door. It said, "Thanks! It's been a gas." Saverin got one the same morning. Someone found a dead body, with shoes we'd all signed at the old High, down the bottom of Morningside Bridge. The notes had both said, "Love Harold." I'd said something to Harold the day before, something very close to "The gun's loaded." Please, Dennis. Old Bargain Harold really got himself into a mess. Harold's dead. You listen.

> *A pause.*

SAVERIN: You want to hear some Steppenwolf?

> *Lizzard, Luke and Saverin leave Dennis alone for an unwelcome rest.*

LIZZARD: I've got this amazing recipe?

SAVERIN: Oh ya?

LIZZARD: I just remember putting M & M's in milk and crunching them up. It's sort of a cereal, like granola or something, but better. Now, what you do is put a bit of milk at the bottom.

DENNIS: Play slapsies, Saverin.

SAVERIN: You're too late, buddy.

LIZZARD: And you add brown sugar. Just a little bit, 'cause come on, you don't want it too sweet, do you? I'm told the morning crowd is just too sweet so, wow, don't overdo it. Give me my M & M's.

Luke gives them to her.

DENNIS: [*desperately wanting attention*] Play slapsies again.

SAVERIN: Dennis.

DENNIS: O.K., forget it. I don't care.

SAVERIN: You don't have to yell at me, do you?

DENNIS: I think I want coffee.

LUKE: Darjeeling, Rosehip, Orange Pekoe, Earl Grey, Lemon Scented, Green, and Hot Chocolate. I used the coffee.

SAVERIN: You feeling alright Dennis?

LUKE: [*to Saverin*] I wonder whether or nay the Afghans will get an invitation to Midnight Mass.

SAVERIN: Oh, I think not. And then again. . .

LUKE: How's your head?

Dennis plays with a knife. He is watched out of one eye.

SAVERIN: Very cold. Occupational hazards!

LUKE: He's a good boy.

DENNIS: What?

SAVERIN: Make sure the doors are locked. Leave the phone off the hook, Luke.

DENNIS: What?

LUKE: Terry got the message. Keep it low?

SAVERIN: Keep it very low.

DENNIS: What?

LIZZARD: [*attracting attention. Appearing to talk aimlessly. Seductively happy, shaking the M and M's box*] You put

your zonkers in with your M and M's and then once in
a while, you gulp them. A big gulp. And you don't light
up when you've got a take 'cause you just don't know.
Could have been an M and M. Wow! So you can never
tell what you're looking through 'cause the zonkers
crunch like the M and M's. But you're eating a porcupine.
The quills'll get you man. Strychnine! [*she laughs*]

DENNIS: Is this aimed at me? [*Leaving the knife on display,
he goes to her*] Is this for me?

LIZZARD: You get all that chocolate in assorted colours.

DENNIS: Hey!

LIZZARD: All the colours of the M and M's Company.

DENNIS: [*as clinic guru*] You're in trouble. Now, watch your
head. Watch your head. Watch it.

LIZZARD: [*gulping M and M's*] You eat four or five from the
top of the box.

DENNIS: Hey!

LIZZARD: I like the greens. Wonder why?

DENNIS: Don't get onto purpose. That's fatal. Stay off purpose.
Luke and Saverin observe.

LIZZARD: You replace the four M and M's with four zonkers.
Close the top and shake 'em all up.

DENNIS: Don't get onto purpose, dear.

LIZZARD: Like dice. Like a rattle.

DENNIS: Just be cool.

LIZZARD: Don't jock off on me, Dennis J. I'll get you something
to write with if you want to take notes.

DENNIS: What was that about strychnine?

LIZZARD: I'm talking about the old zonkers and M and M's
trick. Remember?

DENNIS: I'm your friend. You can trust me. It's not all that
bad, is it?

LIZZARD: You kill me, Dennis. It won't penetrate me, young
bumble.

DENNIS: Easy. Just relax. Sorry I don't have a pen.

LIZZARD: What pen?

DENNIS: No, you don't need a pen. That's right. Just relax.

LIZZARD: Fuck the pen.

DENNIS: Touch my face. See? I'm really here. No dream.
Everything's fine. Just relax.

LIZZARD: Are you crazy, Dennis? I'll bend your fingers back.

DENNIS: You're not crazy. No. You're together, really, I know.
I do this all the time, I can tell. You're going to be fine.
You can't stab yourself with a pen anyway, dear.

LIZZARD: I wasn't talking about pens, was I?

DENNIS: Of course not. You just forget it.

LIZZARD: I was talking about mixing, Dennis.

DENNIS: Never mix. That's the trouble, you can't mix. One
at a time; you fly. Two at a time; you die. Breathe. Don't
forget to breathe. You laugh. It can happen.

LIZZARD: [giggling] Who said anything about dying or —

DENNIS: Did you forget about the knife?

LIZZARD: What knife?

DENNIS: That's it. Forget about it. What's your favourite
colour?

LIZZARD: Green, I guess.

DENNIS: Think green.

LIZZARD: Why?

DENNIS: I warned you, don't think about purpose. Get off that
right now. It's suicide.

LIZZARD: You're giving me the creepies.

DENNIS: Just come on down. You're coming down.

LIZZARD: Get off the mark, Dennis.

DENNIS: I'm only here to help. Just for your benefit.

LIZZARD: [*tries to stand up*] I'm going to have a bath.

DENNIS: [*holding her*] Stay down. You'll be alright. I'm with
you. I'm really here. You can touch me, see? I'm here.

LIZZARD: I want a bath.

DENNIS: You shouldn't be alone. That's what we're here for.
You've got friends, doesn't she?

LUKE: [*cautiously, to Saverin*] I smell a hospital, boobie.

LIZZARD: Dennis, I want to have a bath.

DENNIS: No more talk about suicide. Don't even think about it.

LIZZARD: What?

DENNIS: You don't want to slash yourself. Or drown in the
bathtub.

LIZZARD: Come on, is this a Frat game or something?

DENNIS: What you've done is no game, young lady. Now try
to remember. Were they green?

LIZZARD: Were what green?

DENNIS: Don't worry. It's just dope. Dope. Messes you up.
You'll think of it.

LIZZARD: Dennis, I want to go to the bathroom.

DENNIS: Capsule? Microdot? Christmas Tree? Window Pane?

LIZZARD: [*walks away*] This isn't smart, Dennis.

DENNIS: Don't worry, we'll help you whatever it was. Just be
calm.

Lizzard picks up the toy gun.

LIZZARD: I was just. . .I was only. . .I was just. . .I was only.

DENNIS: What are you going to do with that gun? Come on
down now.

LUKE: Tell him, Lizzard.

LIZZARD: It's just a toy. It's not real. I was just. . .I was only.

DENNIS: No! Put it down. It's all real. You're alright. You're
just fine. We're your friends. You've just bummed out,
a bit. It's alright.

SAVERIN: It's O.K., Lizzard.

DENNIS: You're alright.

LUKE: Just fine.

DENNIS: You can stop worrying.

LUKE: It's all over.

Dennis takes away the gun. A pause.

DENNIS: That's the danger. You've just been through the danger zone. Scary, eh?

LIZZARD: Wow!

DENNIS: Now, tell me you don't want to kill yourself. Come on. Say it. "I don't want to kill myself."

LUKE: Say it Lizzard. We'll believe you. "I don't want to kill myself."

DENNIS: I'm waiting. Your friends are waiting.

LIZZARD: Is this a game or . . . .

A pause.

DENNIS: "I don't want to kill myself."

Dennis repeats the statement over and over with more fervour and no response from Lizzard.

LUKE: [*together with Dennis, encouraging him*] "I don't want to kill myself."

SAVERIN: [*occasionally interjecting with Luke*] "I don't want to kill myself."

DENNIS: [*over and over*] I don't want to kill myself.

LIZZARD: [*Dennis reaches his pitch; she smiles*] I don't want to kill myself.

Pause.

DENNIS: Think of your favourite colour and have a fucking bath.

LIZZARD: [*goes to the washroom*] Green, Baby!

DENNIS: Don't drown.

LUKE: [*to Dennis*] You're even better backwards.

Dennis bathes in false victory.

LIZZARD: [*She comes back from the washroom and walks up to Dennis carrying an oxygen mask attached to a small tank of oxygen*] You are trying, I can see that. Bouncing away there, playing saviour. Very twistabout hauling out those old methods with new twists. Dear Dennis, yes, the customer here is always the leader. That's the idea! That's fine. Most customers never get beyond the leader stage. I think you may be an exception. [*Dennis takes the oxygen*] Now! The customer is usually at the point of freaking when he thinks he's at the point of incredible control. That's alright. The customer is only being exorcized. Catch it, Dennis? Exorcism! Oxygen isn't breath for dopers anymore. It's just another way of keeping up with yourself. Now, before I forget. You pay me. Give me your wallet. [*Dennis gives Lizzard his wallet*] That's a boy. Curves and sliders, Dennis... But no more fastballs. [*She wanders off. Dennis inspects the room*]

SAVERIN: [*in the silence*] Doctor D.?

DENNIS: [*Dennis is speeding*] This place is filthy. I'm the maid, I suppose, am I? Dust on everything. You should be ashamed of yourselves. You should be embarrassed. [*Starts to dust*] Inviting me home to a dust bowl. You live here. You live here and I'm the new maid. It's just incredible. [*He sweeps*] You haven't cleaned the place in weeks, have you? Your socks, Saverin. Filthy. [*He sprays air freshener*] You've left it all for me to clean up, I'm sure. Very considerate of you, dears. Where's my apron?

SAVERIN: Dennis?

DENNIS: Good old Dennis'll clean it up. [*He squirts a plastic*

bottle of detergent] Spill your coffee, don't worry, Dennis
will be home soon.

SAVERIN: Dennis!

DENNIS: Grind the dirt in. He's good at scrubbing. He hates
dust. He hates mess. He'll take care of everything.

SAVERIN: Dennis!

Dennis stops.

I'm not impressed yet. Are you?

A pause.

DENNIS: I'm cleaning up your ass. That's what I'm doing.
Somebody's got to and wouldn't you know, it'd be good
old Dennis standing here, holding the fucking Handy
Andy.

SAVERIN: Dennis. Morality, Dennis? Oh, really? Just who's ass
are we speaking of? Where are the judgements coming
from? All the little values about clean hands and good
and evil and right and wrong, well, that's all bullshit.
Bullshit! You know that already. Just because you think
we've taken the lid off the warm inviting pool, you're
confused, aren't you? Should you dive right in or stand
around the edge? It's not fun and games. Do me a favour.
Just dunk your toe-toe in and try it out for comfort before
you dive right in. Watch the new movie, Dennis. Watch
the normal city twistos with us for the very first time starring new and dangerous personalities. We're exploring
virgin territory, Doctor. So watch your own ass while
you're sucking the sponge. Wriggle it around in the dirt
before you take Spic and Span into the operating room.
Put away the Handy Andy. It doesn't apply. Sit tight and
wait for revelations. And Dennis? Do me a favour. In
the meantime, don't get your head cut off.

A silence. Saverin leaves Dennis to think about it.

LUKE: [*intimately to Dennis*] Now, let's play cheer up. No more long faces. Come on everyone.

DENNIS: [*dejected*] Porny Luke. Who in God's name made that up?

LUKE: I did. Do you like it?

DENNIS: [*musters enthusiasm*] Do you remember how we used to do it? Come on. I'm conducting here. "Do you remember?"

LUKE: Oh. Oh. Mr. Nostalgia rides again. Duck when you hear, "Do you remember—"

SAVERIN: [*to Dennis*] Aren't you tired?

DENNIS: Skits at the reunion.

SAVERIN: Forget it. Luke? He's not ready.

DENNIS: Right after math, we'd run home. Come on, dear.

SAVERIN: It's useless. Forget it.

LUKE: Bring out the Oreos, Den. Where's your old man stash the booze?

SAVERIN: Luke!

LUKE: [*to Saverin*] He's fine.

DENNIS: Get it up, Saverin.

LUKE: Turn on the T.V.

> *Dennis snaps his fingers at the television screen.*

Hey'd you get a load of the tubes on Shelley Fabares. Ooooooooooo-eee. Is she sprouting! Eh, Sav?

DENNIS: [*to Saverin*] Come on, dear.

LUKE: Not on "Captain Bob," asshole. Try "seven."

> *Dennis snaps his fingers again.*

LUKE: That's better. Hey man, "Leave it to Beaver." Eddie Hascal, my hero. Gimme a shot of that.

> *Luke and Dennis sit on the floor with their heads together.*

DENNIS: Close the drapes. Hey Sav, turn it up.

Luke and Dennis mimic an excerpt from "Leave it to Beaver." Lizzard and Saverin, as Mother/Father figures, confer seriously.

LIZZARD: Luke.

LUKE: Hello, Mrs. Cleaver. I must say you look ravishing today. Oh, you've had your hair done, I see. I noticed little Theodore out on the lawn playing. My, how he's growing.

Dennis deeply into the game, splits to another part of the room.

LIZZARD: [*tongue-in-cheek. With bite*] Wally's probably in his room, Eddie. I think he wants to be alone with his new professional football.

LUKE: Why, thank-you Mrs. Cleaver. I'll just quietly show myself up there as Wally has some chemistry homework.

LIZZARD: That's enough, Luke.

LUKE: I promised to assist him with his studies. I certainly wouldn't want to inconvenience you or Mr. Cleaver. [*He joins Dennis*]

LIZZARD: Ward!

SAVERIN: Yes, Dear?

LIZZARD: I'm worried about the boys.

SAVERIN: Why, is something the matter?

LIZZARD: I don't like to be suspicious but I can't help feeling that they're up to something.

SAVERIN: Now, June.

LIZZARD: They've just been too good lately. When I got home from shopping I noticed the floor had been washed. They've never done that before, Ward.

SAVERIN: We can't very well discipline them for being well behaved.

LIZZARD: It just seems too good to be true.

SAVERIN: Well, if it will make you feel better I'll talk to them.

LIZZARD: Thanks, dear.

SAVERIN: Wally! Beaver! Luke! Dennis! Eddie! I'd like to talk to you, boys.

LUKE: Ya, Dad?

DENNIS: Ya, Dad?

SAVERIN: Your mother and I just wanted to make sure that everything was alright while we were out.

LUKE: Gosh, ya, Dad.

DENNIS: Gee, ya, Dad.

LUKE: Beav and I were just messin' around. Making models and stuff. We were —

SAVERIN: You shut up. You're sure now, son. Beaver?

DENNIS: Oh I'm sure, alright. Aren't I, Wally? Real sure.

LUKE: Heck ya, Dad.

DENNIS: Golly ya, Dad.

SAVERIN: Everything under control. Mmmm?

DENNIS: Gee whiz ya, Dad.

LUKE: Course, Dad.

DENNIS: Come on, eh, Dad?

LUKE: Sure, Dad.

DENNIS: Fuck you, Dad.

> *There is a slight pause. Saverin grabs Luke who grabs Dennis who grabs Saverin. They rough and tumble in a war-baby play fight from early days at high school.*

LIZZARD: Hope you're having a good time, boys? Red, Saverin! Red, red, red.

> *The fight gets slightly out of control. They stop in exhaustion in a maze of arms and legs. There is a short silence. Dennis emerges from the centre of the pile holding the straight razor open at Saverin's throat. Luke backs off.*

DENNIS: Gee, Dad. Wally was just showing me how to shave

so I'll know when I grow up and get hairy like you. Gee.
Hey, Dad. *[Moves the razor closer]* Look at me. I bet I
know how to work the razor just like a big person, eh,
Wally?

> *Dennis tries to shave Saverin's face. Saverin doesn't
> move. Dennis draws the razor over Saverin's cheeks.*

Come on, Dad, what do you think?

LUKE: Dennis! *[Takes a step closer]*

DENNIS: *[slashes out at Luke who retreats]* Come on, Dad!

SAVERIN: That's very good, son, but put it away and do some
homework.

DENNIS: No, really, Dad. Doesn't that feel nice? Mom really
loves it when your cheeks are smooth so that she can dig
her nails in and make little trenches. Maybe if I shave
off my fuzz she'll do it to me too. What do you think,
Dad? *[He presses the blade on Saverin's jugular vein.]*

SAVERIN: Go ahead, champ.

> *[Slowly, Dennis backs off]* Very good, Luke. *[Another
> long pause]*

DENNIS: *[holding the razor to his own throat]* Hey, Maybe I
can make my own trenches. Maybe I can dig, dig, dig,
all by myself. Maybe I can save my big brother the trouble. Just a wrist cut? Maybe I can do better. Maybe...I
can...Maybe.

> *Dennis flashes the blade in front of his own throat,
> starting from two feet away and drawing the arc of his
> arm closer and closer to his throat with each swish until
> the motion becomes furious, inches away from gashing
> his jugular vein.*

Maybe...Maybe...Maybe.

> *Saverin and Luke are mesmerized. Lizzard appears with
> a glass of water. She walks up to Dennis. He sees only*

the blade. She splashes the water in his face. Dennis stops.

LIZZARD: [*kindly*] You're lucky. That could have been sulphuric acid.

DENNIS: Maybe.

LIZZARD: O.K. Mother's here, Saverin. Mother's here, Luke. Now, Dennis. Be careful! Don't float away even when you're encouraged. This is serious business. It's not a sock hop.

LUKE: Sorry, very, very.

SAVERIN: [*chants quietly*] "Born to be wild. . ."

LUKE: Camels with the filter? [*offers a cigarette*]

DENNIS: This floor is filthy. Come back here, Saverin.

SAVERIN: He's dead. Did you know?

DENNIS: Fuck it!

SAVERIN: Jerry Mathers. He died. Tripped and stubbed his toe on a mine in Viet Horror. They're trying to bring him back to life.

LUKE: But is Eddie Hascal really Alice Cooper? Or is he dead?

DENNIS: Wally's in his room, Eddie. Remember Lumpy? Remember Clarence. Come back here, Saverin.

SAVERIN: You come here, Dennis. They're all dead, Dennis. All died in running shoes.

DENNIS: Just you wait 'til Larry's father gets home from Pittsburgh. Wally's in his room, Eddie.

SAVERIN: No, he's not. Wally went away to university, Dennis. He died on the operating table. Can't you even play dead, Dennis?

LUKE: We've got a gift for you, old boobie.

SAVERIN: We've been saving it. Sort of a coming of age number.

LUKE: The Reptile Bar Mitzvah.

SAVERIN: So for many years of unfailing service —

LUKE: An undeniable dedication to druggies and such —

SAVERIN: For the cause.

LUKE: The Moose, Kiwanis, Orangeman, Mason of all fucking time.

SAVERIN: Here you go. *[Holds up a gift wrapped box]*

LIZZARD: *[away from them, with a Coke]* You get me.

Dennis leaves the box and walks slowly to Lizzard.

LUKE: A wonderful gift.

LIZZARD: You've almost made it, Dennis.

SAVERIN: Spend some time with Lady Lizzard.

LIZZARD: A hug of congratulations. You've done very well, Dennis J.

LUKE: Go on, Boobie. You deserve it.

LIZZARD: Don't be cautious, Dennis. I don't have to be any more cautious with you than I am with the boys. Eh? We can talk. Hold hands. Share a Coke. One boy to smoke with, to toke with, have Coke with. I'm yours, Dennis.

DENNIS: I don't know.

LIZZARD: Dennis, I'm waiting.

DENNIS: I said, "I don't know." You shouldn't come on to me.

LIZZARD: What?

DENNIS: Right here, in front of everybody.

LIZZARD: Dennis, I'm offering you some Coke.

DENNIS: What? On the floor? In front of everybody. Christ Almighty!

LIZZARD: I think you're a mite confused.

DENNIS: Forget it. I'm not into seeing you spread your legs, does that surprise you?

LIZZARD: What are you on about, Dennis?

DENNIS: Forget it, dear. You can just fucking wait for me. You can just fucking wait.

*A silence. As Lizzard speaks to Dennis, he picks up
the telephone and dials it slowly in his trance.*

LIZZARD: Don't give me any suburbs shit. I've got a line up,
Dennis. I've got a line up because I've got what you want.
Every little jacker has to have it. Don't you? Come over.
Name one thought in your head I'm not in from the neck
down. But that wasn't the offer, Dennis. That wasn't the
offer.

The telephone rings. Saverin and Luke both rush for it.

SAVERIN: That's supposed to be off the hook; out of limits.

LUKE: Is everything going alright?

LIZZARD: Keep it down.

DENNIS: [*on the phone*] Hello, "The Zoo." Mr. Dennis's office.
This is the wizard speaking. [*A pause*] Hello Terry,
dear. . . Music? I'd just love to meet your friends, Terry.
Yes. Why, razz away, Terry if razzing's what you want
to do. Mind? Why should I mind? You be here in half
an hour on the nose and you'll find a scene to really set
you off, that's a guarantee.

SAVERIN: Not tonight, Dennis. I wouldn't suggest it.

LUKE: Let him try, boobie.

DENNIS: [*on the phone*] No. Saverin's just going to be my toad-
ie until morning. [*Slams down the receiver.*]

SAVERIN: Dennis. Do you want a Coke?

DENNIS: [*Into his super jock. The jock of jocks*] Split the Coke
with Luke. I'm the wizard here, let's make no mistake
about that, kids. I don't need pop. Hey! [*to Lizzard*] I'd
say you were "bobby socks and curlers" so put on a pretty
dress. I'll pick you up at 8:30 and take you to the prom.
You can chum around with Dennis the wizard.

They start to leave in disgust. In tears Dennis yells.

Hey! Do you know what I'm going to wear? Do you?

Surprise. I'm going to wear shit from head to toe. That's right, ladies. Shit. Just dripping in shit. The runs. I'm the wizard, Lizzard.

LIZZARD: Do you want to stay and visit the zoo, wizard?

LUKE: The zoo, stinko?

SAVERIN: The zoo?

LIZZARD: Want to stick your face in the lion's mouth?

SAVERIN: Do you want a Coke?

A long silence.

DENNIS: Ya, sure. It's about time. It's about fucking time. Flat.

Dennis very slowly pours the Coke over his own head; total suicide for Dennis. He collapses. A silence. Slowly, they go to him.

SAVERIN: Luke? Lizzard?

Luke carefully removes Dennis's shirt.

Oh my God. Dennis. Dennis. Dennis.

LIZZARD: [*lays Dennis down*] You must have had a long trip. That's O.K. We'll just give you a good scrub, eh, baby? The twilight zone. [*With a sponge, she bathes him*] Scrub all the dried skin. Now, this is a bizarre case for sure, what is your appraisal?

SAVERIN: [*He wears an operating mask. Examines Dennis*] A model O.D.! "A classic example of the flamboyant times that we live in."

They perform a ritual culminating in a mock operation as one of the final stages in the exorcism of Dennis. Dennis wants to laugh but grimaces and stiffens. They get him to walk like Frankenstein.

SAVERIN: Is he dead?

A shape moves through the darkness of the Space. No one notices.

LIZZARD: He finally jumped.

LUKE: He's dead.

LIZZARD: He's done really well. He's going to be fine.

*Dennis has been placed lying on a table by Saverin and
Luke. They bring him gifts. The knife, the scalpel, Coke,
the gift wrapped box, are placed on the table carefully.*

LUKE: You've done really well, Dennis.

SAVERIN: Old Dennis will have a very long sleep. Wake up
a new Dennis. Brand new.

*Mr. Bill Thompson has come in from the street. He's
been watching in the dark. He has a coat over his arm.*

THOMPSON: [*turning on a light*] You do pictures in here?

Chaos. The ritual breaks.

LIZZARD: Hey!

*Lizzard, Luke and Saverin are embarrassed, thrown
off, caught at a crucial and intimate point.*

LUKE: Sometimes. Ya.

SAVERIN: Aren't we closed? [*They quickly cover Dennis up*]
Who left the fucking door open?

LUKE: Red. Red. Red.

LIZZARD: Could you come back later?

THOMPSON: I don't think so.

SAVERIN: Later.

THOMPSON: Hi. Thought I'd drop up and see what you were
up to. We met at the gallery. Are those your friends?
Quite a place. I tried to call. You've left the phone off.

LIZZARD: Great. I'm glad you accepted the invitation. This is
Huck Hound. We entertain Mister —

THOMPSON: Thompson.

SAVERIN: Mr. Thompson.

*They are off balance with Mr. Bill Thompson. Dennis
lays low, but he watches.*

LUKE: Later, Mr. Thompson.

THOMPSON: It's Bill. Which one is Huck?

SAVERIN: Oooooo, that's strictly conceptual, Bill. I'm Wally, this is Eddie. [*Luke*] And over there is our little Theodore. [*Dennis*] Howdy Doody.

THOMPSON: You got a john, Huck?

SAVERIN: [*almost relieved*] Oh, yes we do, Bill. Billy. Do you mind if I call you Billy? Guess which door?

THOMPSON: I don't need the john, Huck. I was just interested. [*Relief breaks. A pause*] Dark room?

LUKE: I operate a Miranda and a Pentax. She's a dainty little model. Or my big butch four by five for studio secrets.

SAVERIN: The Beaver needs to sleep.

THOMPSON: It's getting expensive, you know with this and that.

SAVERIN: [*to Lizzard*] Keep him out of this.

LIZZARD: I took a Cinderella Modeling course. I want to be Marilyn when I grow up.

THOMPSON: I'm not much of a buff. You know what I mean? I've got an instamatic. But I could take pictures of the kids with it. If I had kids.

SAVERIN: So what's been happening?

THOMPSON: Nothing. Give me a feel of your camera. Got a light meter?

LIZZARD: What's been happening?

THOMPSON: Nothing, I've got a lamp like that.

LUKE: Just like that?

THOMPSON: The shade's blue; with peacocks.

LUKE: Red button snaps the shutter. Red.

THOMPSON: They make a pretty good lamp. You got a tri-light in it?

SAVERIN: Check it.

THOMPSON: Mine's a tri-light.

SAVERIN: More expensive.

THOMPSON: You probably got the wrong bulb. Ya. You put in a Westinghouse thousand hour, hundred watt. You need a tri-light. Most people wouldn't know.

SAVERIN: Maybe we screwed it in wrong.

THOMPSON: That can't affect the circuit. You need the right bulb.

SAVERIN: That's a shame. We blew it.

LUKE: What flavour?

THOMPSON: Tri-light. [*Thompson takes a picture of Lizzard. The flash doesn't work*] Red? You don't have much luck with bulbs. O.K. [*A silence*] How much did that cost you, Huck? The picture. How much would you estimate it cost you, off hand? [*He pulls out a wad of bills. They freeze. He tucks the money in his breast pocket*] We can wait to see how it turns out. This used to be a kind of book shop. Then it was a tattoo parlour. Guess what? I was going to get an eagle carved on my bicep.

Luke takes off his shirt.

Changed my mind. Would any of you want a smoke?

SAVERIN: No thanks.

LIZZARD: No thanks.

LUKE: No thanks.

THOMPSON: Really wonderful. It's a sensation now. It used to be boring. I'm a suburbanite. But I come down every weekend and Thursday nights. I was going to go for a brew. They took out Grievdorf's, didn't they? Didn't they? Well?

LIZZARD: Do you want to go outside and do an M and M. And talk —

THOMPSON: I'm chewing a hunk of Spearmint.

LIZZARD: It's O.K., you know. Do you want to take off your coat?

THOMPSON: [*keeps the coat*] What are we doing, relaxing?

LIZZARD: You can call me Marilyn, O.K? Marilyn or Granny.

THOMPSON: Are these your friends? You're cranking out a living down here. It's tough, eh? This is quite a place. I'd
like to help you out. I know this area. What would this
be, about two thousand square feet? Ten dollars a square
foot. You've got your privacy. Do you get it, Huck?

SAVERIN: Hey, Billy.

> *Dennis, fascinated, in the twilight zone, gets up and*
> *creeps around.*

LIZZARD: [*to Thompson*] Would you like to come outside and
talk to me, Mr. Thompson?

LUKE: Fever in the morning. [*He imitates a fire engine siren*]

SAVERIN: I'd like you to meet Marilyn. You've heard her on
talk shows.

THOMPSON: I don't want to gab about it. It's nothing. [*Refer-
ring to Luke's siren*] That's terrific.

SAVERIN: Let me entertain you. Boo dee dop dee.

> [*Thompson laughs*] Where'd you get those lines on your
> face?

LUKE: [*under his breath*] Rude dude.

THOMPSON: [*Takes out a pamphlet. He rolls the sheet into a
tube and sticks it together with his gum. He looks at them
out of a telescope for the next few minutes*] I was coming down tonight. Car broke down on the highway.
There was an old lady with blue-tinted hair jacking up
the ass end of this new Oldsmobile. I couldn't believe it.
I yelled out to her to get her butt out of the traffic. She
was changing the tire like I guess she saw on T.V. Funny
thing. The tire wasn't flat. Old ladies are like that. They
think, you've got your car and you've got your tires. Car
breaks down, you change a tire and this and that. I pulled

over about half a mile down, you know, I was concerned,
I got a '72 Pontiac. I walked all the way back to see if
she was alright to see, Huck?I thought she might have
a heart attack or get hit by a Mack truck. You know
what?

[A pause] It was a guy.Here's me thinking it's a little old
lady and it's a guy. Jesus Christ. In a brand new Olds
with a dress on. Me with my Pontiac and this guy in high
heeled shoes leaning over like a hunchback. I gave him
a good hard talking to. I could have spit.

LIZZARD: What an interesting John.

SAVERIN: No, somebody's been scratching lines in your face,
Billy. [Thompson tears up the tube] Anyway, You can
forget it now.

LIZZARD: Can I get you something?

THOMPSON: It's tough.

LIZZARD: Can I get you some fresh air?

THOMPSON: Hey, Huck!

LUKE: Do you want to take some center shots?

THOMPSON: I don't want to bore myself to death.

SAVERIN: Whatever you like.

THOMPSON: You can have your pamphlets back. I forgot my
contacts. Unless you want to read to me. What were we
just talking about?

DENNIS: [to Thompson, who has totally ignored him] Can I
have a drag?

THOMPSON: Tattoos. I'll give you a cheque to boot.

DENNIS: Can I have a drag off your cigarette?

THOMPSON: I feel like taking my shirt off, it's so bloody humid,
you know. A friend of mine comes here. He said you
played cards.

DENNIS: We share, you know.

THOMPSON: I can't stand smoke in the face. It's funny. I smoke, right? But I can't stand smoke in the face. *[Gives Dennis a drag]*

DENNIS: Can I have a whole cigarette? *[Takes one]*

THOMPSON: I've got a pack with the cellophane still on it. I stopped across the street.

DENNIS: Can I have two? *[Takes another]*

THOMPSON: One for after on. Later, right? It's a real habit, smoking. Nasty. Obviously you've had experience. It takes about six minutes to pick it up and a helluva lot longer to dump. I know what running out of smokes in between can be.

DENNIS: Can I have another cigarette?

THOMPSON: I like menthol when I've got a bit of the grippe. It's really tough if you've got a sore throat.

DENNIS: Can I have one more?

THOMPSON: You'd better not mind the taste of menthol. Everybody's on a rollies kick. It's a fad.

DENNIS: I don't have a match. *[He puts all four cigarettes into his mouth and Thompson uses his lighter]* Thanks.

THOMPSON: I know a guy that does that sometimes. Friend of mine from work.

DENNIS: It's thick.

THOMPSON: Try swallowing.

DENNIS: Sometimes I feel like jamming a whole carton in.

THOMPSON: Cheaper by the carton.

SAVERIN: Billy, I've got an idea that —

DENNIS: Make us tea, brother, brother, brother. We want tea. Darjeeling, Orange Pekoe, Special Breakfast, Earl Grey, or Chinese Green. We would like some tea. I can handle this.

SAVERIN: Well, you know.

DENNIS: Tea, brother.

LUKE: We're out of coffee, boobie. How about some tea?

THOMPSON: Why don't you forget it?

A pause. Dennis and Bill Thompson sit down together. The others watch.

You hungry?

DENNIS: I was really interested in the lamps you were talking about. Like electronics.

THOMPSON: There's a place that sells corned beef. Maybe Marilyn could use a bite.

DENNIS: What's with the Band-Aid, sir?

THOMPSON: I gave myself a nick with the razor.

DENNIS: You did not.

THOMPSON: Just a scratch. I do it all the time.

DENNIS: Incredible.

THOMPSON: Not so bad.

DENNIS: I find that hard to believe, sir.

THOMPSON: Well, it's true, You believe me?

DENNIS: Shaving is dangerous, no?

THOMPSON: I pulverize the old puss every morning. It's habit. I'm pretty careless; I forget what I'm doing. I usually put on a little piece of Kleenex to stop the blood.

DENNIS: I understand.

A pause.

THOMPSON: [*to the others*] Where'd you get these cushions here? The big one.

DENNIS: With our grant. [*Pursues him*]

THOMPSON: You use the cushions, don't you?

DENNIS: That's a lot of shit in the movies where one guy smothers another guy with a big cushion. I've had people push cushions against my face. I can breathe right through the cushion.

THOMPSON: You like posters? *[To the others]* I mean, I know where you can get posters cheap. These old movie posters. There's a great one of Richard Burton in chains. It's out of... out of... some Roman film. A movie about ancient Rome.

DENNIS: A picture of Robin Hood in browns and greens. I have a fantasy about Sherwood Forest, like the perfect subdivision.

THOMPSON: Me? No way. *[Back to Saverin]* I got a pamphlet from the girl a couple of days back. Tuesday. No, Thursday. I was too busy to visit. *[To Dennis]* I could get you a poster of, say, Robert Mitchum.

DENNIS: I'm referred to as the gentle Friar. I want us to be on a first name basis so as to alleviate our relationship of unnecessary friction; to sweeten the atmosphere so to speak. Call me "Friar" or even "Fry." Tell me about yourself.

THOMPSON: Theodore, isn't it? *[to the others]* I might be able to get posters for nothing. I'll see. I can't promise. Maybe we could even make some. Might be fun.

DENNIS: *[eager]* Don't be afraid to burn me. Tell me about yourself.

THOMPSON: *[a silence]* Hey!... I can leave if you really want me to.

DENNIS: Call me "Fry."

THOMPSON: Now, just hold on here a second. I'll leave, I mean, I'm capable of minding my own business if that's what you're saying.

SAVERIN: Billy. Nobody's blowing it really, just enthusiastic —

DENNIS: We're talking here, Wyatt. Meditate... please.

THOMPSON: I'm not stuck. What do you say, Marilyn?

LIZZARD: "I'm going to marry a man who will have some regard for me apart from all that love and stuff." What's that from?

DENNIS: Do you know what it feels like to get rid of all that tension?

THOMPSON: I'll get you the posters.

DENNIS: Let me try to release it. Nasty habits.

THOMPSON: Don't badmouth me, I won't badmouth you. Who wants to feel stupid?

DENNIS: [massages Thompson's scalp] Work it out for me and the show.

THOMPSON: It's tough right now.

DENNIS: I'm just the old curious Friar.

THOMPSON: It kinda gets you down.

DENNIS: Take deep breaths.

THOMPSON: You'd better not do that.

DENNIS: Take big gulps of air.

THOMPSON: Hear me?

DENNIS: In and out.

THOMPSON: You'd better not, pal.

DENNIS: In and out.

THOMPSON: I don't need that. [Stands up quickly, knocking Dennis over] Sorry. [They both giggle for a few seconds] Sometimes I'm so goddamn clumsy. I get really tired of saying sorry. Sorry. Sorry. Sorry. It's sickening.

    Luke and Saverin take Thompson away from Dennis. Thompson is upset. Dennis pursues. Lizzard holds him back.

DENNIS: Do you believe how dusty a place —

SAVERIN: What seems to be the trouble, Billy?

DENNIS: — can get. It's just amazing. The dust —

LIZZARD: Den-nis.

SAVERIN: Billy?

DENNIS: — gets in the air and the air flows in and out —

LIZZARD: Dennis, enough.

SAVERIN: Come on, Billy.

DENNIS: — of all the rooms. Have you noticed that, sir? It gets worse every —

SAVERIN: It's alright.

DENNIS: — year I think. Leaves a film on everything it touches. You can't stop cleaning —

SAVERIN: What's the trouble?

LIZZARD: Dennis.

DENNIS: — even for a short holiday. We've got to keep on lifting the dust. Street cleaners, window washers, garbage collectors. . . carpet sweepers. . . you've got to wash your hair twice a day. . . insane.

>   *Dennis sits down on a cushion and watches. Luke and Saverin are desperately enthusiastic with Thompson.*

THOMPSON: Well, ah, I guess, it's that I feel kind of guilty.

SAVERIN: O.K. Alright.

THOMPSON: I don't even sweat, do you follow me?

LUKE: O.K.

SAVERIN: You've had it too easy?

THOMPSON: Sort of. [*They laugh nervously.*]

SAVERIN: You feel like you need the old trial.

THOMPSON: I feel like an asshole telling you this. I've got to pay something back, eh? And that.

LUKE: It hurts.

SAVERIN: We all have that.

LUKE: We all need someone to bleed on.

THOMPSON: I guess. I wanted to talk to you.

LUKE: Everybody needs a healthy smack down. Figuratively speaking.

THOMPSON: I feel like a piece of shit.

DENNIS: Billy, I understand. I get it.

SAVERIN: We understand, Billy. We've been there so we understand.

LUKE: We'll help you get there. We'll listen to you.

SAVERIN: It'll be alright, Billy.

A pause.

THOMPSON: Thanks.

SAVERIN: Do you want to talk to any of us in particular?

THOMPSON: I don't know. The girl.

Lizzard goes to him. They laugh.

LIZZARD: Sure Billy. We can talk about it.

LUKE: It's O.K., Billy.

SAVERIN: Sure.

LIZZARD: Maybe in the tent. Or over —

THOMPSON: And him! *[Points to Dennis]*

DENNIS: God, it's dusty, Billy.

The others ignore him.

LIZZARD: Come on, Billy.

DENNIS: Billy! Wait for me! *[Pointing to the washroom]* I understand now.

Thompson walks straight past Dennis with Lizzard into the washroom.

SAVERIN: Not a chance.

DENNIS: I can handle it. I can handle it. I won't blow it. You've got to trust me, don't you? I'm under control.

LUKE: Let him try. He's just going to listen.

SAVERIN: Dennis, you should sleep.

DENNIS: I can handle it. We'll have a heart to heart.

LUKE: He can handle it. He can make it. If it works he can make it.

DENNIS: Of course I can handle it. I get it. I'm just going to listen.

LUKE: Go on Dennis, eat some shit, it'll do you good.

DENNIS: Good old Bill Thompson.

LUKE: Where's the drug clinic? Poof! Help the poor bastard.
And then you'd stand in the ocean, you see, towering
about eight miles high over the city. It'd be horrendous.
You'd have this giant chamois and you'd dunk it in the
bay. With one sweep you could wipe the whole fucking
city.

DENNIS: Nobody listens to Steppenwolf anymore.

LUKE: At high noon everyday we'd see this brown cloud streak-
ing down at us. Wiped out. Every speck of dust. Would
that be something, eh?   ·

DENNIS: Hey Saverin.
*Dennis walks into the washroom and closes the door
behind him. A silence.*

SAVERIN: I didn't think he'd go.

LUKE: Oh, come now, we should be very proud of him; tonight's hero for sure. He's amazing.
Laughter and chatter can be heard in the washroom.

SAVERIN: D. is for delectable. E. is for Eddie. A. I wonder what
Mr. Anderson is doing right now. Probably reading a
book on salamanders, listening to his chunky wife snore,
getting ready for some great class he's going to lay on
his present 10B in the five year arts and science pro-
gramme. We should invite Mr. Anderson down for co-
coa. Dennis would like that. He could prove he's done
alright for himself. Dennis moves really quickly. [*Saverin and Luke are speeding like expectant fathers.*]

LUKE: Yas, boss. He's going to be amazing at customer relations
and the complaint department.

SAVERIN: I think we've done alright on the old roller coaster.

LUKE: It will all look different in the morning, boobie.

SAVERIN: Maybe we should dye his hair to help him along. He's so lovable.

LUKE: Green?

The washroom sounds like a noisy classroom.

SAVERIN: I wonder what he'd think if we dug up Shirley-Ann Foebee?

LUKE: Hopefully it would bore him, now. Doesn't it bore you?

SAVERIN: Turn on the machines.

Luke turns on the radio, the stereo and the juke box. Loud rock and roll.

LUKE: Those my friend are the sounds of a satisfied man. Got to keep them happy downtown, you know.

SAVERIN: Turn it up loud. Louder! More. There!

The sounds from the washroom cannot be heard as the sound systems begin to blast.

LUKE: [*Sarcastically, almost shouting*] You sure that's loud enough?

SAVERIN: I like this.

LUKE: What?

SAVERIN: I said, "I like this."

LUKE: Good. [*Luke dances. Saverin walks about. Luke switches off some lights*] So much for Terry and the Afghans.

SAVERIN: What? [*They play with the baseball game.*]

LUKE: You can get lost. Playing this.

SAVERIN: What?

In the semi-darkness they play.

LUKE: Nothing.

Lizzard comes out of the washroom, terrified. Her lips are moving but her words are drowned out by the rock and roll. There is a red stain on her gown. Saverin glances at her for an instant and then rushes to the machines and turns them off.

Breaking glass; screaming and struggling from the washroom. Everyone begins to mumble and shout so that only bursts of words are distinguishable. Lizzard walks to the middle and stands in a trance. Saverin kicks at the washroom door until it flies open. Luke leaps up, searches around and runs into Thompson who walks out of the washroom with blood on his arms. He is carrying a knife and he is dazed. Luke backs off and runs out. Furniture topples. Saverin pulls at Thompson. Thompson drops the knife, falls to his knees and remains huddled on the floor.

LIZZARD: — and I just didn't see it. I mean, who would have thought to look under his coat.

SAVERIN: Jesus Dennis. Oh my God, no. Dennis.

LUKE: Where's my goddamn knife?

LIZZARD: We were just talking. Just talking.

LUKE: Where in God's name —

SAVERIN: Oh. Jesus, help meee. Come on —

LIZZARD: He picked it up. Picked up. A pick up. I was watching him.

DENNIS: [*his voice*] Hold it for — just hold it...Hold it.

LUKE: Saverin!

SAVERIN: Get the fuck out!

LUKE: I can't find it...it's gone...Jesus.

SAVERIN: What did you do?

Dennis walks out from the washroom almost calmly, and Saverin watches him step over Thompson. Dennis is clutching his wound. He staggers across the room, collapses, gets up and kneels beside the bed. Saverin crosses to him, sits and lays Dennis's head in his lap. Luke comes in from the street with his camera out. He looks for an instant and methodically begins to take pictures. Saverin takes the gift wrapping off the package that was going to be given to Dennis. It is a bird cage containing a live yellow budgie. He holds it up. Saverin, Thompson, Luke, Lizzard and Dennis laugh. Luke continues to take pictures.

LIZZARD: He did it to himself. I think I watched him do it to himself.

DENNIS: Hold it. It's not real. Take it easy.

LUKE: Saverin, I'll get —

LIZZARD: Saverin?

LUKE: — someone.

SAVERIN: Dennis! Dennis! It's alright. O.K. . . . Alright.

DENNIS: Hold it. It's not real. Take it easy.

LIZZARD: I didn't look but I couldn't have known. I didn't know. Red. Red. Red.

THOMPSON: So what do I want? It's on my hands.

SAVERIN: O.K., O.K., O.K., alright. We'll make it. We'll still make it.

LUKE: Hold it. Wait.

LIZZARD: Everything's fine. It's fine.

LUKE: Hold it.

DENNIS: We're O.K. We'll be alright. O.K. Alright.

SAVERIN: [*to Dennis*] We'll make it. O.K., O.K., Alright. O.K., alright, O.K. O.K. It's O.K., It's O.K. It's over.

Silence and Darkness.

Border

by
Elizabeth Wray

© Elizabeth Wray, 1981
CAUTION: All rights strictly reserved. Professionals and amateurs
are hereby warned that *Border* is subject to a royalty and is protected
under copyright laws of all countries cover by the International Copyright Convention. Permission in writing must be secured before any
performance or reading is given. All inquiries should be addressed
to the author, 464 Eureka Street, San Francisco, CA 94114.

Border was originally presented as the second part of a three part play entitled *Mobile Homes,* by the Julian Theatre in Spring 1981, with the following cast:

Ace .... Cab Covay

Junior .... Richard Reineccius

Ava .... Laura Tarentino

Directors: Cab Covay and Richard Reineccius

Setting: The Texas-New Mexico border; a gas station/ diner; April, 1980.

Characters: JUNIOR—45; runs the gas station/diner.
                ACE—37; Junior's brother; a conceptual composer; helps Junior with the business.
                AVA—30; formerly a waitress; not yet a rock singer.

A cafe on the Texas-New Mexico border. April, 1980.
On the plate glass window you can read backwards "Bor-
der Cafe." There are a lunch counter, a few tables and
a pay phone. On two carts, off to one side, are an oboe
and tape recording, mixing and editing equipment. Across
the room is a table with an adding machine and papers
on it. On each table and at each place at the counter is
a vase of artificial flowers. Ace stands at one of the carts,
fiddling with the recorders. Junior sits at a table center-
stage. It is 11 p.m.

JUNIOR: Three bottles Kraft Hickory Smoke Barbeque Sauce.
One case Donald Duck Orange juice.

ACE: Stop!

Ace comes over to the table, reaches into the vase of
flowers, removes a small microphone, flips its "on" switch,
puts it back in a concealed position and returns to his
equipment.

You've been fooling with the switches again.

JUNIOR: The hell I have! I don't come near your precious flowers!

ACE: Let's go.

JUNIOR: What do you want?

ACE: Canned vegetables.

JUNIOR: Ten cans Meadowdale White Hominy. One case Ranch
Style Blackeyed Peas. Two cases Van Camp's Pork and
Beans.

ACE: Repeat!

JUNIOR: Van Camp's Pork and Beans. Van Camp's Pork and
Beans. Van Camp's Pork and Beans.

ACE: Continue!

JUNIOR: Fifteen cans Freshlike Veg-all.

ACE: Shout!

JUNIOR: [*Shouting*] ONE CASE MARY KITCHEN ROAST
BEEF HASH!

ACE: Stop! Now what did I say Junior?

JUNIOR: You said: Shout.

ACE: No. I said: Repeat, shout. I was saying repeat, shout about the Freshlike Veg-All, not about the Mary Crocker Roast Beef Hash.

JUNIOR: Mary *Kitchen* Roast Beef Hash. If you wanted the Freshlike Veg-All shouted, you should of said repeat-shout all at once, instead of just shout.

ACE: I was counting on your memory, Junior.

JUNIOR: Well, next time say repeat-shout. Sometimes you're just too vague. You oughta realize that.

ACE: Next time I'll say repeat-shout. But next time don't give me roast beef hash when I want canned vegetables.

JUNIOR: Hash is a vegetable.

ACE: Hash is not a vegetable.

JUNIOR: I buy the food. I oughta know.

ACE: Hash is a carbohydrate and roast beef is a meat.

JUNIOR: Tastes more like vegetables than steak dinner.

ACE: It tastes like junk. That's what it tastes like. I don't know why you buy it.

JUNIOR: It's on the menu, in case you never noticed.

ACE: Forget it. Let's go on to sauces.
      [Pause] Well?

JUNIOR: How do you want them?

ACE: Like always.

JUNIOR: You gotta tell me that. See, that's what I mean about you being vague. *[Pause]* Five bottles Heinz 57 Steak Sauce. *[He makes a slurping sound.]* Nine bottles Del Monte Tomato Ketchup. *[Slurp]* Five cans Hunt's Manwich Sandwich Sauce. *[Slurp]* Twenty-five boxes Chef Boy-Ar-Dee Spaghetti Dinner with Mushroom Sauce.

ACE: Spaghetti is miscellaneous, Junior!

JUNIOR: It's spaghetti *with* mushroom sauce.

ACE: Go on!

JUNIOR: Yeah, well what's Bird's Eye Cool Whip Non-Dairy Whipped Topping?

ACE: Miscellaneous. Just do miscellaneous, Junior. Forget the other. Do miscellaneous. [*No answer*] Whisper-slurp-shout. Do you think you can handle that?

Ava enters and stands in the door, unnoticed by Ace and Junior. She carries a broken fan belt.

JUNIOR: Three bunches Chiquita Bananas. [*Slurp*] ONE THREE-POUND BOX REYNOLD'S WRAP HEAVY-DUTY ALUMINUM FOIL. Fifty packs Juicy Fruit Chewing Gum. [*Slurp*]

AVA: Who runs the gas station next door?

JUNIOR: THREE BOXES ARM AND HAMMER BAKING SODA. [*To Ava*] I DO. What do you want? Sorry, lady . . . what can I do for you?

AVA: I need a fan belt.

ACE: [*flipping off machine*] Perfect! [*He puts on headphones, rewinds and plays back*]

JUNIOR: [*shouting*] Ace, I'm gonna get this lady a fan belt.

ACE: [*listening to tape*] Perfect!

JUNIOR: You got it there? Let's see. You got a foreign car, right?

AVA: It's a VW.

JUNIOR: That's what I thought. I don't have it to fit you.

AVA: Every gas station has fan belts.

JUNIOR: Hard to keep those foreign parts in stock.

AVA: There's only about fifty-million VW's on the road.

JUNIOR: I don't like to mess with foreign parts. I can give you some gas.

AVA: That's going to do a lot of good without a fan belt.

JUNIOR: I could fix you right up if you were a Dodge.

AVA: Aren't there any other gas stations around here?

JUNIOR: Not open this time of night. Of course, if you were on the super highway. . .

AVA: The super highway ran out.

JUNIOR: It starts up again at Tucumcari. [Pause] I guess we could call over to Tucumcari for a fan belt. But how're you gonna get it?

AVA: I'll pay you to pick it up.

JUNIOR: I'd be glad to, if I wasn't so busy. Got my tax forms to finish by the 15th.

AVA: Look, I'm trying to get to San Francisco. I'm in a hurry, you know.

JUNIOR: They always are. [Pause] Well, I'll see what I can do for you. Get my brother Ace there to fix you a cup of coffee. [Exits]

> Ace has taken his headphones off and continues to fiddle with his equipment. Ava makes a long distance phone call at the pay phone.

AVA: Is John Koski there? Is this the service? I've left three messages already. Has he called in? Just tell him Ava called. I'll call back later. He knows me. I'm his wife. No, there's no way he can reach me.

> She hangs up. Pause.

Could I have that cup of coffee? Hey, could I have a cup of coffee?

ACE: Just a minute.

AVA: You've got a funny way of running a business.

ACE: How do you want it?

AVA: Black.

> He flicks a few more switches, then gets her a cup of coffee. She sits down at a table, centerstage.

It sure takes a long time to get a point across around here.

ACE: That depends.

AVA: Things move quicker back East.

ACE: That depends on the point and on what you're crossing.

AVA: I'm about to cross the desert.

ACE: That's not always so easy.

AVA: Yeah. I'm beginning to wonder whether I'm ever going to get across it.

ACE: So. You're meeting someone across the desert.

AVA: No. I'm leaving someone, as a matter of fact.

ACE: *Back* East. For someone *out* West.

AVA: Not someone—something.

ACE: A new life—on her own. The point of the crossing.

AVA: Could I have another?

ACE: The rugged individual! [*Getting coffee*] You've noticed we never say *back* West, just *out* West.

AVA: Well, that's how I feel. Like I'm heading out.

ACE: When you're driving the straight road from back East, out West, what goes through your mind?

AVA: You hope you won't break down in the middle of nowhere.

ACE: I'm recording you.

AVA: I know.

ACE: It's what I do.

AVA: I noticed.

ACE: Not all of you. Just isolated moments.

> *He puts his headphones on and goes back to playing, splicing and mixing. Junior enters.*

JUNIOR: Car's out front. I towed it up.

AVA: What about the fan belt?

JUNIOR: They're sending it. Might take awhile. Ace been taking care of you?

AVA: I got some coffee, if that's what you mean.

JUNIOR: Don't pay him any mind. He's working on his spring concert. Too bad you didn't break down tomorrow. You could of been here for Ace's concert.

AVA: Maybe he'll send me a tape.

JUNIOR: Couldn't do that. All his machines're in use. See, he takes all of them out to the middle of the desert, turns them on full blast and lets them go. Doesn't care if there's anybody there to hear them or not. Says its not important. Well, seems to me it's important. Or else, why bother? So I generally try to round up some folks to go with me. Of course, he always holds it at the worst time of year— right before the 15th, when taxes are due. You got yours filed yet?

AVA: What does he record?

JUNIOR: You name it. Mostly bits and pieces. Conversations, lists, cars, chairs, just about everything. Even the wind. I don't see the point of that one. When you're standing out on the desert and the wind's howling all around you— you sure can't make out the sound of wind on the tape. It's all one, you see. But Ace says that's the point. One of his pure sounds, he calls it. Well, I don't exactly comprehend. Wind on wind, he calls it. Funny, you wouldn't think to look at him he used to be a famous musician.

Pause. Reading the newspaper:

Would you look at this! Food costs up 14.7% in the last 12 months. What was I telling you, Ace. Unemployment up to 6.2%. That's on account of what's happening in Detroit. More and more damn Japanese cars driving through here every day. We got to start supporting our own. But do we? No, instead we herd them all in. The chinks and the wetbacks and our latest—you can read about it right here—the god-damn Cuban Communists.

Yeah, we herd them in, feed them, educate them. Before
too long, some damn Cuban refugee in a three piece suit
is gonna come through here driving some damn Toyota
Corona. I tell you one thing, I'm not pumping any gas
for him.

Pause. He starts figuring at the adding machine.

You'd think he'd help me with my taxes, him being so
smart and all. Not on your life! Thinks he's too good to
act like a regular citizen. Help yourself to more coffee if
you want any. Ace isn't going to wait on you. [*Pause*]
We gotta pay Texas and New Mexico taxes, on account
of Ace there's sitting in New Mexico and I'm over here
in Texas. You're right about on the border line. It gets
complicated. [*Pause*] You fill out your census form?

AVA: No.

JUNIOR: Didn't you get it in the mail?

AVA: No.

JUNIOR: You must of left before it got there.

AVA: Must have.

JUNIOR: Well, you're in luck. I'm an enumerator.

He gets a census form and moves to Ava's table.

Hey, Ace! A census form!

AVA: I don't care about the census.

JUNIOR: That's how a lot of folks feel. I agree with you. It's
a pain in the ass. But the information is important—rep-
resentation in Congress, that kind of thing. Anyhow,
they'll catch up with you sooner or later. You might as
well get it over with.

AVA: No thanks.

JUNIOR: It only takes five minutes. See Ace records all the information, then I fill in the form later by hand. That way
the resident—that's you—doesn't waste time. It's a con-

venience I like to offer my customers.

AVA: Can we just forget it?

JUNIOR: I don't like to mention it, but I did tow your car up to the station for you.

AVA: Yeah, and you'll charge me an arm and a leg for it.

JUNIOR: No charge.

AVA: No charge, hunh?

JUNIOR: I never charge.

AVA: Everybody charges.

JUNIOR: Well, I can't make you. It's just I'd feel better knowing you were accounted for.

Ace comes over to their table, pulls the mike from the vase and switches it off.

ACE: He really would feel better. Maybe she'd feel more comfortable with the machine off, Junior.

JUNIOR: That's OK. I can fill it out right now by hand. OK, what's your name?

AVA: Christ!

JUNIOR: Your given name.

AVA: Ava. Ava Koski.

JUNIOR: Age?

AVA: 30.

JUNIOR: Sex? Female. Marital status? Single, married, divorced, separated, or widowed?

AVA: I don't know. Put single.

JUNIOR: OK, you can relax now. That's all the personal stuff. [*Ava hangs up the phone.*] Next is race. It's pretty obvious you're like the rest of us, but I gotta read all of the other ones to you by law. And you gotta tell me if one-eighth of you is any of them. Anglo-American, Spanish-American, Negro-American, Puerto Rican, American Indian, Samoan, Filipino, Asian-American...

AVA: I'm what you thought I was.

JUNIOR: . . . Eskimo, Hawaiian or Other. OK, now the rest of the questions are about your place of residence.

AVA: I don't have one.

JUNIOR: Then we'll make it your car. How many rooms do you have in your living quarters? Do not count bathrooms, porches, balconies, foyers, halls or half-rooms. [*No answer*] I'll put three. Do you enter your living quarters directly from the outside or through someone else's living quarters? That's for the housing industry. So they can build better housing. [*No answer.*] I'll put: From the outside. Is this living quarter part of a condominium?

ACE: [*into hand mike*] A condominium of cars.

JUNIOR: If you own your home, what is its value?

AVA: It's value is that it moves.

ACE: [*into mike*] The mechanical steed gallops into the new life.

Junior returns to his table.

JUNIOR: I'll check this over. Then you can sign it and we'll mail it off.

Silence. Ava gets another cup of coffee and sits back down. During the following dialog, Ace directs his comments into his mike, then increasingly to Ava. Ava directs her comments increasingly to Ace. There's a quality of performance—for themselves, for each other and for Junior. Junior is entertained by them and then gradually falls asleep.

AVA: Still waiting tables.

ACE: The service profession.

AVA: Five years of serving people crabs and beer! Filling them up.

ACE: Servile.

AVA: A lot of the time, I felt like a whore.

ACE: I appreciate a good place setting.

AVA: I knew where my tip was coming from.

ACE: Two spoons. One for stirring, for skimming.

AVA: A raunchy little joke.

ACE: The other for gouging. Canteloupes, for example. Gouging down to the quick.

AVA: My tight black skirt.

ACE: Two knives. One dull one for patting and spreading the butter across the buns.

AVA: The way my breast flattened when I leaned over to serve the kids' plates.

ACE: The other for cutting. For separating the fat from the rump cut. For severing the tiny ligaments in the tenderest breast.

AVA: Getting them drunk and taking their money.

ACE: Crystal glassware. Reflecting the cutlery.

AVA: Still, I liked the drunks the best. At least they knew what they wanted.

ACE: A rim so finely blown that your wine-dipped finger sings along it like the faint song of a chain saw coming at you from 50 miles deep into the woods.

AVA: I hated the nibblers. The nibblers and the sippers. They hardly knew they were alive.

ACE: And a plate of fine white porcelain china. Where you see a perfect reflection of yourself. Leaning over your well-appointed trough, you see your lips curl slightly, your front incisors jump. [Pause] Out here there aren't many customers.

AVA: No, I guess not.

ACE: That's why I came back. [Pause] Have you noticed the visual insistence out there?

AVA: The visual insistence?

ACE: Television, billboards, neon. All of it.

AVA: I read somewhere that we have the most visual culture of all the industrialized countries.

ACE: Conspiracy. The leading conspirator is the television industry. They have systematically bred the death of the imaginative listener. The imaginative listener's buying accounts for only 10% of the records sold each year. Proportionately insignificant.

AVA: Rock and roll must account for the other 90%.

ACE: Rock and roll is the opiate of the inarticulate. Also, it's breaking down the membrane structure of the ear canal.

AVA: Yeah? Well, can you dance to your so-called music?

ACE: Music and dancing are no longer the point. The task is to reawaken the aural imagination.

AVA: I guess we've got different ways of going about it. [Pause] Did you play in a symphony or something? [No answer] Well, I'm in rock and roll myself.

ACE: Do you hear that? [He takes his mike to a window, opens it and sticks the mike out.] Wind. The primary sound. It creates and destroys.

AVA: I had a friend once who loved the wind out here. I looked her up in San Antonio. Nobody had heard of her.

   Ace leaves the window open and returns to his machines.

ACE: Like anywhere else, you learn to fill the space. Of course, there are certain threats.

AVA: It sounds empty. Like it could swallow you up.

ACE: You come to see life as on-the-road and off-the-road. I've chosen to live off-the-road. You're of the opposite persuasion. Which is what makes you of interest to me.

AVA: I'm never going to make San Francisco by Monday.

ACE: The unplanned stopover. I've almost completed my symphony. Whereas, you're just beginning yours. That symphony called "A New Life." [*Pause*] Of course a symphony is never really complete. Like a life. The remaining sounds I'm after are rather hard to get out here in the middle of nowhere. As you put it. Aptly. The remaining sounds are animal sounds. The remaining sounds are always animal sounds. Certain animal sounds are easy to get—the coyote, for instance. And the crow. Others are more difficult—the snake, the hyena. They're hard to get because they're hard to get around. Hard to get around. And once gotten around, they're hard to get out. Out of one's system, I mean. They're hard to get rid of. Hard to forget. Then there are the animals that are nearly impossible to record. Those animals that don't sound like themselves. Or don't sound like you might imagine they might sound. Like the bat. Have you ever heard the sound of a bat?

AVA: I didn't think they made sounds.

ACE: Oh yes.

Ava goes to the phone to make another long distance call.

AVA: Is this The Boarding House? Could I speak to the manager? [*Pause*] Hello? This is Ava Koski. [*Louder*] Ava Koski! I'm a friend of Joel Bernstein's. [*Louder*] Joel Bernstein! He set up an audition for me at your club. [*Louder*] An audition! [*Pause*] This is long distance. All right, I'll hold.

JUNIOR: [*asleep and moaning*] Tickets! Tickets!

Ace quickly fiddles with his switches and puts his headphones on.

ACE: Where are you, Junior?

JUNIOR: . . . booth.

ACE: Where? A booth? Where?

JUNIOR: . . . tickets! . . . tickets!

ACE: What tickets? Junior! [*Ace goes over to Junior and shakes him violently.*] Wake up, Junior! Wake up! Tell me your dream!

JUNIOR: Don't. . . hey, cut it out! Leave me alone!

ACE: I want to know your dream!

JUNIOR: I don't know. I was selling tickets. . . something. Something important. That's all I remember.

ACE: Think!

JUNIOR: That's all I remember! You're not supposed to wake me up like that!

ACE: You were fading.

JUNIOR: I don't want you to waking me up like that any more, Ace. [*He exits.*]

AVA: [*into phone*] Hello. Hello! [*To Ace*] You sure take advantage of him.

ACE: That's how families are. Didn't you know that? He takes a certain pride in me. Goes along with the lack of education, I suppose.

AVA: Some people make use of their education.

ACE: Well, don't mind me—take some courses. An acting class, perhaps. To improve your song delivery. Oh yes! One cup arduous study, three cups of meaningful experience, ten years of reading movies magazines, another ten watching American Bandstand, a dash of luck, a pound of gall. Shake them up with a heavy downbeat and PRESTO!!! A rock and roll star!

AVA: [*shouting into phone*] Hello! Hey!

ACE: Hey! You never know! It could be you!

AVA: You're goddamn right! [*Pause; she slams down phone*]

ACE: Can't get through?

AVA: No.

ACE: You'd better get used to it.

AVA: What?

ACE: Out there. The connections are always jammed. That's always the problem when the life is led on the road. You never get through.

AVA: Is that why you stopped being a "famous musician"? You couldn't get through?

ACE: You could put it that way.

AVA: You couldn't play the game. Couldn't play to win. So you came back home.

ACE: I had projects awaiting me.

AVA: Yeah, like waiting tables. That's probably what'll happen to me.

ACE: A desert mission.

AVA: Who am I fooling? [*Starts to exit*]

ACE: Here. [*Hands her a mike*] Take this with you.

AVA: What for?

ACE: Protection. It will absorb some of the desert sounds.

AVA: I'm just going to stand out front awhile.

ACE: Be sure you listen. Listen closely to what the desert's saying. Otherwise, it could kill you.

She takes the mike and goes out front. Lights fade a little inside and come up outside, in front of the cafe. Ace puts his headphones on. Ava holds the mike at her side. The wind has picked up. She stands still for a few moments.

AVA: [*listening*] It sounds like it's swallowing up everything. [*Hums a tune. Stops. Listens. Sings.*] I had learned to play it / Close to the vest [*Listens. Sings.*] Not to be so anxious / To be the first to confess. [*Pause*] I don't think this wind is going anywhere. It's just going. Like me. Just going. Why do they bother putting up fences out here?

While Ava has been standing out front, Junior has walked up to Ace, had some words and walked out again. Ava stands still a few moments. Ace takes off his head-

*phones, flicks some switches and removes a large clay pot
and 15 glass jars from behind the counter. He brings the
pot and jars over to the carts. As he's doing this, Ava
comes back inside.*

ACE: They hadn't left Tucumcari yet, so Junior's going to get
the fan belt himself. [*Pause*] It was my idea that Junior go.

AVA: How much longer am I going to have to wait here?

ACE: I must admit, I was selfishly motivated. I wanted a chance
to talk to you, alone.

AVA: I don't feel like talking.

ACE: Suit yourself.

*Ava gets herself another cup of coffee. Ace starts drop-
ping jars into the clay pot and recording the sound of their
breaking. Annoyed, Ava sits back down at her table. After
Ace has broken several jars.*

AVA: You're driving me crazy!

ACE: You didn't want to talk.

He breaks three more jars.

AVA: All right! Let's talk.

ACE: Parts of my concert are calculated to bring about a direct
and predictable response.

AVA: You really like upsetting people, don't you?

ACE: Upsetting, yes. Or perhaps, redirecting. For instance, the
sound of glass breaking alone [*He breaks another jar*] is
simply disturbing. But the sound of [*He flicks a switch
and we hear crickets*] crickets [*pause*], glass breaking [*He
breaks a jar; pause*], and more crickets [*He turns off the
tape*]—is another matter entirely. Such juxtapositions
tend to restructure the mind, you might say. [*Pause*] Out
here one is reminded of the difference between things.
Life is led on the border.

AVA: It gives you a kind of suspended feeling.

ACE: A bird on a wire.

> *Pause. He flicks a switch which sends wild animal sounds into the room, barely perceptible at first but growing gradually louder. He switches the mike in the flower vase back on.*
>
> *During the following dialog, he spreads a place setting around Ava as she's sitting at the table.*

ACE: There are noticeable differences between this table and that one. Each entity has its own peculiar laws. Junior has his laws for instance, and I have mine.

AVA: I bought some beer in Oklahoma. This awful watered-down stuff. Baptist law, they said. I was glad to get to Texas and drink real beer again.

ACE: The difference between the plains of Texas and the New Mexican desert is that while the plains are unpredictable, they're generally kind. The desert is unpredictable and mean.

AVA: Back East. Out West.

ACE: The border position is in practice a lawless place, governed neither by the laws of one state or the other.

AVA: My life could take me anywhere.

ACE: It is the habitat, the place of the unjudging observer.

AVA: It could take me nowhere.

ACE: The border position is a privileged position, allowing for a certain clear perception. You can see in two directions.

AVA: East. West. Middle of nowhere. Nowhere.

ACE: There's a fine line, a tightwire, between on and off the road, between direction and misdirection.

AVA: Maybe I should stay here. Set up a crab house.

ACE: In choosing a life off the road, you choose living with the menace.

AVA: Drive out every night and hunt for sandcrabs on the

desert. Stand on the desert, listening for crabs.

ACE: Consider the road signs: Watch for Falling Rock, Keep Off Soft Shoulders. [*Pause*] There are no true directions.

AVA: A sand crab scratches in the sand.

ACE: The sand crab is surrounded by a circle of animals. By animals breathing.

AVA: The sand crab looks for an escape.

ACE: The sand gives way. The animals close in.

AVA: The sand crab digs upwards.

ACE: The sand pours in on it. The animals dig in.

AVA: [*beginning to panic*] What are those sounds?

ACE: Desert sounds.

AVA: What are you doing? I don't want any food. I'm not hungry.

ACE: [*standing over her*] Animal sounds.

AVA: [*starting to get up*] Is there any more coffee?

ACE: [*preventing her*] Bad for your nerves.

AVA: I'm not hungry.

ACE: I am.

AVA: I'll get up. I'm in your place.

ACE: We're both in place. My dinner is almost complete.

AVA: There's nothing here to eat.

ACE: Lean over the plate. [*No response; threateningly*] Lean over! [*She does.*] What do you see?

AVA: Nothing... [*Ace leans toward her*]... the plate.

ACE: Look closer. My concert is almost complete. I need only a few more... animal sounds. Of the type that are nearly impossible to record. The type that never sound as you imagine they'll sound. The fascinating kind. Like the bat. I've yet to record the bat. They say its sound is not unlike the human scream. The human female scream. The human scream of certain healthy young females.

She is leaning over the plate. He leans over her and picks up the knife and fork. The knife is sharp. He holds them on either side of her head.

The further off the road, the greater the hunger. The stranger the desire. What do you see?

AVA: My reflection.

He jabs the fork into the plate, silently, as if into the piece of meat that is her reflection.

ACE: The stranger the desire, the greater the satisfaction. What do you see?

AVA: Myself.

He cuts the imaginary meat that is her reflection. She screams, low in her throat. He returns to his machines with the mike that was hidden in the vase. He rewinds and plays back her scream over the speakers.

AVA: You creep! [*She picks up a chair and runs at Ace. He moves out of the way. She breaks it over a machine.*] Goddamn creep!

ACE: What the hell are you doing!

AVA: [*hitting the chair over the machine again and again*] You stupid creep! You goddamn stupid creep! [*etc.*]

Ace tries to restrain her but she threatens him with the chair. She knocks the cart over, picks up the machine and throws it to the floor. *** *Ace is in agony. He crumples to the ground, moaning. Ava keeps trashing the machine. Gradually Ace's moaning turns to laughter. He grabs mikes from table vases and records Ava's rampage.*

*** *Or, more practically, for production AVA could rip the tape from the machine that recorded her scream, push and knock the carts around, and perhaps overturn one of the cafe tables.*

ACE: The death of the machine! The end of the era! The fall
   of the West! Death to the machine! [etc.]
   Junior enters in the middle of this.
JUNIOR: Miss Koski! Miss Koski! I got your fan belt on for you.
   Ava stops, exhausted.
ACE: Death to the tyrant! Free the aural imagination!
JUNIOR: Shut up, Ace! [*To Ava*] Seems like I had one over in
   the shop all along.
AVA: [*to Ace*] You're heading nowhere!
   She grabs her bag and exits.
JUNIOR: [*calling after her*] Hold it, Miss Koski! You gotta sign
   your census form.
   *Junior goes over to his table and begins figuring his taxes
   again. He uses the adding machine. Ace puts the mikes
   back in their vases. He take's a jew's harp from one of
   the carts, sits down and begins to play it.*
JUNIOR: I don't know why you wanna bother people like that,
   Ace. You know every time you do, they get mad. This
   one sure told you a thing or two! Ha! Serves you right.
   [*Pause. Ace continues to play the mouthpiece as Junior
   figures*] I've told you a thousand times we got a business
   to run here. We're here to fill them up and send them on
   their way. Down the road. It's not much, but it has its
   importance. Hell, I wish she'd of signed her form. [*Pause*]
   You wanna finish recording the food list? [*No answer*] You
   never acted crazy before you left here. They probably
   screwed your mind up in Los Angeles, or one of those
   other cities. I don't mind everybody saying: Your brother's crazy. How many of them's got brothers who played
   in famous symphony orchestras. Still, you shouldn't of
   left in the first place. You should of stayed right here like
   me. By the side of the road. Watching things. Living the

peaceful life.

Ace plays the jew's harp. Junior figures on the adding machine. The lights fade out.

Forecast
A Parable

by
Elizabeth Wray

© Elizabeth Wray, 1982
CAUTION: All rights strictly reserved. Professionals and amateurs are hereby warned that *Forecast* is subject to a royalty and is protected under copyright laws of all countries covered by the International Copyright Convention. Permission in writing must be secured before any performance or reading is given. All inquiries should be addressed to the author, 464 Eureka Street, San Francisco, CA 94114.

Forecast was first presented at the Intersection Theatre in November 1982, with the following cast:

Woman .... Priscilla Cohen

Man .... Ellery Edwards

Director: Elizabeth Wray

Place & Time   Peru, 2050

Characters   POTATO FARMER—small, thin, dark woman, around 30.

ASTRONAUT—tall, athletic, blond man, around 35.

SCENES

1. Prolog
2. Work
3. Remembering/Imagining
4. Watching. Sleeping
5. Storytelling
6. Building a Fire
7. Nesting
8. Not Knowing
9. Nightsoil
10. Changing Weather
11. Epilog

PROLOG

Woman plants potatoes. She hears something, puts her ear to the ground. Man enters. Woman is on guard.

MAN: I'm from the United States. My capsule crashed...Do you speak English? My capsule crashed [*makes sound of crash*] over there. I'm hungry. [*Indicates hunger*] Food... potatoes....

He reaches toward potatoes on the ground. She groans and knocks him down, pulling a knife on him. He retreats, scrambling out of the way. They watch each other carefully. Neither moves. He points to the sky.
Rain [*Makes sound and gestures of approaching thunder storm*]...Storm.

He looks at the sky and remains looking, transfixed. Finally, she returns to her planting, cautiously. She stops working, looks to the sky, looks at the man. She throws him a potato, which he starts to devour.
WOMAN: Hey! [*Man looks up*] When is the rain? [*He looks at her amazed that she speaks his language.*]

WORK

WOMAN: Forecast. C'mon. Forecast, goddamnit.
MAN: I'm waiting for my french fries.
WOMAN: I can't plant until I know the forecast.
MAN: Country style french fries. And leave the skins on.
WOMAN: There's not much food left.

No response. She throws him a potato.
MAN: Double order.

She throws him another potato.

MAN: Temporary deterioration. Strong breezes ahead.
WOMAN: Yeah? Hmmmmmmmm. Maybe I should wait.
MAN: Large branches in motion. Whistling in telegraph wires. . .
WOMAN: There aren't any branches.
MAN: It spices up the forecast.
WOMAN: There aren't any branches because there aren't any
   trees. Face it.
      She returns to planting.
MAN: Umbrellas used with difficulty.
WOMAN: Umbrellas! Ha!
MAN: Umbrellas!!!!!
WOMAN: Ha!!!!!
MAN: [*undertone*] Umbrellas.

REMEMBERING/IMAGINING

      She squats with a stick, drawing a map in the dirt.
MAN: Got things all figured out?
      She groans at him.
MAN: You know what color my eyes are?
WOMAN: Doesn't matter.
MAN: It matters.
WOMAN: Not to me.
MAN: Yeah, I bet you think you got things all figured out.
      *She continues figuring in the dirt. He cracks a stick. She
      puts her ear to the ground. He throws sticks down in front
      of her.*
MAN: Doesn't do any good to try to figure things out. Things
   change.
WOMAN: Very deep. [*Pause*] You'd think somebody who spent
   most of his life in outer space would have more to say.
MAN: I know where we're going.

WOMAN: You do not.

MAN: Yes, I do. I've imagined it many times.

She beats sticks together.

MAN: What color are my eyes?

WOMAN: I don't know.

MAN: Imagine.

WATCHING. SLEEPING.

They both keep watch. She watches low to the ground. He looks to the horizon. She thinks she hears something, puts her ear to the ground. He puts his ear to the ground. False alarm. He yawns. He falls asleep. She watches. He wakes up screaming.

MAN: Opening. . . black hole. . . fire . . . .

WOMAN: Wake up. Wake up. You're dreaming. Wake up.

MAN: Can't breathe. . . watch out. . . ship's opening up . . . .

WOMAN: Stop it! You're dreaming. Look at the ground. It's all right. Look at it.

MAN: No.

WOMAN: Look at it!

MAN: No!

WOMAN: You were dreaming about before.

MAN: We had to abandon ship.

WOMAN: Now you're here. All right? The ground is underneath you. It's not going anywhere.

MAN: I'm scared.

WOMAN: Go back to sleep. I'll keep watch.

MAN: You won't go to sleep?

WOMAN: No.

MAN: Promise?

WOMAN: I promise.

She watches. He sleeps. He wakes up. She sleeps. He
watches. She wakes up screaming.
WOMAN: Falling! Fire bombs! Falling!
MAN: It's OK. It stopped.
WOMAN: Make them stop falling.
He pushes upward with his arms.
MAN: Only stars up there. See for yourself.
WOMAN: I was dreaming about before.
MAN: There haven't been any bombs for a long time. I wish
    you'd look at the stars. Looks like a picture postcard.
    Nightsky over moonlit bay. If you looked at it, you
    wouldn't be scared any more.
WOMAN: I'm going to try to sleep.
MAN: Red sky at night. Farmer's delight.
WOMAN: It's not really red, is it?
MAN: See for yourself.
WOMAN: It couldn't be red.
MAN: You'll never know.
WOMAN: You won't go to sleep?
MAN: Don't worry.

STORYTELLING

WOMAN: [*frog*] Ribit.
MAN: [*whistles bobwhite*] Bobwhite.
WOMAN: Ribit. Ribit. Ribit. [*Etc.*]
MAN: Bobwhite. Bobwhite. Bobwhite. [*Etc.*]
MAN: [*crow*] Caw. Caw. Caw. [*Etc.*]
WOMAN: [*dog*] Argh. Argh. Argh. [*Etc.*]
MAN: [*small plane*] Putta. Putta. Putta. Putta.
WOMAN: Putta? Putta? Putta? Putta?
MAN: Putta. Putta. Putta. Putta. [*Larger plane*] Vrrrrroooooom.

Vrrrrrroooooooom. Vrrrrrrrrrrooooooooooooooom.
WOMAN: Argh. Argh. Argh. [Etc.]
MAN: Vrrrrrooooooom. Whoooooooosh. Vrrrrrooooooooom.
Whoooooooosh. [More threatening] Nyyyyyrrrrrrrrrrrrr.
Nyyyyyrrrrrrrrrrrr. Nyyyyyrrrrrrrrrrrr.
WOMAN: Argh. Argh. Argh. [Wolf] Auwoooooh. Auwoooooh.
Auwoooooh.
MAN: Nyyyyyrrrrrrrrrrrr.
WOMAN: Auwoooooooh. Auwoooooooh.
MAN: Auwoooooooh.
MAN AND WOMAN: Auwoooooooh. Auwoooooooh. Auwoooooooh.

BUILDING A FIRE

> *The man looks out. The woman plants potatoes. She*
> *stops, looks at him.*
WOMAN: Say something.
> *No response. She continues to stare. He continues to*
> *look out. She returns to her planting.*
MAN: I was imagining all the ways to leave here.
> *He looks out. She continues planting.*
> *She gets a sack and spills it at the man's feet. It's full*
> *of dried, black potatoes.*
WOMAN: Fuel.
MAN: These?
WOMAN: It's getting cold. We need a fire.
MAN: We can burn these potatoes?
WOMAN: That's why I dried them out.
MAN: They look like charcoal brickettes.
WOMAN: What's that?
MAN: What we used to barbecue hamburgers.
WOMAN: Hamburgers?

MAN: Cow. Ground up pieces of cow.

WOMAN: Yech!

MAN: They were good.

WOMAN: To me they look like ears. In the shed they looked like a big pile of ears. Cut off by the soldiers of men who didn't want to be overheard.

MAN: Yuck! I'm glad I didn't grow up in your country. It's made you too paranoid. That's no way to live your life. With your ear to the ground.

WOMAN: It's the way it is.

MAN: Well, the way it is is pretty boring.

WOMAN: What do you want?

MAN: I want to go home.

WOMAN: How?

MAN: I don't know. I haven't figured it out yet. It would help if you could get behind the idea a little bit.

WOMAN: You're free to go.

MAN: What about you?

WOMAN: This is my home.

MAN: This! Home! Ha! That's a laugh! You don't remember much do you? This is no fucking home, lady! Homes were. . .

WOMAN: What?

MAN: Full. . .yeah, full. . .full of things.

WOMAN: What things?

MAN: Warm things. . .like. . .

WOMAN: We're building a fire, aren't we?

MAN: No! I mean like love.

WOMAN: Ha!

MAN: You're blind, you know that? You refuse to let the world in. [*Picks up two blackened potatoes*] These are your eyes.

WOMAN: There's no room for love any more.

MAN: [*picking up potato*] This is your heart.

WOMAN: [*grabs potato from him and bites into it*] See! The toughest part of the body! The heart isn't the place where love grows.

MAN: Where is it then?

WOMAN: [*throws potato back into fuel pile*] Let's light the fire.
>   *They light the fire. Silence. She reaches out her hand to him. He reaches out his hand to her. They clasp hands.*

WOMAN: What color are my eyes?
>   *Slowly they look into each others' eyes. Stare. Then slowly look away. Silence.*

MAN: Say something.
>   *No response. He looks at her. Silence. He returns to looking out.*

WOMAN: I was thinking it's too late for children.

NESTING

> *The man drags out a large, nest-like piece of his space capsule.*

WOMAN: What the hell is that thing?

MAN: Part of my capsule. I found it out there, over that rise.

WOMAN: What's it for?

MAN: Does it have to be *for* something.

WOMAN: We could use it.

MAN: It's my goddamn capsule. This is very special.

WOMAN: It would make a good potato hut.
> *He climbs in the capsule.*

MAN: Get in. I want to show you something.

WOMAN: What?

MAN: Something special.
> *She gets in.*

MAN: Now lie down.

WOMAN: I don't want to.

MAN: C'mon.

> *She lies down. So does he.*

MAN: Well?

WOMAN: I don't like it.

MAN: Why?

WOMAN: Things could fall on you.

MAN: What things?

WOMAN: Bird shit.

MAN: Have you seen any birds lately? [*Pause*] Now look up at the sky. Are you looking?

WOMAN: I'm looking.

MAN: Now I'm going to teach you how to daydream.

WOMAN: Is that what you did in outer space?

MAN: No. That's what I did when I was a boy in my country.

WOMAN: A child's game.

MAN: More than that. All the dreams came true.

WOMAN: How?

MAN: You start out imagining yourself leaving your body.

WOMAN: That's impossible.

MAN: Just try imagining it. You just sort of float out of your body and go somewhere.

WOMAN: Where?

MAN: Just go. You'll find out where.

> *They begin rocking slowly, back and forth, in the capsule.*

MAN: Floating. . .floating. . .

WOMAN: [*following his lead*] Floating. . .

> *It is peaceful. They are dreaming. They repeat the word floating from time to time, as they continue to rock the capsule. They rock in wider and wider arcs until they are*

near the point of tipping over.
WOMAN: . . . floating. . . falling. . . falling. . .
MAN: . . . falling!!!!!
The capsule tips over, spilling them onto the ground.
They lie in each other's arms. Silence.
WOMAN: Smell there.
MAN: Wet pine.
WOMAN: Smell there.
MAN: Trout. Smell there.
WOMAN: [*singing*] Ahhhhh ah ah ahhh
                    Ahhhhh ah ah ahhh
MAN: What's that?
WOMAN: An old song.
WOMAN: Ahhhhh ah ah ahhh
                    Ahhhhh ah ah ahhh
    Silence.
MAN: [*singing*] Ahhhhh, ahhhhhhhhh, ahhhhhhhhhhhhhhhh,
    ahhhhhhhhhhhhhhhhhhhhhh
WOMAN: What's that?
MAN: A song from my grandfather's time. C'mon. I'll teach it
    to you.
    They stand up.
MAN: Ahhhhhhh, ahhhhhhhhhh, ahhhhhhhhhhhhhhhhhhhhh,
    ahhhhhhhhhhhhhhhhhhhhhhhh
    Shake it up baby
WOMAN: [*following along*] Shake it up baby.
MAN: Twist and shout
WOMAN: Twist and shout
MAN: C'mon c'mon c'mon c'mon baby
WOMAN: C'mon baby
MAN: C'mon and work it on out
WOMAN: Work it on out

MAN & WOMAN: Ahhhhhh, ahhhhhhhhh, ahhhhhhhhhhhhhhh, ahhhhhhhhhhhhhhhhhhhhhh

NOT KNOWING

WOMAN: You say all your dreams came true?
MAN: Is that what I said?
WOMAN: Did the poor people's dreams come true?
MAN: I didn't know any poor people.
WOMAN: You didn't know?
MAN: I didn't know.
WOMAN: Did you know that your country arms the soldiers in my country?
MAN: No. I didn't know.
WOMAN: You didn't know?
MAN: I didn't know.
    She grabs her knife and points it at him.
WOMAN: I should cut your heart out.
MAN: Why?
WOMAN: For not knowing. [*She throws the knife into the ground. Silence.*] When the soldiers come, you'll know.
MAN: When the soldiers come, I'm going home.
WOMAN: They'll kill you.
MAN: They couldn't. It would make a stink in my country.
WOMAN: They'll throw you in the potato shed. You'll rot there. Your country will never know.
MAN: I'll tell them who I am.
WOMAN: Who are you? You look like a potato farmer.
MAN: Will you come with me?
WOMAN: I should cut my own heart out.
MAN: You will come with me?

NIGHTSOIL

> *The man and woman squat near each other, relieving themselves.*

MAN: It never worked in my country.

WOMAN: What?

MAN: Recycling. Nobody had time. *[Slight pause]* Too busy recycling soldiers, I guess. *[Pause. Laughs. Stops. Keeps laughing.]*

WOMAN: What?

MAN: Nothing. *[Keeps laughing]*

WOMAN: *What?*

MAN: I was just thinking my buddies should see me now. Doing my duty with my girl in the middle of nowhere.

WOMAN: What's so funny about that?

MAN: See, in my country men and women shit separately.

WOMAN: Why?

MAN: I don't know. It was just the custom.

WOMAN: Why? It ends up in the same potato bed.

MAN: We had some stupid customs.

CHANGING WEATHER

> *Thunder. The woman looks at the sky. The man figures in the ground with a stick.*

WOMAN: I think we'll have more rain this year.

MAN: Mmmmmmm.

> *Thunder.*

WOMAN: When I was girl I believed the thunder was the voice of God.

MAN: I went to church every Sunday till I was 7. Then I read

about the German massacres in my great grandfather's
time. I never went to church again.

WOMAN: Why?

MAN: It felt like a part of my past I wanted to get away from.
Thunder.

MAN: Maybe that is the voice of God.

WOMAN: But you didn't get away from it.

MAN: I kept a scrapbook of all the wars, even the little ones.
My Lai. El Salvador. I wanted to be aware...

WOMAN: No one gets away from the massacres.

MAN: I knew that my country was involved in some of them.
But it was hard to know for sure. The wars never felt real
to me.

WOMAN: How could they? You were 500 miles up in space.

MAN: Until I found myself here. [*Digging in dirt*] This dirt may
be covering a mass grave. Thousands of your countrymen
gunned down. Not so long ago. Rotting. Bulldozed over.
[*Pouring dirt in her hands*] Little rotting baby brains oozing
out. . . .

WOMAN: Stop.

MAN: We live on them. We eat their flesh.

*She grabs his hand, stops his digging. They are on their
knees in the dirt. Thunder. They look to the sky.*

EPILOG

*The man squats in the dirt pulling up potatoes. The
woman watches the sky.*

MAN: What else?

WOMAN: Gale wind. Donkeys hide. Chimney pots explode.

MAN: Chimney pots?

WOMAN: Chimney pots.

MAN: Explode!

WOMAN: Explode!

MAN: Ha!

WOMAN: Ha! [*She goes to the capsule and sits in it; to the man:*]
Once upon a time there was an astronaut who was always
looking up.

MAN: [*looking at her*] Once upon a time there was a potato
farmer who was always looking down.

He pulls a carrot out of the ground. They are amazed.
They devour the carrot, laughing.

The Professional Frenchman

by
Mac Wellman

© John Wellman, 1983
CAUTION: No performances or readings of this work may be given without the express authorization of the author or his agent. For production rights contact: Helen Merrill, 337 West 22nd Street, New York, NY 10011.

The Professional Frenchman was first presented by the Brass Tacks Theatre of Minneapolis, Patty Lynch, Artistic Director, on February 10, 1984, with the following cast:

Blaise .... Howard Dallin

Jacques .... James M. Detmar

Sam .... Mark Haarman

Femke .... Anne Devitt

Mevrouw .... Mez van Oppen

Director: John Richardson

IN ORDER OF APPEARANCE:

BLAISE, an enterprising Belgian businessman.

JACQUES, an enterprising Professional Frenchman and proprietor of *La Belle Epoque*.

SAM, an enterprising American businessman and football enthusiast.

FEMKE, wife of BLAISE.

MEVROUW, mother of BLAISE.

GIRL SCOUT, a voice in the wilderness.

The action of *The Professional Frenchman* occurs at the home of BLAISE and FEMKE DUYKINCK in the Northern Virginia suburbs of Washington, D.C. just after Thanksgiving dinner.

The snowstorm that builds throughout the first two acts is of great violence. The sudden respite from bad weather in Act Three should come as no surprise to one familiar with the vicissitudes of climate peculiar to the region.

The little statuettes of Washington, Lincoln, and Reagan alluded to in Act Two should, of course, be in striking evidence in Act One.

The house itself should be furnished elegantly, with taste, but in the somewhat severe fashion of Common Market Europe.

The author desires the "look" of the play to be obsessive, confined: a series of Cornell boxes, all set off the by howling fury of the storm.

Neither the GIRL SCOUT, nor the DUYKINCK's daughter Saskia, ever actually appears on stage.

An asterisk indicates a point in the text where a subsequent line begins, thus overrunning the first.

THE PROFESSIONAL FRENCHMAN is a valentine for Yolanda.

ACT ONE

Late afternoon at the home of Blaise and Femke in suburban Arlington, Virginia. Blaise's mother, (Mevrouw), Jacques and Sam have joined them for Thanksgiving dinner. Femke busies herself with the dishes. Saskia, her daughter, is hanging around in the next room, apparently refusing to take a nap. Saskia never appears in the play. The scene begins in the middle of an animated discussion.

BLAISE: Precisely in the event of such a catastrophe.

JACQUES: But that is absurd.

BLAISE: Monsieur Petit, you are, like all
    Of your race, an idealist and a
    Somnambulist.

SAM: Femke, the turkey was out of sight.

JACQUES: Such an event would no doubt
    Trigger a nuclear war.

SAM: Old Jacques here's green with envy.
    See? He's not saying a thing.

BLAISE: But I assure you the King
    Is an admirable fellow.
    Charming. Forthright. A visionary.
    And as Madame Sesostris has
    Written. *Some laws are written
    And some are not.* Profound.
    Madame Sesostris, among her other
    Talents, is astrologer to Golub.
    Golub has not only exposed the
    Terrors of the Bolshevist camps.
    But has predicted the rise of a
    Brilliant new quasi-monarchical
    Republic, here, in the Americas.
        Sam burps.

SAM: Oh, pardon me.

FEMKE: [*to Saskia off*] *Absoluut niet!* Back to your room,
    Saskia! It is still time for your
    Nap.

SAM: Golub's an old hypocrite.

BLAISE: Madame Sesostris is also the
    Washington representative of
    The Romanov Pretender. He is

The custodian of a most unusual
Collection of drillings. But, *helas,*
The Romanovs are tainted by the
Events of their pitiable downfall.

FEMKE: Saskia!

BLAISE: One might propose as alternative
The House of Orange. By the way, Sam,
Have I showed you my dueling pistols?

FEMKE: [*to Saskia.*] Is that your silver spoon?

BLAISE: Being Belgian I would prefer our
Own royal family. But my wife and
Mother, being Dutch, would oppose me.
For me, I find the House of Orange
Vulgar and undignified. But very rich!

SAM: Rousseau it was who said: *France
Is geographically monarchical.*
Well, in the same terms, America
Is geographically anarchical...

BLAISE: Madame Sesostris has great influence
On Capitol Hill.

SAM: The profound idiocy
Of those unfortunate souls who
Imagine that legislators are men,
Laws are paper,
And nations may be constituted
With ink.

BLAISE: You see, Sam, we agree!

SAM: Hell, when America goes
Communist we'll be the best
Damn Communists in the world.

FEMKE: [*to Saskia.*] Are you still biting your
Silver spoon?

BLAISE: It is perfectly clear, Russia
Is an anachronism. It is
Even now falling apart.
But to the East! The Mongol hordes!
Femke shakes her head.

JACQUES: Blaise, you have a penchant
For melodrama.

FEMKE: He will not even go to the
Chinese restaurant!

BLAISE: Historical truth always wears
The apparel of melodrama.

JACQUES: A dictum Madame Sesostris would surely
Contradict.

BLAISE: Madame Sesostris is a highly intelligent
Person, *sans doute.*

FEMKE: She says history is an unending
Tragedy.

BLAISE: And a mystic as well.
History is not the least
Bit tragic. But it is sad.
Unhappy people imagine their lives
Tragic, when they are merely tiresome.
The equation does not hold. *Madame,*
Can we get you something? Coffee?
Brandy? Are you tired? Would you
Like to nap?

MEVROUW: Thank you, Blaise, but no.

JACQUES: The catastrophe may not so easily be
Avoided.

BLAISE: But I was going to say:
The Americans are an
Inventive people, perhaps

They will discover some
Force capable of protecting
Us from the nuclear devices.
What do you think, Sam?

SAM: Does anyone have the
Time?

FEMKE: I am putting the child to sleep.
Are you coming, *Maman.*

BLAISE: Sam, tell us what do
You think?

SAM: I think America,
Sadly, is a country
That has fallen out of
Love with the truth.

MEVROUW: I would like to stay
And listen. May I have
A glass of water?

BLAISE: Sam, don't you think
Europe is finished?

    Sam goes to get a glass of water for Mevrouw. Femke follows.

I am convinced. Why,
There's so much in this
Country. So much waiting
To be developed. For the
Finishing touch of civilization.
I find it quite remarkable.
People here are quite naive.
Particularly about foreign matters.
Isn't that so, Jacques? You too!
But, mark my words, I predict
A Chinese invasion, first of

Russia, then of Europe. Bang,
It's finished there. But here!
All the things I believe in,
All the most precious of them,
Can find fallow ground here.
It is amazing how resourceful
People are! The ingenuity! The
Passion for new ideas, for new
Products, inventions. Of course
There is naiveté. Stupidity also.
But the terrible canker of European
Socialism, that has not worked its
Poisonous evil here. We are free!
If you work hard you can make money.
So much money it is amazing. Why,
In Belgium I could not afford a
House like this. This is a big house.
Femke, is the coffee ready?
     Femke who had just entered frowns and goes out again.
It is so
Even for you, a sentimentalist
Like you, eh Jacques?
JACQUES: It is true. Business is very good.
BLAISE: *Maman,* we are talking about the
     Life in America. About how good
     It is.
MEVROUW: Oh yes. It is good. Very good.
JACQUES: It seems people do nothing else
     In Washington, but go out to dinner.
MEVROUW: Only the bread is not good.
BLAISE: Bread!
     We can bake our own bread!

It is foolish to judge a country
On the basis of what bread it eats.
You are foolish, *Maman*.
MEVROUW: And it is very cold.
BLAISE: Cold! Bah! Jacques, where is Sam?
    Maman, Sam will tell you about cold.
JACQUES: I would not like to think of France
Overrun by hordes.
BLAISE: I see it coming, *mon ami*.
We must make a new home.
A safe home. I'll show you.
    He rushes out. Pause.
JACQUES: Blaise's house is very
Elegant. This carpet.
I have never seen a
Carpet like this one.
It has a peculiar sensuous
Quality.
MEVROUW: I'm sorry.
My English not too good.
    Sam enters with the water which he hands to Mevrouw.
SAM: Cleveland plays Oakland today.
    Femke enters looking confused.
SAM: It's a big game.
FEMKE: Have you seen a small silver bracelet?
MEVROUW: I would not like to be
Married to a man like
Blaise.
FEMKE: Oh, *Maman*, what foolishness.
JACQUES: Sam, don't you think Blaise
Has a remarkable sense of
Taste?

SAM: Quite remarkable.
   Blaise enters with his pistol.
MEVROUW: *Nom de dieu!* [*Crosses herself.*]
BLAISE: This is my protection.
SAM: Browning automatic pistol.
   Looks at it.
   Forty-four caliber?
BLAISE: Nine milimeter. [*Sam nods.*]
FEMKE: Will you put that thing
   Away. You're frightening
   Your mother.
SAM: Beautifully made.
FEMKE: Put it away, little boys.
   Blaise puts the gun in the drawer.
JACQUES: I have a dish I must describe
   To you, Blaise. It is very novel.
   Elephant's feet. I thought that with
   The new administration
   It might catch on. As you know
   The late Secretary dines frequently
   Chez nous.
   During this Blaise begins playing with his pistol again.
   Now with *pieds d'elephants* the
   Crucial thing is to use only feet
   Of young elephants, as the older
   Ones are quite unpalatable;
   Next one must purge them
   In warm water for at least
   Four hours. This is to render
   Them free of gross impurities.
   As you can imagine the feet
   Of elephants do not walk

In shoes and stockings, so
Much in the way of filth
Becomes embedded in them.
SAM: And elephants do not often
Wash their feet.
JACQUES: Actually, that is incorrect.
Elephants are a fastidious species,
Ask anyone who knows.
FEMKE: Put the gun away, Blaise.
BLAISE: Such a child. [*He does so.*]
JACQUES: It is simply that an elephant
Walks on the earth with great
Crushing weight. He cannot
Help being so destructive, but
The point is, his feets become
A bit corruptible in the process.
SAM: That's because he can't scrub
His toes.
JACQUES: Precisely. Now after the feet
Have been thoroughly purged,
You remove the skin and
Bones, then cut each. . .
BLAISE: Jacques, this is preposterous.
After you remove the bones
What is left? It is absurd!
JACQUES: Blaise, an elephant's foot is much
Larger than a human foot, and the
Flesh of the creature is quite
Succulent.
You must then blanch. . .
BLAISE: At any rate
I think it is a very foolish idea.

Sam begins doing pushups. No one pays attention.
If you concoct a special dish
Of ass's ear, for instance, now
Then you might have something.
But the Republicans surely will
Not want to dine on the feet
Of their symbolic beast, eh Sam?
Sam is preparing for his game.
Isn't that right?

SAM: I don't know. I think
Jacques' got a point.
Only I would prefer
Serving Republicans' feet.

JACQUES: But I thought I had explained.
There is insufficient flesh
On the foot of man.

SAM: Have you ever taken a good
Look at a Republican foot?
Whole lot of meat there.

JACQUES: It would not taste good.

SAM: Fancy, fat foot.

MEVROUW: Everyone is laughing.
Everyone is so gay.

BLAISE: Who here has tasted human flesh?
Pause. Sam gets up.

FEMKE: Blaise's
Sense of humor deserts him
At the most remarkable times.

SAM: I hope it has not deserted him
Now.

FEMKE: [*Getting up. To Blaise.*]
Will you please come say goodnight

To the child?

SAM: I'm going to watch football. [*He goes out.*]

BLAISE: Why must she go to sleep? It is
Early.

FEMKE: Please, Blaise.

BLAISE: I mean it seems to be your
Philosophic position that a
Person ought not to be so
Free. In America we are free.
You must try to understand
That. We are free to do
As we please. Now, Sam.
He must go watch football
So he goes. He does not ask.
He goes. It is the American way.

FEMKE: I think it is very impolite.

JACQUES: Blaise's point is a true one,
But I do not understand
American football.

MEVROUW: What are they talking about.
Femke?

FEMKE: *Pied d'Americain.* [*She goes out.*]

MEVROUW: I would not like to be married
To a man like you, Blaise.

BLAISE: *Maman*, she has no sense of humor.

MEVROUW: You should go to her, Blaise.

BLAISE: Yes, I will go. [*He does so.*]

JACQUES: You know, *Mevrouw*, when I first
Come to this country I see pictures
Of these American footballists and
I think: *these people are indeed
Some different kind of creatures.*

It is a foolish mistake. Myself,
I am not interested in *Le sport.*
> *Pause.*
This is your first visit to America,
Mevrouw?
MEVROUW: Yes, my first.
> *Pause.*
JACQUES: What are your impressions?
MEVROUW: It is true.
JACQUES: Pardon, *Mevrouw.* I meant
What are your ideas
About America?
MEVROUW: It is much the same as I had
Expected from seeing all the
Movies. Only I had expected
Things to be a little bigger.
JACQUES: The buildings downtown on the
Mall, they are very large, no?
MEVROUW: Oh, very large. And white.
I like the roads.
The roads are very wide.
JACQUES: You must come to my bistro.
MEVROUW: Some things are the same
As in Belgium.
JACQUES: I am very proud of my..
MEVROUW: The rabbit here, for instance,
Is the same as Golf, at home...
JACQUES: Pardon?
MEVROUW: The Volkswagen Rabbit. Only
We have one they do not have
Here, called...
JACQUES: *La Belle Epoque* is the equal

Of any restaurant, in its class,
In Bruxelles.
MEVROUW: I forget. In Brussel
But I have only seen pictures of the
1958 Oldsmobile 98. But here there is
One on this very street. It has much
Decoration. There are silver *croutons*
All over it. The louvres are, pity,
No longer real. As they were...
No, I am thinking of the Buick.
Also a remarkable automobile,
Only I have not seen one. Now,
This Oldsmobile is very dirty so
The owner must not wash it.
I am surprised so many fine
Automobiles here are so poor-
Looking. They look like wrecks.
I also saw a Ford Fairlane 500.
1959 model. With overhead cam
Fuel-injected super V-8. 0 to 60
in 5.5 seconds. A most remarkable
Machine, indeed. In fine condition.
The owner is a young man on the
Street near here. He installed
The supercharger himself, but
I'm not sure it is done properly.
A nice boy. Very polite.
But the bread is not good.
JACQUES: No *Mevrouw*, I tell you, if I had
The money I would start my own
Bakery: make real French bread.
You could sell so much. But, *helas*,

I have so much to do as it is now
With *La Belle Epoque*. It is very difficult.
Sam rushes in.

SAM: Sipe to Newsome. 46 yard touchdown pass! Whoopie!
He leaps. Goes out.

MEVROUW: Sam is a nice man, only I can't
Understand when he speaks. He is
A little like my friend with the Ford.

JACQUES: It is American football. Extremely violent
Sport.

MEVROUW: Is it?

JACQUES: Very boring sport. Each team hunches over
The ball. At a given signal they all
Jump in a heap. Whoever makes the
Greatest *frappe* wins the ball.
A great mountain often results
From all the charging bodies.
I have seen it with my own eyes.
Beep! A whistle is blown, then the
Players slowly get up and behave
As though nothing was done.
So it goes. Crash. Stop. Crash. Stop.
It is a totally incomprehensible sport.

MEVROUW: Many things are difficult to understand
Here.

JACQUES: But Blaise is wrong. Europe is not
Finished, I hope.

MEVROUW: My young friend
Tells me how
Bad people want
To bus school children.

JACQUES: Oh, yes, that is bad,

Very bad here. One
Is mugged in front
Of one's own house.
My customers tell me
How dangerous it is.
But even in Amsterdam,
I tell you, *Zeedijk*,
You know, which was
So lovely, is all crime.
Drugs.

MEVROUW: It is very sad, I think.

> *Enter Femke.*

FEMKE: *Maman, here you are. It is late.*
> *Don't you want to lie down?*

MEVROUW: Blaise and I are talking.

FEMKE: Don't you mean Jacques?

MEVROUW: You make mistakes too, Femke.

FEMKE: Jacques, I don't know why you
  Have to be so stupid. Can't you
  See an old woman must rest?
  Why don't you do something useful?
  Get up. Help. The dishes are washed.
  You just sit there. Where is Blaise?
  Sam is watching his idiot football.
  You keep an old lady up when
  She should take her pill.
  Where is Blaise?

JACQUES: I thought he was with you.

MEVROUW: Maybe Blaise's watching football.

FEMKE: *Maman*, you silly. He would not
  Do that. Europeans cannot
  Understand American football.

As she speaks Blaise stomps in.

BLAISE: Yes we do.

FEMKE: Where have you been? Saskia is asleep.
    She wanted you to read her a story.
    But you didn't come.

BLAISE: It's snowing.
    I make a big snow-angel.

MEVROUW: What is a snow-angel?

JACQUES: Who will want a *pousse-cafe?*

FEMKE: *Maman,* are you all right?

BLAISE: You lie in the snow and wave
    Your arms and legs, like so.

MEVROUW: I would like to see.

FEMKE: No, *Maman,* it is late.

MEVROUW: Blaise, we are talking about
    busing.

FEMKE: So no one will help. Fine. [*She goes out.*]

BLAISE: You know, when I was in Vienna.
    I was an excellent football player.
    I have a very strong leg.

MEVROUW: Listen, Jacques. This is a good story.

BLAISE: When I was eighteen I can kick
    The ball very far. Sixty-five meters.
    With either foot.

FEMKE: [*offstage*] IT IS GETTING COLD!

BLAISE: So we are practicing. One day
    Our manager, Lothar, he comes
    Up and says *Duykinck, here*
    Are some Americans. They want
    To talk to you. I can't
    Understand what they want.
        Sam appears at the door.

They say...

SAM: Howdy Mister Duck-ink, my name is Jenning
And this guy is Mitch...

JACQUES: Oh, Sam.

BLAISE: So they open a box and hand to me
A funny-looking leather ball, shaped
Like *aubergine,* and they say:
We are from the Houston Cowboys,
Mister Duck-ink, how far do you think
You can kick this? So I take the
Ball and kick it about seventy meters
Into a little wood. And the one guy
Say to me *Mister Duck-ink how would*
You like to come to America, huh?
   Femke enters with a centigrade conversion card.

FEMKE: It is eight degrees fahrenheit. What is that?
   Studies the card.

BLAISE: But I was young. Foolish...
So I say: *Thank you, but no.*

SAM: You missed your chance, Blaise.
   Sam and Blaise go out.

FEMKE: It is thirteen degrees of frost.
That is cold! [*She goes out.*]
Maman...

MEVROUW: Yes, I am coming. Still, Jacques,
I think it is a terrible thing not to
Let the poor children ride a bus
To school. Distances are so far.
And there are very few sidewalks
In this part of Virginia.
   She ambles out. Pause. Femke bustles in.

FEMKE: Listen, Jacques, I am telling you

I don't want you trying to get
Blaise to loan you money.
JACQUES: But Femke.
FEMKE: Sneak around all you want,
All you want, I don't care
But we do not have the money
To waste on a silly bakery
For fancy people. Do you hear?
Blaise stretches the truth. We
Have many debts and no money.
You see this big house and alarms
And you think "Blaise is rich."
It is not so.
　　Mister Pickett has not called
In months. We can't sell a thing.
JACQUES: I'm sorry, Femke, I didn't know.
FEMKE: If you are Blaise's friend you will
Understand what I am saying and
You will stop this foolishness. . .
　　Pause.
Perhaps one day you can explain
That "catastrophe" you and Sam talk about.
JACQUES: Femke, you are my friend too.
FEMKE: Then we understand one another?
　　He shrugs.

ACT TWO

　　*An hour later. The stage is divided into three playing
areas: a kitchen with table and chairs to the left, a dark-*

ened TV room to the right, and in the center and up a large bay-window through which a portion of the yard is visible through a dense, swirling snowstorm. A single snowman stands a few yards back. The only light in the TV room comes from a large TV, which faces upstage. Sam and Femke stand facing one another in the kitchen. No one else is visible.

SAM: Not now.

FEMKE: And why not
     May I ask?

SAM: Half time's
     Nearly over.

FEMKE: You and your idiot football.

SAM: Raiders are out in front
     After that fumble recovery.
     Cleveland has what they call
     A porous defense.

     As before. In the brightly-lit kitchen. The company is seated around the table, enjoying coffee and brandy. Sam and Femke are standing exactly where they were at the end of the last scene.

SAM: Pardon me, where are the
     Facilities, *alsjeblief?*

BLAISE: Down the hall, first door. . .

FEMKE: He can't use that one.
     Remember?

BLAISE: True, the room is temporarily
     Incommoded.

FEMKE: My husband uses the WC
     To do his smelting.

BLAISE: Take the elevator down to the
     Second level. Open the door

On the right as you come out.
Not the other one, please.
MEVROUW: What is "smelts"?
JACQUES: *Je crois que un* smelt
Is a fish.
FEMKE: Please, Jacques.
        Sam goes out.
BLAISE: Saskia is crying.
FEMKE: Coming. [*She goes out.*]
MEVROUW: Now will you show me the snow
Angels, Blaise?
BLAISE: *Maman,* the snows have already
Covered up the angels. But maybe
We will construct a snow man...
Een echt Amerikaans sneeuwmannetje.
MEVROUW: That would be nice.
BLAISE: But first Jacques and me
Must talk.
MEVROUW: Did I ever
Tell you about Papa's
Voyage to Spitzbergen?
BLAISE: *Maman,* go help Femke.
MEVROUW: Later I will tell the story.
BLAISE: *Tot ziens, moeder.*
MEVROUW: Jacques, my son has an un-
Pleasant personality. It worries me.
Perhaps it came from the Hunger Winter
During the last months of the war when
The English and Americans had not yet
Beaten the Germans. It was a hard time.
All we are eating is tulip bulbs and
Some few potatoes. Blaise was a child.

It must have injured him.
> *She begins to go out.*

JACQUES: Later we will hear about Spitzbergen.

MEVROUW: And make the snowman.

JACQUES: Of course.

MEVROUW: You are a good man, Jacques.
A bit stupid, but good.
> *She goes out.*

JACQUES: Blaise, I have been thinking about
This business of the loan for our new
Bakery, and I am not sure it is the
Right time for such a project.

BLAISE: But why not?

JACQUES: Perhaps it would not be wise to
Take on an additional risk, just now.

BLAISE: But
You cannot get such a rate of interest
At any bank.

JACQUES: I am not doubting you, Blaise.

BLAISE: As you wish. You would do well
To think the matter over, my friend.
But it is your decision.

JACQUES: I am apprehensive.

BLAISE: You must have faith, Jacques.
Have you been talking with Sam?
> *Pause.*

I tell you. Things are perfectly sound.
Certainly better for investment than at home.
People are optimists here. People believe in
New things here. You must accept new ways,
Jacques. Everything happen very quickly.
If you jump on the boat you don't get left

On the dock, as in Europe. You can sell
Anything here and someone will buy it.
It is competition. That is good for people, in
Europe you must ask *this* association and
That association and apply for a spot on the
Waiting list and then it is too late or too soon.
Pause.
I get new ideas every day. I am melting
Down metal in the bathroom and casting
Little art objects. It is a hobby. Of course.
But maybe I can sell them. People who
Want a little statuette can find one here.
I have several models. It is experimental.
General George Washington. Lincoln. Reagan.
Now in Europe I would need a license for
The metal and a license for each mold.
Where did Sam go?
Imagine! A license for the Abraham Lincoln
Mold!
Is he come back? Sam, I mean.
JACQUES: I think he must be watching football.
BLAISE: But I want to talk to him about politics.
He is gloomy so we have very fine fights.
It makes me feel very good to argue
With such an astonishing antagonist.
You will see!
Sam!
*Blaise goes out. Pause. Jacques looks out the window
at the snowman.*
JACQUES: Jacques *le sot*. Jacques the fool!
You would think
If you didn't know

But of course you know.
But of course. Grind his bones
To bake your bread. Bread is
The perfect body of the ideal
Perfected. Mindless. Heartless. Sexless.
Better to work. Better to bake the warm
Rising bread of society and solitude
Doubled in the dough rising of a whole
Wheat loaf. I am the perfectly realized
Self-begotton contraption. Traption.
Keep the trap shut, old man. Trapped.
Better. Work. Work and more work.
The service of an ideal.
The dream of perfect teeth. . .
The dream to replace the self with an
Other. I am an other. You would think
If you didn't know, mister snowman,
Voyant, the dream of perfect teeth
Rending the perfect duplicate loaf.
Monsieur Le Neige, mon semblable, mon frere.
   Pause.
Dites moi, Monsieur Le Neige,
Comment allez vous?
   Bien, et vous? Monsieur
Le Francais Professionel?
   Dites moi, Monsieur Le Neige
Man, why is it you stare
So fixedly from your remote
Part of the world? Because
Mister Professional Frenchman,
I see many wondrous things.
Because I have a heart of ice

I do not turn away. Ah, cynic!
You are like Sam, a grumbler.
I see a marriage with no love.
I see age without wisdom, youth
Without innocence, talk without
Dialogue, dialogue without sense.
Money without value, a house
Without the sense of being a home.
Without home-*iness, comme ca.*
I am horrified.
    And most horrifying of all
These apparitions is you.
        You call me an apparition, monsieur!?
But I protest.
        Of course you protest *mon cher.*
You own a French restaurant
Of high repute and questionable quality
In the glittering capital of an empire
Whose favorite food is...
Le cheeseburger...
    Pause.
Unspeakable.
    Enter Femke.
FEMKE: Did I hear someone talking?
JACQUES: I am conversing with the snowman.
FEMKE: How strange you are.
JACQUES: Thank you, ma'am.
FEMKE: I wanted to apologize
    For what I said earlier.
JACQUES: No trouble.
FEMKE: It was none of my business.
JACQUES: I spoke with Blaise.

The deal is off.
FEMKE: Thank you Jacques.
I am very worried
About finances.
Blaise will not let me
Understand anything.
I have no idea...where,
Or rather, *how* we are
Doing...Financially.
With a young child
It is extremely difficult.
And I want everything
To be just perfect, for
Saskia. She must know
How good life can be.
JACQUES: Still, I think children are happier
In Europe.
FEMKE: How can you say that?
JACQUES: But the old people are sadder.
FEMKE: But *Maman* is quite happy,
Don't you think?
JACQUES: Ah, but she is here.
FEMKE: Jacques, I think people here
Are capable of being greatly
Happy. Only they are so
Busy making all that money
It takes to be busily happy.
Americans like to be busy and
Happy at the same time. Children
Here are the same. They sell
Newspapers, clothes, the parents'
Jewelry, etcetera etcetera. Happy.

Pause.

I see what you mean. Sad.

Very sad.

She sits down and starts to cry. Jacques throws his
voice into various objects in the kitchen: a coffee pot,
a bread box, a cupboard.

JACQUES: Why is Femke weeping?

FEMKE: I have much to give thanks

For.

JACQUES: Don't be so Dutch.

Dutch always talk like the Jews.

Nothing is for pleasure only.

Nothing is for caprice, for the

Hell of it. Everything is for

A higher purpose. It makes you

Extremely difficult people to

See into the hearts of, like wood.

Pause.

Blaise is Belgian.

Pause.

Belgium is a disgusting place,

It's true. Sun never shines there.

But the people don't try to serve

Higher purposes when they eat

Sleep and make love. They just

Sleep eat and make love. But they

Are not a pretty people, no.

Pause.

But Jacques is *un sot.* He knows nothing

but food. Who wants to talk about

That? Hence he is not invited to

Parties. He talk to himself too much.

Pause.
Have you talked to Sam?
FEMKE: He won't talk to me.
Now's not the time.
I'm in love with him.
JACQUES: Among my many talents
Are voice-throwing and
What did you say?
FEMKE: You act surprised.
JACQUES: How Dutch you are.
FEMKE: How cruel you are.
JACQUES: What am I to say?
FEMKE: Sometimes your accent
Is very American.
JACQUES: People are coming.
It is the ventriloquism.
FEMKE: You didn't want to hear that.
I shouldn't have told you.
JACQUES: What am I supposed to say?
FEMKE: You are mixed up with all this
Shit of deprogramming, aren't you?
Mevrouw enters.
JACQUES: *Mevrouw,* shall we go
For a walk in the snow?
Look, a wall of snow
Is coming at the house.
How interesting!
MEVROUW: Like at Spitzbergen.
Jacques gets up.
JACQUES: Are you coming
Mevrouw? [*To Femke*]
MEVROUW: Are you coming

Femke?
Femke stalks out, passing Sam who enters noncha-
lantly, with a yo-yo.
SAM: It's funny, but I can't watch it.
It's too exciting, I just can't stand
Watching it. That's why I'm here,
And not in there, watching.
MEVROUW: What is he saying?
SAM: Cleveland has a quarterback named
Brian Sipe. He's a story in himself,
Because he's a genius who breaks all
The rules and came from nowhere, but
He specializes in winning unwinnable
Games in ways that defy logic, reason,
The whole hoary body of football common-sense,
Whatever the hell's ass that is! But never
Emotion. They're filled with terrible emotion.
He loses a few that way too. It always
Comes down to the last few seconds, he
Throws a long pass that is caught by
One of his receivers in the midst of a
Swarm of furious defenders. Or it is not.
    Blaise, where's Blaise?
    When you see Blaise tell him he
Put up his snow fence on the wrong
Side of the house, it should be out there.
On that slope, which is unprotected.
See the snow-devils whirling around
Out there? At the stadium in Cleveland
It was *one degree* Fahrenheit at the start.
Wind chill made it feel like 37 below.
    I grew up in Cleveland. But my

Only connection with the place is the foot
Ball team. No friends. No family. Nothing but
A few snowflakes wheeling about in the
Eternity of a blue sky big enough to hide
Everything and beautiful enough to hide
Nothing.

I used to be a professional grumbler,
A demon-monger, a straightener-out of
Crooked souls. But now I'm nothing. *Nothing.*
Nothing will come of nothing, they say.

The Cleveland team is called the
Browns after their first coach Paul
Brown. I went to school with his
Son Peter Brown, but I didn't know
The man. The best player the team ever
Had was a very formidable fullback
By the name of Jim Brown.

Paul Brown wore brown shoes, brown
Suits, brown ties, brown overcoats.
People were afraid to speak to him.
He did not have a reputation for
Friendliness. Or mercy...

He wore a brown hat.

Cleveland winters look like this. All the
Time. Cleveland receives less sunlight than
Any other major American city.

I am fond of places like that. When time
Runs out for a civilization it finds solace in
Pictures of pretty faces and bodies. Pretty
Cities too. But if the passion's gone the
Pictures don't mean a blessed thing.

Cleveland is not a pretty place. Nor

Is New York City.
The New York Giants are my other favorite
Football team.
Pause.
MEVROUW: I don't understand a word he says.
But it is quite remarkable.
Pause.
Are we going to build the
Snow man?
JACQUES: *Mevrouw,* someone has already
Builded one.
MEVROUW: Is that so?
SAM: Back to the game. [*He goes out.*]
JACQUES: Sam, wait.
MEVROUW: Such an unpredictable person.
Curious how people behave...
JACQUES: They don't seem to know, always,
What they are doing.
MEVROUW: Do you know what Blaise
Does?
JACQUES: I have very little idea of what
I do.
Pause
But is it so important? To know?
MEVROUW: As I spoke I had second thoughts.
Soon Femke will come in here and
Tell me it is time to lie down.
JACQUES: She is very anxious to take care
Of people.
MEVROUW: It's not what I want.
JACQUES: Beg your pardon, *Mevrouw?*
MEVROUW: I said it's not what I want.

JACQUES: She is doing her best.

MEVROUW: I did not say she was not doing
Her best. It is sometime irritating.
She treats me like an invalid, but
I need excitement. Or I get sick.
It's true.
    Pause.
Shall I tell you about Spitzbergen?

JACQUES: Perhaps we should wait for the others.

MEVROUW: It is impossible, obviously, with such
Selfish people, to get them all to stay
For a time, in one room.

JACQUES: It is the function of food. *Mevrouw.*

MEVROUW: Jacques, you are a nice boy, but
You should not act so stupid,
Particularly when you are not.
It is. . . it makes a disagreeable
Impression. But I want to say
What I find so interesting about
These people, my son, too, is that
All of them seem to have suffered
So terribly but it is difficult to
Discover how the suffering came
Or what it is. Or what its name
Is. But perhaps I'm not clear.
    *Sam and Blaise dressed heavily outdoors building
snowmen. It is difficult, in fact, to tell them from the
snow-people, one of whom is Jacques. All the dialogue
is a voice-over.*

SAM: You'll have to dig out the drive
The way you set up the storm
Fence, Blaise. We'll never get out.

BLAISE: You are such a *moraliste*.

SAM: I am talking about snow.

BLAISE: America is such a wonderful
  Country, if only Americans were
  Not so foolish.

SAM: What is of value in America
  You despise.

BLAISE: Your new president understands
  More than you.

SAM: Freedom for the few.

BLAISE: Freedom is only of use
  To the few.

SAM: Freedom is not a
  Commodity.

BLAISE: What humbug you talk
  Sam.

SAM: What have you got in the
  Basement?

BLAISE: I told you not to go in
  There.

SAM: Got my signals crossed.
  Looks like a warehouse.

BLAISE: Use your imagination.

SAM: I try to avoid that.
  It creates monsters.

BLAISE: My wife is in love with you.

SAM: She has good taste.

BLAISE: It is an awkward situation

SAM: I'm on the lam
  So I can't afford
  To be a threat.

BLAISE: Sometime you will explain

What, precisely, you were up to.

SAM: I told you: battling demons.

BLAISE: You have such a metaphorical
    Way of talking it is not easy
    To grasp your significance.

SAM: My lawyers
    Assure me
    If I gab
    I'm fucked.
    Jacques was involved: ask him.

BLAISE: I always thought you work
    With computers.

SAM: No. I said
    De-programming.
        The Snowman starts moving. They pay it no heed.

BLAISE: All I know is here I can be
    Free. In my own way.
    The values that are important
    To me are possible here.
    Europe is finished. Done.
    I have told you— and I am
    A deep student of foreign
    Affairs, as you call it—
    The future of the Euro-Asian
    Land-mass belongs to the
    Chinese. Europe as we know it
    Has lost all its moral character,
    And is incapable of stopping the
    Spread of. Panmongolism. The huns...

SAM: What values do you
    Represent? Do we
    Represent? Tell me that.

BLAISE: You are like all these German
　　Students who practice
　　Symbolic self-mutilation
　　In order to be more pure
　　Than the Nazis, their parents.
SAM: You don't understand the
　　New World.
　　　In the Old World
　　Socialism is a lie,
　　A totalitarian charade.
　　Old Golub has a valid point.
　　　But here, in the
　　Wilds of both the Americas,
　　Where space and time
　　Do not always seem to
　　Behave properly, where
　　People go crazy from the sheer empty immensity
　　IT'S NEVER BEEN TRIED, AND IT'S GOT TO BE
　　　TRIED...
BLAISE: Rubbish, romantic rubbish...
SAM: Let me speak. You think freedom
　　Is a wonderful thing. I say true
　　Freedom, the kind that blows
　　Up and down these continents
　　With the trades, is a terrifying force
　　That cannot be reduced to your
　　Simple European notions of a
　　Respectable Perfect Rational System.
　　　Long pause.
BLAISE: So, that's what I say.
　　Freedom is not for
　　Everyone. Freedom is

For the few. We agree.
Snowman pats both on the back. They begin to walk to the kitchen door.

SAM: I have to explain football to you.

BLAISE: We must all make our own peace
With the world and the stuff of its filth.
Snow is white and looks clean
But is filth. Life is filth.
They go in to the kitchen where Femke is sitting with Mevrouw. They pass by ignoring the women. Femke is smoking. She gets up.

FEMKE: It's a mystery to me why
I have to be in love
With such an idiot.

MEVROUW: If he were not an idiot
Would you love him
More?

FEMKE: I don't know. Hush! [*Listens.*]

MEVROUW: She's asleep. . .

FEMKE: I shouldn't smoke.

MEVROUW: It pleases you. . .

FEMKE: It causes cancer.

MEVROUW: Soon I will tell my
Story about Spitzbergen.

FEMKE: It's like trying to hold
Water.
In your hand.
Sam enters at full tilt.

SAM: Cleveland just kicked a 49 yard
Field goal. They lead 12 to 7. . .
Sam runs out. Pause. Femke fetches a snow shovel from the corner near the door and toys with it during

her speech.

FEMKE: I have such powerful feelings.
There is so much I want to
Destroy, *Maman.* It's not right.
I know, I know...
You have to believe in love and
Have faith in people like Blaise
And Sam. That's all there is.
But I feel so powerless and
Even as I speak I am sick
Of my feelings. Once I had
An affair with Sam. Before
I got pregnant. Now it seems
I have trouble getting over it
But it was no problem then.
Blaise knows about it, he must,
But he never mentions it, I have
To put up with a quiet sort of abuse.
It's my way of paying. But I am
Sick of both.
I want to go very far away.
Maybe back home. I go to church
Sometimes. To be alone, but if I were
Alone I would be more unhappy.
Should I go on?

MEVROUW: It is better not to talk about
Some things, I think. Femke,
You are a big talker, but
Only to yourself.
So nobody listens.

FEMKE: Saskia is...
Very young.

MEVROUW: What is that
    You are holding?
FEMKE: A snow-shovel.
    Sneeuwschop...
MEVROUW: May I see it?
    *Hands the snow-shovel to Mevrouw who pushes it
    slowly around the room.*
FEMKE: Saskia wanted to go out
    Today: "To wash the snow."
MEVROUW: It must be difficult to push
    So much snow from one place
    To another. It makes me tired
    To think of it.
    Replaces the shovel in the corner.
FEMKE: You should lie down now.
MEVROUW: I am prepared for that.
    She lies down on the floor. Pause.
FEMKE: What are you
    Doing?
    Maman?
MEVROUW: I am fooling.
    Sam enters. He does not see Mevrouw on the floor.
SAM: SO YOU
    WANT TO SPEAK TO ME
    IT'S TIME FOURTH QUARTER
    FUCKING OAKLAND SCORED A
    TOUCHDOWN 2:22 TO GO
    CLEVELAND GOT THE BALL ON THEIR
    OWN TWENTY YARD LINE
    DOESN'T LOOK GOOD
    OAKLAND'S AHEAD 14 TO 12
        BRIAN SIPE IS RUNNING OUT

OF MIRACLES I CAN'T STAND IT
   YOU WANTED TO TALK
   SO TALK...
      i'm a proud man you had
your chance and now you give
me a hard time and act like i've
done something horrible it's you baby
i loved you remember but you
were playing games that's it
so stop making a fool of yourself
you understand it's crazy i woulda
done anything for you see that arm
i would have gone and cut that arm
off for you but you you were playing
playing playing see where it's got
you mewling brat by a man like that
that crazy mother-in-law house in
the sticks out there it's fucking cold
baby cold it's fucking ultima thule
      the fucking hard ass end
of the world baby and as for
blaise you know what he is femke
he's a fucking cat-burglar that's what
the whole fucking basement is full
of loot swag i've never seen
anything like it he's melting down
gold baby gold in the basement
it's your own damn house and you don't
even know what's going down it's pathetic
i know i'm nothing
but i was big one time baby big
i deprogrammed some of the biggest

spider heads going real lulus
i spun webs of intrigue out of
the most unlikely polyester doubleknit
wasn't a demon in town didn't
know to stay clear of old sam
here.
   i snuffed out monsters in the dreams
of the power elite and royalty
   just because a lot of jew lawyers
pitch in to botch up a case one
fucking lousy idiotic case
and i'm out on the street with
the bums selling pencils is it fair
i ask you.
FEMKE: You say horrible
   Things, Sam.
SAM: i can't stand it
   Begins to go out, then notices Mevrouw smiling at him.
   Oh, hello, *Mevrouw. Tot ziens.*
   Starts again.
FEMKE: Stop, please just stop.
   I think we are grown up people.
   We do not need humiliations.
   It proves nothing. I am sorry
   For what it's worth.
   I should not have
   Done many things
   To you. I acted badly
   But, it's the winter
   Now, and we have
   Been friends, so why
   Can't we be gentle

With each other
For a time? I don't
Want to be a bad
Person. Blaise thinks
I'm a fool, maybe
You do too. But I'm not.
Maman, has her story to
Tell about Spitzbergen.
Nobody will listen.
Will you?

> *Pause. Sam sits down.*

SAM: I'm tired of warring against
The obvious. It sticks in my
proverbial craw.

I'm here, foolishly,
Because a friend of mine,
Jacques, is a friend of
Yours: that's all.

I make no demand.

At some point the
World will end. Until
That moment we must
Live as if we were
Going to live forever,
Does that sound right?

I know a man who
Truly lives aphoristically:
He makes up his mind
Every morning to behave
As if that day were his
Last. He wills himself
To do it.

I tell you, no
Human being ever
Lived more wretchedly.
I know you despise me
Because you think
I used you, but
At least, I do not
Worship death and if
I acted foolishly it was
Because I wanted to
Live life *well*. With
Someone like you. You.
What the hell is she
Doing lying on the floor?

MEVROUW: I am resting.

FEMKE: But Blaise likes you.

SAM: Oh, Christ...
You don't speak,
You emit...

He storms out.

FEMKE: I feel numb.

MEVROUW: [*getting up slowly*] I am so glad I came to
America. It is like a
Trip to St James Campostela.

FEMKE: I won't tell you to
Get up if you don't
Want to.

BLAISE: Have you seen Jacques?
I thought he was with me
Out in the snow, he was
Throwing his voice into trees,
Stones, I would hardly hear

Him for the wind. Piff. Paff.
He vanished. So, I go up
To the snowmen we are making
To doublecheck if one of them
Is Jacques. But no. He had
Been throwing his voice into
The snowmen, it was quite
Convincing. Then I step on
One of the alarm sensors in the
Lawn, that's why you hear
That terrible loud noise, eh?

FEMKE: We didn't hear anything.

BLAISE: Damn, maybe it doesn't work!
Goes to the wall phone. He dials. Pause.
I'm calling the security company.
You pay good money for those
Devices, and then they don't even work.
John recommended the sensors,
You know John, the neighbor there. [*Gestures.*]
CIA man with the big dog that
Chased you? Remember him? Nice guy.

FEMKE: A real nice guy.

BLAISE: So where is Jacques?

FEMKE: Maybe taking a walk.
You know Jacques.

MEVROUW: I go look for him.
She goes out.

FEMKE: He might freeze to death
Out there.

BLAISE: What can I do? I am
No *deus ex Machina.*
Perhaps everyone wants

A *pousse-cafe*, Femke?
No one answers. [*He hangs up.*]
FEMKE: It's a holiday, remember?
BLAISE: I have a new idea for a
    Way to make money.
    What do you think of
    This: when Pickett calls. . .
FEMKE: Blaise, I have to talk to
    You.
BLAISE: It is about the statuettes.
    I promise to clean up
    That mess with the smelting.
    It creates a nuisance, eh?
    No, it's not that. Okay,
    I go look for *le sot.*
FEMKE: I am taking Saskia
    Back to Ghent.
BLAISE: Aha. . .
FEMKE: Tomorrow. Or the day after.
    Long pause.
BLAISE: Maybe I can make you
    Change your mind.
    Enter Mevrouw.
MEVROUW: Jacques is watching
    Footballs with Sam.
BLAISE: WILL YOU TELL US YOUR
    STORY ABOUT SPITZBERGEN
    NOW, *MAMAN?*
MEVROUW: In a while. I want to see the
    Conclusion of the American
    Football match. It is like
    War.

Or like pictures of a flower
Opening up. Bing. Bang. Bam. [*Gestures.*]
She goes out.
BLAISE: No story, I'm afraid.
FEMKE: If you touch me I'll scream.
BLAISE: You are so easily provoked.
Perhaps, I should have
Reminded you more often
That certain parts of the
House are off limits, Femke.
Begins to dress for outdoors.
FEMKE: I meant it, Blaise.
BLAISE: We are going for a walk.
*Sam and THE PROFESSIONAL FRENCHMAN in the
TV room watching the fateful conclusion of the Browns-
Raiders game. Both are bathed in blueish TV light. Sam
peers at the game through his fingers. It should be unnec-
essary to point out that Jacques's accent in this scene is
completely American.*
JACQUES: It do pay the bill.
SAM: Indeed it do.
JACQUES: I dunno, Sam.
SAM: I know, I know.
Field goal'd win it. But
Even if it's only twenty
Fucking yards, damn, it's the
Windy end of the field.
Cockcroft'll blow it;
He missed a real dink
Of a sixteen-yarder earlier.
JACQUES: So what are we gonna
Do now? I mean like

I'm real tired of being
What I am, you know?
SAM: *Weighs down on you?*
JACQUES: Weighs me down
　　To fucking China.
SAM: *Here we go.* [*Turns his chair around.*]
　　Can't watch...
JACQUES: SIPE'S BACK TO THROW.
SAM: BACK TO THROW?!
JACQUES: NEWSOME'S GOT IT...
　　NO, IT'S BEEN
　　INTERCEPTED!
SAM: INTERCEPTED!? [*Wheels about.*]
JACQUES: They blew it!
　　I told you!*
Hot damn!
SAM: Horseshit. I
　　Don't fucking
　　Believe it.*
　　He went and
　　Threw it
　　Into a
　　Crowd.
　　I don't believe it.
JACQUES: Oakland's the team of the future!
SAM: Forty-six seconds to go
　　And he goes and throws
　　It into a fucking crowd.
　　I don't fucking believe it.
JACQUES: You lose.
　　　Holds out his hand palm up. Sam produces a ten-dollar
　　bill from his wallet and lays it on Jacques.

SAM: Incredible.

JACQUES: You live by the pass,
    You die by the pass.

SAM: [*Curls up in his chair.*] I'm gonna be
    Ill.

JACQUES: [*Stands and looks out the door.*]
    Here she comes. *Mevrouw...*

SAM: Looks like
    You'll have to start
    An Argentine bakery.

JACQUES: What's an Argentine bakery?

SAM: All the rolls and croissants elect
    The big loaf as dictator and he
    Responds by sending them all out
    On killer squads.

JACQUES: Leastwise I got me a job.

SAM: Everything on your menu
    Is made from Rice Krispies,
    Motherfucker.

JACQUES: You're just pissed because I
    Knew Oakland was a sure thing.
        Mevrouw ambles in.
    Monsieur Al Davis c'est le grand
    Maitre de la football. C'est le bon!
    A la victoire allez les spoils!
    N'est-ce pas? Sam has no instinct
    For winners. Blaise now,
    Blaise has *le winning-instinct,*
    Is it not so, *Mevrouw?*

MEVROUW: I am not sure I understand.

SAM: Take my advice, *Mevrouw.* Never
    Gamble against professionals.

They are merciless.
*They laugh. Pause. Sam speaks in a strange, demon-
iacal, deep voice.*
You have to beat them
Into submission. Once
You get a man down
In America, blessèd America,
You have to fucking pound
Him into the clay, you have
To finish him off. Destroy
Him. Pulverize him. Be-
Cause if you show a man
Any mercy. Any kindness.
If you leave him with any
Small part of his self-respect
He'll never forgive you, he'll
Make you bloody well pay
For every fucking thing you
Ever did. For him.
  Never give a man a second chance.
When you get the opportunity
To eat a human being
Swallow him whole
Or grind him to
Pulp, but never NEVER
Leave the tiniest bit
Of living humanity left
Or you'll be sorry for it.
  You can bet your ass
Reagan won't. Reagan-Reagan
The First. Year One of Reagan-
Reagan. Just like Bokassa.

A perfectly honed human machine.
Only Bokassa was too mild.
He didn't eat up all the children.
He left some. We had it all,
    Rusty, we had it all.
We fine-spirited humanitarian people.
But we succumbed to our sense of
Mercy. We had the Nixons of
The world beaten and begging.
And we took pity and gave them
Mercy. It's going to snow a
Hundred years and Reagan
Will have no mercy, you can
Be sure of that. We'll all be
Buried so deep in the ice-box
Of history no one will ever
Know we existed. Never.
    Brian Sipe had mercy, he
Had too much imagination.
Mevrouw, do you know your
Son has feasted on human flesh?

JACQUES: Shut up, Sam.

SAM: Ask him about Ougadougou.
Ask him about Intertop and
About Bokassa.

    Out the window one Snowman is throttling another.
    Pause.

MEVROUW: It is called "long pig."

    Pause.

SAM: Never show mercy, never...

JACQUES: *Mondieu! Mondieu!*

    Jacques and Mevrouw seated at opposite ends of the

kitchen table. Outside the snowstorm is swirling about.
Inside it is very dark, and eerie shadows—as of wings—
flit about. The TV in the other room is on, but the sound
has been turned down. A voice-over of Mevrouw telling
her Spitzbergen story begins as she stands up, in a puddle
of light, and beams. The voice-over continues for a time,
then quiets as the subsequent scene commences with the
departure of Jacques into the outdoors.

MEVROUW: [*voice-over*]

THEN Smeerenburg, a narrow strip of sand caught between the icy water of the fjord and a lagoon over-
grown with birdlife;

REMNANTS of train-oil ovens can be seen; the founda-
tions of settlements rising up from the marshy ground;

IN three-hundred and fifty years Nature has destroyed
much of its former glory; but despite these traces of
degeneration it is a unique feeling to tread in the foot-
steps of the seventeenth-century whalers.

SPITZBERGEN, or Svalbard, as the Norwegians call the
island, literally means "cold coast."

THE Dutch seafarer Willem Barentsz and his men rediscovered Spitzbergen in 1596. Permanent daylight en-
hances our feelings of safety in a territorium that is the
domain of the polar bear; it is a happy thought that
one of these monsters cannot enter our camp under the
protection of night. The locals are annoyed when the
supplies of hamburgers, pies, cakes, and other food
stuffs disappear into the stomachs of the Dutch.

THE tourist ship is met by a weird-looking group, giving a surrealistic theatre performance. The group of
musicians is so drunk they can only keep their balance
by leaning heavily against the strong breeze, playing:

"When the Saints Go Marching in. . ."

ON the way back Willem Barentsz spotted land to the South. It was 17 June 1596 and after several centuries the island of Spitzbergen had been rediscovered. Between the end of the 16th century and the middle of the 17th century more than ten thousand Dutch whalers set off for the whaling grounds in the Arctic Ocean.

IN September last year the expedition returned with a wealth of garments, leather goods, boots, tufts of hair, clay pipes, tools, and food scraps;

HOWEVER, the hibernation of the seven ended in disaster. One after another died in the Arctic winter. The surviving men continually face the task of burying the dead in the frozen ground at Smeerenburg. Out of driftwood, washing ashore from Siberia, they construct coffins. The remaining two survivors were withheld a stylish burial: they died shortly one after the other.* Within a fortnight of their lonely death, a Dutch ship arrived on the horizon. This fact could be derived from the diaries the survivors at Smeerenburg had meticulously kept till their bitter ends.

OUR first impression, standing between the train-oil ovens at Smeerenburg, is of a god-forsaken place where no man can survive, an icy wind brings tears to your eyes and makes you shiver in the penetrating drizzle. The island is encompassed in wet cloth.

AFTER 1600 whale fishing ceased because whales had grown scarce. The whales fled to the pack ice and kept hiding there.

BECAUSE at low tide the water level in the lagoon is about three feet above the sea it seems sufficient to dig a small channel from the lagoon to the sea. And in less than an hour we have this job fixed.

AFTER that we happily sit and enjoy a couple of gins.
A short time later we are startled by a murmuring noise
that soon becomes a roar. To our dismay we see that
the water from the lagoon, streaming to the sea, has
turned our small channel to a 15 feet wide river.

WE must now throw up a dam to stop the water from
devastating the bird sanctuary.

VERY popular on Spitzbergen is the story of the Austrian
tourist who in the region of the Magdalena-fjord poked
his head out of his tent in the morning, to have it
promptly chopped off by the paw of one of the polar
bears.

Out in the storm. Jacques with difficulty approaches
Sam and Femke. Blaise has been knocked cold and is
prostrate in the snow. Femke holds a hammer. The snow
is swirling about so much that it is nearly impossible to
tell the people from the snow-people.

SAM: How soon
Can you
Get the two
Of your packed?

FEMKE: His eye's open.

SAM: Out cold and
Snowblind. [*Bends over Blaise.*]
Out cold. . .

FEMKE: So much snow. . .

SAM: It only moves when
It's standing still.

FEMKE: It's so magical tonight.

SAM: Great things have small beginnings, my dear.
As he drags Blaise toward the house he meets the

slowly plodding Jacques.

JACQUES: God is good, it seems,
To children, fools, and
Americans.

FEMKE: Hello, Jacques.

JACQUES: What is happened to Blaise?

SAM: Spat into the wind,
So a house fell on him.
Out cold.
Give us a hand, Jacques.

FEMKE: His eye's open!

The house late at night. Again the TV is on, again silently. Mevrouw tiptoes in wearing a long nightshirt, slippers, and nightcap. She begins mouthing the Spitzbergen story, from the beginning. As she starts, the voice-over picks up where it had left off, and runs to the conclusion. Thus, she is out of synch with the tape, and after it ends she continues to recite, in absolute silence. After a short time there is a slow blackout.

MEVROUW: [*voice over*]

HAVING a shower at 60 degrees is suddenly a deep and satisfying experience.

NORWEGIANS are much nicer people than we initially thought.

THE return to our camp was like a cold shower.

THE destructive blizzard had finally succeeded in flattening our camp; we finally succeeded in using a treetrunk as tent-pole.

THE illusion that King Winter would relax his grip on the climate in North-West Spitzbergen until the Dutch expedition would have returned home was cruelly disturbed.

THE wintry atmosphere remains our steady companion, like the traditional iron ball to the leg of a convict.

LOUWRENS Hacquebord suddenly yells out: "Bear, bear!" Through our binoculars we see a huge polar bear clambering from rock to rock with slow, athletic steps.

ONE can almost feel the tension.

THE bear gets closer and we try to discourage it by producing noises on jerrycans, pots and pans.

LOUWRENS even fires into the air.

THE bear looks startled and tries to find out where the bullet went.

IT makes for the tents, where the hamburgers are.

LOUWRENS waits, his gun ready.

WHEN the bear is too close for comfort he fires his first shot, hitting it in the heart.

THE beast rears, roars for pain, turns abruptly, takes a few steps and falls face down.

AFTER approximately ten minutes it moves one of its paws.

HOWEVER, after the last convulsions the polar bear does no longer move.

TOMORROW a representative of the Norwegian government will arrive for making an official report. We'll see what will happen.

DURING their investigation such questions arise as: "What was the cause of death of the whalers on Ytre Norskoya? What were their ages? Where were they going? Where had they come from? Were they all men? Were they all human beings?"

ACT THREE

*The next day, bright sunshine streaming in the kitchen
window. Blaise, Jacques, and Mevrouw are seated around
the table eating breakfast. Blaise's head is bandaged.*
BLAISE: Who said I am worried?
MEVROUW: She hit him with a hammer.
JACQUES: *Mon dieu, un marteau!*
BLAISE: As though to inflict
     Injury.
          Pause.
JACQUES: It is a very interesting
     Petit dejeuner.
BLAISE: Old Belgian pastry.
     It is called "Vlackebos."
          Pause.
JACQUES: What means "Vlackebos"?
BLAISE: Because Sam says I am a cat-burglar.
     I have no wife. I have even a young
     Child, a mother even. But no wife.
MEVROUW: What is "catburglar"?
BLAISE: The Dutch are no good.
JACQUES: It is a difficult concept, Mevrouw.
MEVROUW: Blaise will now begin
     Telling Dutch jokes.
BLAISE: It's a pity. I can't
     Think of any.
MEVROUW: I will think of one.
JACQUES: Maybe she has gone to visit
     The supermarket.
BLAISE: She has run off with her
     Old lover.

JACQUES: But, I tell you, Blaise.
    America is a country
    Full of old lovers.
    Everywhere you meet
    Them, but it is a
    Passing phenomenon.
    They go away, because
    Everyone goes away.
    Usually for no reason.
    Lovers in the street.
    Lovers in the attic.
    Lovers on the viaduct.
    Lovers in the bistro.
    All of them *old* lovers.
    Not agèd, just old.
    None of the old lovers
    Make love, as elsewhere.
    They simply *co-exist.*
    It fills America
    With delicious pain
    As in the old movies
    And cigarette commercials.
    But it all passes.
    It means nothing.
BLAISE: I devote my life to a
    New life here, I learn
    A new trade, everything;
    See what Fate befalls
    Me! ME! A man of some
    Importance, *helas.*
MEVROUW: It is because you are a
    Unpleasant person, Blaise.

JACQUES: She means you burgle.

BLAISE: I do not burgle, I told her.

Pause

MEVROUW: She will come back, Blaise.

Femke is a good girl, she will.

BLAISE: I am made ridiculous.

MEVROUW: Jacques, can you

Throw your voice

Into the teapot? [*He does so.*]

JACQUES: You should write her a letter.

BLAISE: I will not do it.

MEVROUW: You are difficult to understand.

When you are not entertaining

Strangers you are silent.

BLAISE: I am her master.

MEVROUW: She is your mistress, Blaise.

JACQUES: You should write her a letter.

BLAISE: It is essential

That the origin of sovereignty

Show itself to be beyond the

Sphere of human power, so that

Even Men who appear to

Influence it directly are only

Creatures of circumstance.

MEVROUW: Even as a child he talked

In this way.

BLAISE: It is an unwritten rule.

JACQUES: Perhaps Femke desired the rules

To be expressed clearly, openly,

As in a written constitution, no?

BLAISE: Things written will never never have more

Than the appearance of wisdom. Thus, he

Who believes himself able by *writing*
Alone to establish the truth or falseness
Of doctrines is A GREAT FOOL, so!
MEVROUW: Find a lawyer and make a divorce.
Pause.
BLAISE: She hit me injuriously on the head
Avec un marteau.
JACQUES: *Un marteau sans maitre.*
BLAISE: See, *Maman,* how
The French are an indigestible people
When they are not discussing *la cuisine.*
MEVROUW: I must go to Saskia now.
It is good being a mother
Again.
She goes out. Pause.
JACQUES: You should not have hidden your true
Occupation from Femke. You are not
Intelligent.
BLAISE: Sam may go to the police.
JACQUES: I don't think so.
He is also a criminal.
Americans do not like people
Who attempt to make them
Think otherwise than they want to
Think. Criminals like you. And
Sam. You think. Americans are
A happy people. God loves them.
We must do the thinking for them.
Pause.
We and the Germans.
BLAISE: I cannot go to the administration.
Pause.

People who work in the administration
Are demons. They infect the air.
*Doorbell rings. Pause. Blaise attempts to get up but
is unable to do so. He looks puzzled.*
Ah, Jacques. . .
Doorbell rings again.
Moment.
JACQUES: Something is wrong.
Doorbell rings long and loud.
BLAISE: I am unable to stand.
Jacques, perhaps you
Could answer the door.
*Jacques is similarly afflicted. Mevrouw comes in and
goes to the door. It is a Girl Scout selling cookies, but
she is not visible to the audience.*
JACQUES: Blaise, I did not want
To say anything, but I
Also am unable to. . . arise.
GIRL SCOUT: Would you like any
Girl scout cookies?
MEVROUW: [*to Blaise*] What is "cookies"?
BLAISE: Jacques, what is
"Cookies"?
JACQUES: *Biscuit. . .*
Mevrouw tastes one.
MEVROUW: Is she in the army?
BLAISE: *Maman,* don't be so inquisitive.
GIRL SCOUT: Would you like to buy some
Girl scout cookies?
Pause.
BLAISE: Answer *no.*
MEVROUW: Answer no.

Pause.

BLAISE: *Maman*, don't stand there in idiocy.
Your comprehension of the language
Is quite sufficient to tell the girl
Scout that we are not in the least
Desiring to purchase her damn cookies.

JACQUES: *Mon dieu*, Blaise, I am
Absolutely immobilized.

GIRL SCOUT: Lady, if you want some cookies I
Can leave 'em. Here. You can decide.
Later. When you learn the language.
Tomorrow even.

BLAISE: Say "No thank you."

MEVROUW: No thank you, *ma fille.*

BLAISE: Give her the box, *Maman.*

MEVROUW: When Blaise
Begins in such a harsh manner
I become quite agitated. It causes
Me to forget all words of your
Language. Mine too. *C'est dommage.*

GIRL SCOUT: Good bye, lady.

MEVROUW: Good bye, the cookie of which I tasted
Is indeed magnificent.
Girl scout goes out.

BLAISE: *Maman*, can you see the snow
People?

MEVROUW: The sun is shining, Blaise, everything
Is melting.

BLAISE: Can you see the snow
People still there?

MEVROUW: They are no longer resembling
Human people, Blaise.

BLAISE: I am totally unable
  To move my lower
  Portions, Jacques.
  Maman's pastry is
  Of course very delectable to the palate;
  It is, however, of a massive ponderation.
  I have become stone-bottomed.
JACQUES: I had a wager with myself that if
  The sun came out Femke
  Would return. As if reborn.
  My intuitions are acute, my sense
  Of preview has led me to witness
  Many strange and monstrous events.
BLAISE: Sit and talk with me, Jacques.
JACQUES: I am unable to do otherwise.
MEVROUW: The sky is beautiful
  I will go see if Saskia
  Wants to play.
      She goes out.
BLAISE: Over the hill is the Agency.
  The Agency can make the
  Snow go away. John our neighbor
  Says there are immense invisible devices
  Capable of changing the climate;
  It can be done easily he says.
JACQUES: Perhaps they have so dramatically
  Changed the weather to announce
  The new presidency of Mister Reagan.
  This enforced sitting is hard thing.
BLAISE: You are truly unable to move
  As well?
JACQUES: I, in fact, have feigned

Comfort. If I was
Able to move
I would fall.
BLAISE: The same with me.
Pause.
Perhaps we have died.
JACQUES: I think Femke will return.
BLAISE: Perhaps our souls have left our
Bodies and become lost. Out there.
JACQUES: Astral projection is an unproved
Hypothesis, Blaise.
BLAISE: Perhaps our souls have become
Somehow lodged in the upper air.
I have not felt such weight
Since now. It is disturbing.
Pause.
No one must know.
JACQUES: But, why!?
BLAISE: *Maman* will be distressed if she
Discovers the secret of her pastry.
JACQUES: First you lie to your wife,
Now you plot a subterfuge.
BLAISE: It is no subterfuge.
JACQUES: It is subterfuge.
Pause.
More coffee?
BLAISE: Yes, I would like some.
JACQUES: The coffee is excellent.
BLAISE: Femke had the beans ground.
JACQUES: At least we have
Coffee.
BLAISE: We should be grateful.

JACQUES: An healthy man assumes
     Much.
BLAISE: Too much.
     Pause.
     When I recover the use of my legs
     I will change my life, Jacques.
     In America one can be anything
     In the world. One may become a god.
     A lawyer. A spy. A newspaper
     Seller. A tobacconist. It is not
     So easy back home. Here one may
     Become even a Dissident, like Golub.
     In many countries it is forbidden.
     It is an envious position to be
     In, I tell you.
JACQUES: One can be a pre-
     Seer, as your excellent friend
     Madame Sesostris.
BLAISE: Yes. One can be a Secretary of State.
JACQUES: A president.
BLAISE: Still I think *we* have something to
     Contribute. We are not useless. Especially
     When we are able to move freely about.
     And our wives have not run off
     With deranged American deprogrammers.
     It is enough to give one the gout.
     Jacques, do you think it is the gout?
JACQUES: It cannot be, Blaise.
BLAISE: Perhaps it is a special malady
     Known only to us. Perhaps. . .
JACQUES: Perhaps it is
     "The Thanksgiving Disease"! Ha!

BLAISE: What about poor Saskia?
How will she eat, and my
Mother, how will she eat?
JACQUES: It is a vile fate.
I have some feeling,
Here, in my hams.
BLAISE: I must call Pickett and arrange
To dispose of my inventories,
If I am to be invalided I must
Have cash.
JACQUES: I am still unable
To move.
BLAISE: Can you hear anything?
JACQUES: No, I hear only us.
BLAISE: *Maman* has fallen
Asleep.
JACQUES: Saskia will be
In danger.
Jacques gets up.
BLAISE: Jacques!
*Jacques strides swiftly out. Pause. He returns and sits
as before.*
BLAISE: You walked!
JACQUES: No one is there.
They are gone.
BLAISE: You are re-covered.
JACQUES: Only a little.
Now I need rest.
BLAISE: I must find a new life.
JACQUES: It is of necessity a hard lot.
BLAISE: Perhaps *Maman* has poisoned us.
JACQUES: The thought has occurred to me

Blaise, but I don't think so.

BLAISE: Ah, I see them. *[Looking out the window]*

JACQUES: Where are they?

BLAISE: By the mountain of snow,
Throwing snowballs at cars.

JACQUES: I am feeling better.

BLAISE: The enormity of Fate.

JACQUES: I could provide you with
Papers. And, for a time, a job.

BLAISE: I did not really eat human flesh.
Pause.
It was a test. In the Congo.

JACQUES: Of course not.
Long pause.

BLAISE: A family is a large responsibility.
What if one should be immobilized?
It is a delirious thought, Jacques.
But I have hope.

JACQUES: I have some tricks here.
Puts on a fool's cap and produces a whistle from his pockets. Throws his voice into the ice-box.
I am a large
Rectangular
Oblong of
Snow-white
Coloration:
What am I?

BLAISE: You are Jacques
Being the ice-box;
Please stop.

JACQUES: Things have their secret essences
Which may be evoked by thought.

He blows on the whistle.
Each of the herbs has not only
A name but an essential spirit.
It is the secret of cooking by enchantment.
He blows on the whistle.
BLAISE: Are you being a fool?
JACQUES: I am entertaining you
     With an entertainment.
BLAISE: Why are we speaking English?
     Slow blackout begins.
JACQUES: I was not aware that
     We are speaking English...
BLAISE: We are not speaking French!
JACQUES: One must not be hasty.
BLAISE: Talking to you is to talk
     To a complete imbecile...
JACQUES: I was making a joke, Blaise.
     Puts away hat and whistle.
     Mevrouw is quite correct:
     You have a disagreeable
     Personality.
BLAISE: I tell you.
     I have the ear of the late Secretary.
     He possesses the ear of Golub.
     Golub possesses the ear of
     Madame Sesostris who, in turn,
     Possess the ear of the would-be
     Secretary. Jacques, I promise.
     I will tell them *Ban the French*.
     And in especial you must ban
     The Professional Frenchmans.
     Pause.

　　Maman's pastry is of a Dutch
　　Construction, I fear.
JACQUES: I can move my
　　Toes, Blaise.
BLAISE: It will last five hundred years.
　　　Pause.
　　How can you recognize
　　A group of Dutchmens
　　At a cafe? [*Pause.*]
　　　They are the ones
　　With one coke
　　AND FIVE STRAWS! HA!
　　　Pause.
JACQUES: Can you get up?
BLAISE: I am not going to try.

Fin. End. *Einde.*